Jacobean Revenge
Tragedy
and the Politics
of Virtue

Jacobean Revenge Tragedy and the Politics of Virtue

Eileen Allman

DELAWARE

Newark: University of Delaware Press
London: Associated University Presses

Associated University Presses
440 Forsgate Drive
Cranbury, NJ 08512

Associated University Presses
16 Barter Street
London WC1A 2AH, England

Associated University Presses
P.O. Box 338, Port Credit
Mississauga, Ontario
Canada L5G 4L8

The paper used in this publication meets the requirements
of the American National Standard for Permanence of Paper
for Printed Library Materials Z39.48-1984.

Library of Congress Cataloging-in-Publication Data

Allman, Eileen Jorge, 1940–
    Jacobean revenge tragedy and the politics of virtue / Eileen
Allman.
        p.   cm.
    Includes bibliographical references and index.
    ISBN 0-87413-698-9 (alk. paper)
    1. English drama—17th century—History and criticism.   2. Revenge
in literature.   3. Politics and literature—Great Britain—
History—17th century.   4. Political plays, English—History and
criticism.   5. English drama (Tragedy)—History and criticism.
6. Virtue in literature.   I. Title.
PR678.R45A55   1999
822'.309353—dc21   99-18960
                                                                              CIP

To the memory of my mother
Emma Jorge

and my grandmother
Viktorija Zgomba

Contents

Preface

Cultural materialist and new historicist critics have persuasively argued the premise that no text is separable from the culture that creates it and that is, in turn, created by it; that, further, a text's readers are equally implicated in the historical moment of their reading. Criticism, they maintain, is not and has never been a transcendent aesthetic practice. Where the only absolute truth is the truth that no truth is absolute, all criticism is political, and the critic, obliged to acknowledge the biases and thwarts of any reading, is free to use that reading in the service of a contemporary political agenda.

Current feminist scholarship in Renaissance studies has been profoundly influenced by materialist/historicist tenets and methods. Early feminist attempts to link the past to the present tended to ignore or to blur historical distinction: such studies have since been repudiated for building on theoretically unchallenged assumptions. Feminist scholarship of early modern England has now largely adopted the practice of concentrating on the specificity of the historical moment, examining all texts that provide information about women's lives within the cultural context in which they were lived. These studies have uncovered a rich vein of factual and speculative material, with the result that texts gone stale from generations of critical exposure are again vital, while others once underrated or ignored are valued and foregrounded. Nonetheless, the linking of past to present remains a dubious venture. No matter how many texts are available for study, we cannot ignore the accidental quality of history's leavings. Even if we were able to access all human, and even nonhuman, consciousnesses and generalize from that totality—I imagine some transhistorical, transpecies computer (God?)—the result would not necessarily be anything more than an infinite number of fragments interpreted in an infinite number of ways by temporally compromised readers.

Dilemma: If we posit a human faculty that transcends the historical moment and reaches across time and space to others possessing that same faculty, we are in danger of underestimating

9

difference and appropriating the past. If, however, we deny that premise and assume that we are collectively and individually locked in a prison of contingency that insists we deny the existence of anything outside it and prevents us from comprehending its very nature, we are in danger of celebrating a radically destructive solipsism. When we embrace what separates us as humans—whether it is time or gender or race—we risk dismissing *a priori* any effort to forge connections across the spaces that divide us. Our own efforts to write and speak of the inevitable failure of human language are, of course, doomed to fail before we make them. Yet we do continue to write and speak, using language to heal division by expressing it.

As a contemporary reader—female, American, middle-aged, liberal humanist by training, educated at a New York City public college and teaching at the same and not-same college—I am aware of the contingencies involved in my discussion of gender in Jacobean revenge tragedy. I do not assume that my understanding of Jacobean revenge tragedy, even a single line of a play, would be the same as that of a merchant's wife in the original audience, or of a male colleague at the college where I teach, or of a postcolonial African novelist. I do, however, entertain the possibility that enough similarity exists in the species to allow us in some way to scale the walls between us. Even if the belief that a human faculty can escape the endless play of *différance* is no more than a wishful and politically motivated illusion, it is an illusion that has acquired the force of tradition: we find its record in theologians' claims to transcendental truth, in mystics' accounts of states of ecstasy, in poets' assertions of vatic inspiration, even in readers' experiences of temporal dislocation. When an illusion takes part in the everyday structure of cultural belief, it exists in the material world and affects that world as if it were itself material. Perhaps what connects a text's author(s) and its readers—across time and culture—is just that: the belief, conceivably wishful and fallacious, in a transcendent human faculty.

In the ever complicating debate among theories and practices of reading, I find myself in sympathy with Marilyn Williamson, Carol Thomas Neely, and Peter Erickson in their partial acceptance of materialist/historicist assumptions. Confronting the term *ideology*, Williamson acknowledges that "both author and reader are inscribed in discourses, social formations, and material conditions of a historical moment," but she resists "giving up a partially self-made subject and the author" (1991, 148). Neely, too, draws her lines: "I have not abandoned my conviction that the plays had an author. . . . I do not think that character need be subsumed entirely under 'textual strategies,' that 'desire' or 'sexuality' can be satisfactorily explained as simply an aspect of class conflict, or that individual subjectivity is absolutely controlled by the dominant ideology" (1991, 3). While disagreeing with humanist premises, Peter Erickson nonetheless seconds Harry Berger's affirmation of new criticism's practice of close reading (1991, 13–16).

This moment of reevaluation after the revolutionary headiness of poststructuralism offers the possibility of renegotiating critical terms along less sectarian lines, seizing the chance to merge ideas that have been represented as irrevocably separate and, in the process, abandoning accusation and righteousness for a cooler assessment of the critical past's contributions. With Williamson and Neely, I accept the inscription of text and author within a moment of time but reject the reflex elimination of subject, author, and character; with Erickson, I believe that close reading of passages remains a vital tool of criticism. Last, and perhaps most retrograde, I cannot, *de facto*, abandon the human faculty that believes it can glimpse a world outside time.

Acknowledgments

It is a special pleasure to acknowledge the help I have received in writing this book. I am particularly grateful to two good friends and colleagues: W. Speed Hill for his invaluable advice on shaping and placing the book and Carol Sicherman for her careful reading of some sections and, even more, for her unflagging professional and personal support. To Carol, too, I owe my participation in the Westchester Women's Writing Group, whose generous, receptive regulars provided an ideal audience for early drafts of my book.

Stanley Chojnacki's 1996 Folger Library seminar, "Men, Women, and the State in Renaissance Europe," was a rare gift in the later stages of my thinking and writing. My thanks to Stan and the seminar members for their encouraging response to "Tyrants." To Martin Elsky, coordinator of the Renaissance Studies Certificate Program at CUNY Graduate School and University Center, I am in debt for the gentle nudge to apply for the seminar; to the Folger Consortium, the grant-in-aid I needed to attend; and to the library's remarkable, committed staff, their maintaining the Folger as an oasis of civility.

Additional assistance for the book came from Lehman College in the form of a grant that allowed me to hire Denise Sands Baez as a research assistant. I am indebted to her for her assistance in preparing the manuscript. Thanks, too, to Eugene Laper, the indefatigable and uncomplaining head of Interlibrary Loan; I could not have managed the research without him. To my Lehman students, whose ambition and courage humanized my professional life for a quarter of a century, I am profoundly grateful.

Last, first, and always, from research to copy editing, my husband, John Allman, steadied the boat with words and wit. To him, to our daughter Jen, to Lucy, Chloe, and Beau, I owe more than thanks can compass.

Jacobean Revenge
Tragedy
and the Politics
of Virtue

1

Gender, History, and Jacobean Revenge Tragedy

Misogyny and Male Rivalry

I began this study with the intention of reading Jacobean revenge tragedy oppositionally: exploring the relationships among the genre, the historical moment in which it flourished, and the simultaneous and, I believed, linked assault and praise of women. While the subject remains the historical knot of gender and authority in revenge drama, my understanding of the issues it raises has changed in significant ways.

First, the plays' idealization of virtuous women, a cultural stance now widely accepted as the mirror image of misogyny, cannot, I conclude, be dismissed as inseparable from contempt and equally disempowering and dehumanizing.[1] It is easy, even comfortable, to reject as an act of male ventriloquism the dramatic representation of women who take pride in their virtue—who have, to quote Desdemona, the "authority of [their] merit" (*Oth.* 2.1.145–46)—and speak from that strength.[2] The virtuous heroine, in that view, is a male fantasy given material form by playwrights and foisted on women, real and fictional, who are esteemed only because they have internalized the script. The presentation of praiseworthy women then becomes no more than male tyranny exercising the "benign" rather than the "violent" option of patriarchy (Erickson 1991, 24).

Certainly the playwrights of the age, with one known exception, were men, and they wrote words and commanded gestures for women, or, to complicate the issue properly, for boys adopting female gender. Playwriting, by definition, is a ventriloquist's profession. Drama, in Elizabeth Harvey's words, is ventriloquism's "quintessential paradigm" (1992, 2). Playwrights stuffed words into everyone's mouth: university men wrote lines for clowns and fools; sons of glovers for noblemen; white Englishmen for Moors, Romans, Tartars, and astral spirits. The exception, Elizabeth Carey, ventriloquized a biblical world of both women and men. A playwright has the extraordinary, threatening power to reshape culture simply by representing it.

Yet while the scripts of these professional ventriloquists depict men and women as essentially different, they do not always differentiate characters' responses to their dramatic situations according to sex. In revenge tragedy, some men and some women serve tyranny; some resist serving it; some first opt to serve it, then return to abandoned principles. Characters of both sexes struggle, or refuse to struggle, to keep their sense of virtue in the face of a pervasive and omnivorous cynicism. Some lament their impotence to correct injustice; some sharpen their tongues to further its cause. The origin of that general disempowerment—the tyrant—is male, but his maleness, an isolated and absolute claim to mastery, sweeps men and women alike into ignominious postures of subjection.

When we turn specifically to the ventriloquism of female characters, we find admiration expressed for those who actively defy tyranny, not for those who passively accept martyrdom at its hands. In the portrayal of women's rejection of corrupt state power, the gender lines usually drawn between the political and the domestic, the public and private blur.[3] The respect accorded these characters, albeit in some instances partial and ambivalent, is not founded on a male insistence that women constrain themselves in culturally acceptable postures of chastity, silence, and obedience. The unequivocally idealized heroines of the tragedies—Castiza of *The Revenger's Tragedy*, the Lady of *The Second Maiden's Tragedy*, Lucina and Eudoxa of *Valentinian*, Matilda of *The Bloody Brother*—are indeed chaste, but they are decidedly not silent, nor are they obedient. They are not circumscribed by what Marilyn French has termed the inlaw principle, that is, a "wispy" female benevolence that complements and is subordinate to male power (1983, 24). They assume and exercise, often publicly, a forceful and unswervable moral authority over the minds and actions of male and female figures in their plays. They also exercise dramatic authority over the audience: our eyes follow them; we wait for their words; their choices and decisions matter to us.

Contempt and idealization may form the defining extremes of the Jacobean attitude toward women, but in revenge tragedy they are not inextricably linked and they are certainly not the same. Female characters are idealized not when they still their voices but when they raise them, when they cast off their presumed social subjection and assume authority. As Constance Jordan observes, even "dramatically misogynist literature can have a feminist dimension; by depicting women as forceful rebels, it can convey their capacity to think and to act" (1990, 19). That capacity remains disconnected from officially sanctioned state power, yet under the domination of revenge tragedy's tyrants, women and men alike are politically impotent. To reconstruct female action purely as a function of male power is to deny women the agency that the plays—ventriloquized by men—accord them.

Agency does not, of course, imply a socially and culturally independent subject. As Giddens argues, human agency can be understood only in connection with an acting subject who exists in time and space (1979, 2). Yet while historically, discursively constructed, the subject is nonetheless capable of agency because the "I" makes choices, even if they are necessarily limited by language and circumstance (Scott 1992, 34). The doubly constructed subjectivity of revenge tragedy heroines—they are the fictions of their authors' constructed subjectivity—is represented as an "I" that has choice and, therefore, agency. The heroines use the language of religious piety to authorize themselves; they choose paths that affect them and their fellow characters; they act on and accept the consequences of those choices within the limitations of their scripted time and space.

To reverse the emphasis of my first premise, misogyny in Jacobean revenge tragedy is not exclusively the dark, candid obverse of idealization, the extreme consequence of men's need to control women. In fact, the plays represent it as equally integral to men's need to control other men. Second, therefore, I do not discuss the relationships between women and men in isolation from those between men and men.[4] In any culture where signs of dominance and subjection are gendered—i.e., the majority of human cultures (Trexler 1994, 1)—men use the verbal and physical signs that indicate dominance over women to assert themselves against other men. Because a tyrant's rule is insistently based on dominance, men find themselves not only sharing women's place in the social hierarchy but also forced into postures culturally assigned to them. The majority of men occupy nonphallic positions in society. Their voices are silenced, their social and familial authority is usurped, and their sexuality is controlled.

Certainly misogyny has deep roots in human biology and culture, but in revenge tragedy it is the flower of male rivalry. When a man is defeated by another man, he is both unmanned and feminized; that is, he is stripped of cultural signs of dominance and forced to assume those of submission. Yet even though he has been coded female, his body and the meaning he has been taught to attach to it remain male. For the loser, then, femaleness is not a separate and distinct sex but a denial of maleness—an infliction and a stigma, a sign of loss—that can readily be displaced onto women in the form of misogyny. So it is, too, with the victor. The common ground required for competition is the shared belief that signifiers of femaleness humiliate and degrade men.

In revenge tragedy, the insistent strain of misogyny is, in fact, most frequently voiced by male characters who either tyrannize other men or are tyrannized by them—Vindice and the Duke or Lussurioso, the King and Amintor, Bosola and Ferdinand. That the male rivalry in these plays arises between a tyrant, who wields absolute authority through his position, and a subjected man grants the tyrant an initial and seemingly insurmountable advantage in their struggle. In the subject's decision to retaliate or, as in Amintor's case, not to retaliate, the plays acquire an explicit political dimension.

Although frequent and intense, misogyny is not, however, the exclusive male response to tyranny in revenge tragedy. Some men refuse the terms of the tyrant's attack, disempowering him by severing the connection between gender and the political signs of dominance and submission. Affranius in *Valentinian*, Govianus in *The Second Maiden's Tragedy* (who, however, does at first assume that women are temporizing and fickle), and Antonio in *The Duchess of Malfi* do not transform subjection into misogyny. Instead, like the women to whom they are linked, they reject the tyrant's sexual and political claim to authority by affirming obedience to the divinely derived principles that, in theory, sanction his dominance. Authority, then, is relocated to a world of virtue where anyone, again in theory, can claim it. In that leveling assumption of spiritual equality,[5] authority is both degendered and depoliticized, or, more accurately, repoliticized to disempower the tyrant and to empower the subject. Protestantism's, especially its radical sects', emphasis on individual conscience, reinforced by the revolt against and continued opposition to Catholicism, puts religion in post-Reformation England always in potential conflict with the state.

Degendering authority in order to overturn a tyrant means deauthorizing maleness, severing the automatic connection between dominance and maleness not only in the tyrant but also in the subject. It allows men and women both, by asserting obedience to a higher authority, to assume, recognize, and obey that authority in themselves and in one another. To state the case narrowly, it means that men can obey women. There is great reluctance in characters to break the social codes that govern their sexes' conduct—the Lady and Govianus, for example, are both horrified by his unmanly faint and amazed by her unfeminine suicide by sword—but they discover that resistance to tyranny often propels them over the lines of custom and culture.

The third shift in my understanding of the subject, then, involves a commitment to examining instances, in both revenge tragedy and in the culture of its flowering, where the binary of gender is deconstructed even as it is affirmed, where the interwoven codes of dominance and submission are violated, often grudgingly. To focus on difference between maleness and femaleness, whether in the overdetermined misogyny of Jacobean drama and society or in the paralyzing current replay of male tyranny and female victimage, is to ignore or distort evidence of sameness and to deny potentially liberating grounds for common cause.[6] Within the plays, characters of both sexes maintain their culture's belief in the essential difference between men and women, but they must confront the similarity of their subjection under tyranny. While some do respond by exaggerating sexual difference into misogyny—and, in Aspatia's case in *The Maid's Tragedy*, misandry—others abandon the discourse entirely.

This argument for focusing on similarities as well as on differences between men and women is not meant to dismiss or dishonor the suffering that oppressive authority, traditionally white and male, has inflicted on those constructed as inferior. Special kinds of humiliation have been and are visited upon women and upon other groups who share the gendered codes of their subjection—colonized peoples, homosexuals, masterless men.[7] Women of early modern England could be tortured and burned alive as witches; brutalized by fathers, brothers, and husbands; and denied the right to legal recourse for injuries done them. Yet the fact that the signifiers of subjection have a life of their own and separate from one group to attach to others—even to members of the culturally privileged group—not only validates the sexual binary but undermines it by separating gender from sex. The man who is viewed as weak and inferior and then termed "effeminate" reinforces the connection between women and inferiority. Yet because he is also a biological male playing the social role assigned to women, the essentialism of the binary is challenged.

Not even patriarchy, the term applied to a social system based on the presumption of inherent male superiority, can be equated directly with maleness but is rather "gender-complicated" (Claridge and Langland 1990, 3) and "multivalent" (Erickson 1987, 116; 1991, 23). A perfectly functioning patriarchy is an impossibility, its use as a term of political invective self-defeating. To focus on it is to divide the world into executioners and victims, to use Kristeva's terms, an opposition that can be more reasonably understood as potentially functioning *within* "each identity, each subject, each sex" (1986, 210). The executioner is not the exclusive role of monarchs, magistrates, males, and Europeans. Anyone can play.

Catherine Belsey has observed that Viola, as she speaks to Orsino of her father's daughter, is neither Viola nor Cesario but a third subject who is neither male nor female (1985, 187). Perhaps there can be no freedom from any social confinement by category or analogy—of gender, race, class—unless, as Kristeva says of third generation feminists of both sexes, we learn to see opposition itself as metaphysics (1986, 209). In Jacobean revenge tragedy, characters profess faith in that metaphysics, but their actions belie it.

The Unshackling of Analogy

According to the orthodox hierarchies of Renaissance England, authority and maleness were mutually reinforcing lines in a network of intersections. Recent scholarship, however, has irrevocably altered the notion that a single theoretical frame can contain the jostling vitality of Tudor and Stuart England, or indeed of any culture. The elegant symmetries and cosmic harmonies of E. M. W. Tillyard's Elizabethan World Picture, while privileged as orthodox belief, were daily violated, ignored, overridden, reinterpreted, and contradicted by English life. In theory and, at all levels of society including the royal pinnacle, in practice, sexual essentialism and its analogic link to the rules governing political hierarchy had become troublesomely problematic.

Potential for turmoil was inherent in the culture's structures of belief. Based simultaneously on antithesis, which creates a vertical structure of authority within a category, and analogy, which provides horizontal connections between those structures, English society could pull apart at any number of points of intersection. Sexual difference, one of the vertical axes, forms a hierarchy based on the male/female binary; class, family position, education, and race form additional hierarchies.[8] Theoretically, the apex of each hierarchy is analogically connected to all others, with maleness and monarchy equivalent and mutually supporting positions of dominance. Yet while a vertical axis grants authority, the horizontal lines of analogy may contradict it: Elizabeth and Essex offer a famous instance of clashing authorities, with fatal consequences for Essex. The richness of the age's drama is in part a result of these perilous intersections. Othello, Venice's great general, is a Moor; Hamlet, a prince, is also emphatically a son and stepson. The English social fabric, then, was not so much a neat intersection of mutually reinforcing lines as a series of misalignments and exceptions that placed the primary support structure of the society—and its conflicted human members—under intense stress.

With the dizzyingly rapid shifts in the economic and demographic bases of English society, the inevitable gap between theory and practice widened threateningly. The rise of capitalism, the destruction of rural life, the swelling of urban centers, the discovery of human societies functioning outside the boundaries of Europe's established categories of knowledge—all these interrelated changes created an England that subverted the theoretical social order in ways that seemed dangerously destabilizing. Conservative reaction to that instability was equally and predictably forceful. The hierarchical paradigms whose function it was to define and organize social positions were reaffirmed. Voices as different as monarchs and radical Protestants called for a return to strict, if differently drawn, lines of authority. There was a general harking back to a nostalgically created once-upon-a-time when social boundaries were clearly marked and vigorously patrolled, and people functioned within them, theoretically for the good of all. The rapidity and unpredictability of social change, however, continued to strain the points of intersection where, according to the rules of analogy, hierarchies met for lateral support. The greater the turmoil, the more violations of the theoretical social order; the more violations, the stronger the reactionary impulse to strengthen that order.

At the troubled, shifting border between the sexes we find Renaissance theory and practice clashing with particular intensity. Biological sex and social gender were, in theory, continuous; in the political context, whether in family or state, that meant that males commanded and females obeyed. According to the paradigm, God and Nature gave men the right and responsibility to dominate women as well as all others constructed as beneath them on the vertical axis, like children, servants, and non-Europeans, with analogies drawn among those groups. Arguably, women define the category of submission. Dympna Callaghan, for example, asserts gender as the "pivotal and paradigmatic opposition in the structure of antithesis, a condensation of other hierarchies" (1989, 11). Men actively impress themselves on women and, through women, on the world; women passively accept and bear the impress. In this scheme, no less than the world's balance hangs on women's fulfilling their part of the binary bargain.

Women were, in fact, accused of willfully refusing to fulfill their duty and made scapegoats for the violent upheavals in English life. Increasingly banished from the public to the private spheres, used as commodities in the economy's burgeoning capitalism, denied subjectivity and voice, they were repeatedly and publicly exhorted to fashion their behavior according to their ordained role and punished for offenses like shrewishness and gadding. Because women were identified as both cause and effect of social disintegration, they also had the potential power to reverse the effect and restore society to its alleged former strength. If women would only hold their tongues and keep their places, all would again be well. Ideally, they would comply with male wisdom of their own volition, but if they would not embrace subjection freely, then men had the responsibility to force it on them.

The very need to articulate and enforce the old antitheses, however, suggests how difficult the tumultuous, unruly present was to control. Predictably, the effort to put women in their place, and so impose on them the burden of weaving the woof and warp of antithesis and analogy into seamless cloth, was only partially and randomly successful. The increase of commentary on external signifiers like dress as validators of authority and the regular calls for the policing of those signifiers demonstrate how separate the hierarchical theory granting authority had become from the practice. Theory may have held that women were inferior theologically, intellectually, psychologically, and physiologically; that men therefore had to keep them under tight legal, economic, political, and familial control. Practice, however, was often at odds with theory, and theory itself was under attack.

The analogy between sex and authority was most glaringly violated at the very top of the political hierarchy. The presumption of an uncomplicated, unchallenged patriarchy in Renaissance England cannot withstand even a cursory study of the long reigns of Elizabeth I and James I. Neither came to the throne in a direct patrilineal way. Elizabeth was the third and last child of Henry VIII, and the second daughter, to succeed him. The closest male Tudor progenitor for James was his great-great-grandfather Henry VII. The Stuart line was perpetuated by daughters, Margaret Tudor and Mary Stuart. James's foreign birth, an infelicitous feature of his accession, was the direct consequence of his inheritance through the exogamous female line.[9] Patriarchal rules of succession allowed for such inheritance, of course, and so while it may have been disquieting for the English to be governed for seventy-three years without the royal title passing reassuringly from father to eldest son, the social structure could absorb the irregularity.

Elizabeth and James, however, unsettled the analogic foundation of their authority further by presenting their royal personae as androgynous. While androgyny is a divinely transcendent state of being appropriate for sovereign majesty, and not uncommonly claimed by Renaissance princes (Marcus 1986, 58), as a concept it is, as Constance Jordan reminds us, "inimical to patriarchy" (1990a, 28, 15). Whether we view androgyny as a "spirit of reconciliation between the sexes" (Heilbrun 1973, x) and elevate that reconciliation to a spiritual "moment of allegiance to a larger concept of self than merely self" (Kimbrough 1990, 6–7); whether we see it as a return to a stage of childhood development that precedes the "socio-symbolic contract" on which the separation between the sexes is founded (Kristeva 1986, 209–10); or whether we see it, with Jordan, in a social context as the "bigendering of each sex" that leads to social equality (1990a, 28–29), androgyny functions as a flat denial of essentialism in sex and gender. It is not the equivalent of bisexuality or of asexuality, nor is it the equivalent of hermaphroditism, a bodily union of the sexes viewed as monstrous (Belsey 1985, 189).[10] It is a state of being that is simultaneously immanent and, within Renaissance structures of belief, transcendent, an enactment of both sexes in one person and, through that enactment, a recognition in both androgyne and audience that the difference between the sexes is not a simple matter of biology.

We have no way of knowing whether androgyny was Elizabeth's personal or philosophical inclination, but, with her sex a blatant violation of patriarchal intent and her half-sister's career a grim example of female rule, it was clearly a political necessity. When it meant adopting a male persona to deny her biological weakness, androgyny clearly enhanced her effectiveness as a ruler. By laying claim to the inherently masculine authority of the monarchy, she could assume that persona and all the rights accorded the head of a patriarchal state, from arranging marriages to waging war. When expedient, Elizabeth asserted and enacted that maleness: she blurred the sex behind her royalty by using the androgynous "Prince" rather than the feminine "Princess" and, increasingly during her reign, the fully male "King" rather than "Queen" as her title of authority (Marcus 1986, 56–57). Nonetheless, she was ostentatiously female. Gorgeously costumed and habitually flirtatious, she bared breasts and belly—Montrose calls it "erotic provocation" (1983, 34)—to visiting ambassadors and invited courtly adulation well into her old age.

For Elizabeth to put solid ground beneath her royal authority, she had to find sanction for it in the woman's part of that androgynous joining as well as in the man's. The artful solution was what became the Cult of Elizabeth, which gave her femaleness a positive force of its own.[11] Constructed to appear at a mythic remove from the compromising politics of male domination, the Cult of Elizabeth used the queen's hyperbolic virginity as the linchpin in a chain of new hierarchies. Because virginity involved women voluntarily controlling their allegedly voracious sexual appetites, it was an area of female power granted them by and within patriarchal theory and often honored with the highest compliment: it made a woman male.[12]

Virginity, then, allowed Elizabeth to erect an edifice of female-based androgynous power that could exist as a separate and parallel authority structure within the patriarchy. Despite Protestant attempts to displace the Catholic veneration for virginity by exalting the married state, Elizabeth could still build on virginity as a traditionally allowed locus of female power.[13] Virginity also had very practical advantages. By claiming the virgin's allowed control over her own body, she could block any plans to marry her into the reassuringly female and subordinate family roles of wife and, as was fervently hoped, mother. As long as she was the Virgin Queen, she owed obedience only and directly to God and not to a man who, representing God, would stand between her and the governing of England. Her sister Mary's marriage to Philip of Spain, a costly and humiliating mistake, was no doubt educational.

Virginity was not the only area of female authority that Elizabeth assumed into her androgynous monarchy. The Cult of Elizabeth was a coalition of culturally recognized female icons, with the queen as center and reification. By presenting herself as any one of a legendary army of good women from biblical and classical lore—widely celebrated in the ongoing polemical tracts of the *querelles des femmes*—she connected herself to all of them and to the transcendent and divine realms they figured. Nor did she stop at sacred sanction for her womanhood. From the natural world, she absorbed into her public self the figure of Dame Nature and presented herself as exhibiting the best of Nature's gifts to women—beauty, strength, youth, fertility—maintaining her title to these attributes even after they had become obvious fictions. In the specifically and centrally human realm that mediated between the divine and the natural, she gave female form to the authority of education, wit, cultivation, and political acumen.

And so, while Elizabeth's androgyny asserted her possession of the male authority of kingship and the qualities identified with it, it also created an equal and viable authority based on her biological sex. Under her direction, her femaleness was more than invidious not-maleness. If, in the political structure of hierarchies that she inherited, Elizabeth's authority was compromised, in the mythological structure she created, she was the perfect monarch. Androgynous not simply by way of compensation—denying her femaleness and claiming maleness—she created a system that gave her full authority as both male and female. As an androgyne, she could play any role her state and survival required.

Sometimes the role required her to deny the female authority she had created. Appearing on horseback at Tilbury dressed, in one account, "as armed Pallas," she addressed the English army before the anticipated battle with the Spanish Armada, announcing that she had "the body but of a weak and feeble woman, but . . . the heart and stomach of a king, and of a King of England too" (Somerset 464).[14] Certainly that statement, as Belsey says, uses her voice "most famously to deny her femininity" (1985, 180). Yet the context demands closer attention. At Tilbury, she was not the queen receiving ambassadors, meeting with ministers, or dallying with courtiers. She appeared in a military role as head of the English army. Like Shakespeare's Henry V before Agincourt (his identity, however, unlike hers disguised from his men), she began by confirming her soldiers' fears: I am a woman and therefore physiologically unapt for war. In the same announcement, however, she rhetorically prepared them for better news: I am also a king, and "a King of England too," with the courage to lead them to victory. By acknowledging her assumed weakness, Elizabeth deflected attention from it, as Marcus says, disabling "her audience's resistance to the invisible truth that follows"

(1986, 56). If she did indeed appear as armed Pallas, her physical representation reinforced the verbal paradox. She could be both a woman and a man by being neither and both, by creating the suggestion that she was Athena, the wise, divine, androgynous warrior whose palladium had protected Troy. And so what Elizabeth confessed, she unconfessed; what she gave to her male heart and stomach, she dressed as a female god.

The intended cumulative effect of costume and rhetoric on her troops was equally double: she asked them as chivalrous men to come to the defense of a helpless woman while simultaneously challenging them to be as manly as their king. Elizabeth's androgyny was pragmatic. As a woman, she could inspire chivalry when she claimed weakness, veneration when she claimed spiritual superiority. As a man, she could dominate and challenge men by claiming a kingly heart and stomach. Her strategy for maintaining political control could and did include demeaning women; it could not and did not include demeaning men. While maleness was problematized and arguably undermined by servitude to a woman, Elizabeth made sure that it was also recognized and admired. From the moment she pronounced her coronation ring the symbol of her marriage to her people, she cast her subjects, and especially the courtiers who closely attended her, in the collective role of chaste and faithful spouse. For a man to serve Elizabeth was to be subjected to her, but it was also to play the male part opposite England's still unravished bride. Her object was to maintain her royal authority, and that meant keeping control of the people around her, making sure the roles played opposite her were always to her advantage.

While Elizabeth accepted and used the essentialism of her society's ideology, then, her androgynous persona denied it, weakening the foundation of male domination. The creation of such an implicitly dangerous new structure of authority might not have worked politically if it had not worked poetically. As important as the construct itself was the method of its dissemination. Elizabeth not only fashioned herself in a public way as the center of a national theater, but, from her coronation through her queenly progresses and court ceremonies, she also demonstrated an extraordinary ability to involve others in that theater. Within the carefully proscribed limits of the genre she established, she invited the creative artists of her realm to collaborate improvisationally with her. Her invitation to participate in the queen's self-creation engaged the men of her court and country through their ambition, their courtliness, their spirit of competition. The result could be challenge and subversion: Montrose points to a subtext of male opposition to female rule in *A Midsummer Night's Dream* (1983), and Frye exposes the violence of Spenser's reproductions of Elizabeth in *The Faerie Queene* (1993, 97–147). Yet, in the usual way of subversion, those challenges also reiterated and reinforced the icon they sought to topple.

Elizabeth's combination of domination and coquetry was not without problems. It resulted in, indeed depended on, her maintaining a high level of male frustration. Witness, for example, Simon Forman's famous dream of breaking that intricate knot by impregnating the little old lady in the garden. And, indeed, when her aged body made it impossible for men to play the game with unfeigned enthusiasm, when Essex cut the knot by attempting to seize the power that she would not unambiguously give, she could no longer maintain her authority in the same way. In her last decade as an increasingly isolated old woman pursuing unpopular foreign and domestic policies, the high gloss of Elizabeth's cult began to fade. With a male inheritor who had begotten sons waiting across the border, the female authority of Elizabeth's androgynous structure began to dissolve, her mystical male body alone commanding respect.

Courtiers and ambassadors visited James in Scotland, with statesmen as highly placed as Cecil and Harrington courting, secretly of course, the next king by letter; *Basilikon Doron* became a "bestseller" (Wormald 1991, 51) in England. Clearly, it was unnecessary to pay more than lip service to Elizabeth's stale and now embarrassing assertions of virgin strength and beauty. As England chafed under her longevity, the androgynous art form of the realm's female monarch was an ideal fading in the bright sun of male hope. Yet her mythic creation was so deeply embedded in the national psyche, so identified with the England she had governed for close to half a century, that it would linger and indeed revive after her death when no longer she but James would prove the grievous disappointment.[15]

The royal claim to androgyny, with its inherent challenge to the essentialism of patriarchal theory, continued after her death. James's self-styled androgyny, however, did not honor women as Elizabeth's honored men. It did not have to. His emphasis on male privilege and his isolation from women, whenever he could manage it, rendered his rhetorical assumption of women's biological capacities a hostile appropriation. When he presented himself as sire and wet nurse—"A loving nourish-father" (James I 1918, 24)—to England, he was not affirming female nurture.[16]

Like his claims to absolute authority, androgyny made him a god, as Jonathan Goldberg says, "*sui generis*, self-contained as a hermaphrodite, an ideal form" (1989, 142)—but a specifically male god who had absorbed, in order to eliminate, women. His androgyny was exclusive rather than inclusive, seeming, in fact, a yearning for both parthenogenesis and divine autogeny.[17]

Certainly James emphasized his maleness, claiming all the rights of his biological sex. Pointedly reversing Elizabeth's coronation vow to be the bride of her people by assigning that role to London at his coronation and declaring himself England's husband and master in his first address to Parliament—"I am the Husband, all the whole Isle my lawfull Wife; I am the Head, and it is my body" (1918, 272)—James cast himself as the natural apex of all hierarchies, an analogic convergence. His insistence on the given rights of men and his strong, misogynistic opposition to women assuming authority seemed to underscore the return to a strict patriarchalism with the head of state ruling as dominant male. Yet while he offered an anxious patriarchy the proper sex at long last, he also metaphorically transformed the men of England, accustomed to playing Elizabeth's male consorts, into submissive and obedient wives, bodies to his head.

Because King James's sex conformed to patriarchal theory, his claim to androgyny was inherently more disturbing than Elizabeth's. It was subtraction by addition: the presumed superiority of the male compromised by the addition of the female. Nor did his royal behavior and public attitudes conform to contemporary English traditions of male gender. In adopting *beati pacifici*, for example, "Blessed are the peacemakers," as a personal motto, James assumed a culturally female attribute (Jordan 1990, 8). For those Englishmen who had, during Elizabeth's reign, defined manhood in military terms, the king's pacifist foreign policy, especially toward Catholic Spain, seemed cowardly and womanish. James honored maleness, but as it was defined by him and in him, certainly not in the shape of hero-adventurer relics of a former age like Sir Walter Raleigh. He used his position to intensify the cultural assertion of male domination, but he revised the definition of male gender, thereby recreating the conflict between royal authority and maleness that he was supposed to resolve.

The most problematic revision occurred in his public displays of love for male favorites. Perhaps, as Goldberg observes, James's claim to androgyny was a transparent veil for his sexual preference for men (1989, 142); certainly his behavior blurred the sexual binary on which the theory of patriarchy rests.[18] Francis Osborne speaks of the king's "love, or what else posterity will please to call it" for his favorites, his "kissing them after so lascivious a mode in publick, and upon the theatre, as it were, of the world," that many wondered what occurred "in the tyring-house" (Ashton 1969, 114). Simonds D'Ewes, in a diary record of a conversation, calls that love by the name Osborne claims to leave to posterity:

> Of things I discoursed with him that weere secrett as of the sinne of sodomye, how frequent it was in this wicked cittye, and if God did not provide some wonderfull blessing against it, wee could not but expect some horrible punishment for it; especially it being as wee had probable cause to feare, a sinne in the prince as well as the people, which God is for the most part the chastiser of himself, because noe man else indeed dare reprove or tell them of ther faults.
>
> (Qtd. in Bergeron 1991, 183)

English court gossip in general supports D'Ewes's assumption although usually, as with Osborne, the demonizing word *sodomy* is avoided. *Corona regia*, written in the Spanish Netherlands, was more forthcoming with the accusation, and James responded by attempting, unsuccessfully, to have its author identified and punished (Sommerville 1991, 59).

With the traditional definition of male gender rewritten from the throne of England, heterosexual men found themselves again in positions of subjection that were uneasily comparable to women's. No matter how much men of the court might demonstrate authority by manipulating the king's sexual attentions and favors, their construction of male gender was no longer mirrored at the top of the hierarchy that gave the king authority over them. Under Elizabeth, their maleness had remained normative. Now they were themselves Other, and not without political repercussions for James and his claim to absolute authority. He had reopened the division between sex and authority that Elizabeth fought to close. Again a subject could find grounds for disobedience to his monarch. Osborne's example of Sir Henry Rich, who lost an opportunity for advancement by "turning aside and spitting after the king had slabered his mouth" (Ashton 1969, 114), offers an instance. Rich's understanding of his sex and gender had cultural and, he would have assumed, divine sanction; the monarch's laid claim to divine sanction and, moreover, had direct political implications. In Rich's disgusted and defiant public response to James's overtures, we see a courtier who—like Essex

and like the rebels of revenge tragedy—used the divided structure of authority to refuse subjection.

That the marginalization of heterosexual men placed them in
their relationship to the king on culturally equal, if not identical,
ground with women boded both good and ill for women. The
seemingly tyrannical rule of another man could create a male
backlash of sympathy and respect—a balancing philogyny already present in the iconography of Elizabeth's female rule—and
a willingness to allow women to speak in the public arena, in
part as a signifier of the unnaturalness of political authority. Yet
because the equality of position was based on a diminution of
men's authority, it could also create a defensive exaggeration of
men's difference from women and a hypertrophe of women's
alleged weaknesses, in short, misogyny. The coexistence of opposite responses, with the possibility of their being housed in the
same person at the same or at different times, is what we find in
the male rivals of revenge tragedy.

The pressure of royal approval and example, albeit dubious and
ambiguous, supported misogyny. Certainly Queen Anna could
not sustain Elizabeth's affirmation of women. She was not allowed
into the political arena; she was eventually not allowed into the
king's private quarters. She governed her own court, an important center of patronage in the arts (Barroll 1991, 205–8), and
she used the masque to establish her own subversive political
presence in the court (Wynne-Davies 1992, 86), but to King James
she was a necessary and barely tolerated adjunct. The women of
the court were equally reduced: gifted women like Arbella Stuart
and Mary Wroth were forcibly restrained from asserting the political and artistic rights of their birth, while gossip constructed the
queen's ladies as vainer, sillier, and more extravagant than Elizabeth's. An ambient disdain for the female sex, of course, puts
pressure on women to behave like the unthreateningly foolish
creatures that they are assumed to be. In James's court, a woman's
place was apart from men, her function to procreate at the will
of her husband and to spend, or appear to spend, her time gossip-
ing benignly in the spaces allowed her life.

The resurgence of misogynist discourse in Jacobean England,
then, can be understood as resulting from very specific historical
causes: the king's overt antifeminism, the defensive male response to James's problematizing of heterosexuality, the queen's
peripheral participation in political life. Steven Mullaney (1994)
has persuasively argued for misogyny's relationship to mourning
for Queen Elizabeth. Misogyny was also, however, the result of

the apotheosis of female virtue in the Cult of Elizabeth. The political need for Elizabeth to stress her purity had widened the cultural split in the category of women. If during her reign she had taken the allowed power of virginity and used it to construct her own separate power structure, she had also reinforced the view that women unlike her were inherently wicked and licentious. Not even she herself could escape the force of that division, repeatedly falling victim to rumors of promiscuity. The necessary presence of female evil as the defining other half of Elizabeth's purity left the culture's misogynistic assumptions intact while a woman's presence on the throne had made its public expression unacceptable. All the stronger for its underground life, then, misogyny could reemerge as much in reaction to the queen's long control over sexual ideology as to the new king's male absolutism.

Had James become a loved and respected king, maleness and authority might have reunited in English society, with misogyny functioning as an extreme but unchallenged cultural attitude. Biology, however, did not prove enough. Bullied by petitioners, prodigal with money and titles, dominated by favorites and sycophants, unwilling to assume the quotidian duties of the monarchy, James quickly became an unpopular figure.[19] He was king of England by the thread of analogy that connected maleness and monarchy, and he had problematized the analogy. The climate was propitious for nostalgia. The good old queen and the mythological structure of virtue she had magnified into a national art and identity began to revive as justice, righteousness, and virtue appeared to vanish from the court. If the anticipation of James had undermined Elizabeth's authority in her last years, her haunting of James's reign returned the favor. The mythology of Elizabeth, floating free of her deteriorating natural body and her personal dominance, could attach itself to brave and virtuous women. For Esther Sowernam in 1617, her virtue was a model for both sexes: "Elizabeth, our late Sovereign, not only the glory of our Sex, but a pattern for the best men to imitate, of whom I will say no more but that while she lived, she was the mirror of the world, so then known to be, and so still remembered, and ever will be" (Henderson and McManus 1985, 231). Created as a theatrical form, the cult that had glorified female virtue was particularly useful in the representation of women in revenge tragedy, the darkly nostalgic genre devoted to the exposure of injustice, favoritism, and corruption.[20]

Under both James and Elizabeth, the patriarchal foundation of the social edifice—biological, heterosexual essentialism—was more sand than rock. In the final analysis, cultural maleness was politically more effective than biological maleness. A female monarch who could display herself when the occasion arose as aggressively and confidently militaristic was a more satisfying Renaissance monarch than an indolent and pacifist king. "Tom Tell-Troath" writes of those who "wish Queen Elizabeth were alive again, who (they say) would never have suffered the enemies of her religion to have unballanced Christendome, as they have done within these few yeares." "For who would have thought that wee should have lost, but rather infinitely gained, by changing the weaker sexe, for your more noble, to be our commanders" (Ashton 1969, 218, 220). When a woman, a member of the "weaker sexe," can be seen as the better "man," the analogy between sex-gender and authority is anything but firm.

Jacobean Revenge Tragedy: Tyrant, Revenger, Heroine

Like cultural traders, the plays and players of Jacobean England trafficked in the ambient uncertainty, furthering and containing change as they reflected it. The drama's popular genres, while representing the time's unruly mutability, also offered audiences fictions that seemed to control and contain it. Revenge tragedy had become popular during the latter years of Elizabeth's reign, but in the early to mid-Jacobean period that Fredson Bowers titles the "Reign of the Villain and the Disapproval of Revenge" (1940, 154–216), the genre achieved a particular and noteworthy blend of politics and sex, revolution and rape.[21] Concentrating evermore intently on crimes of personal violence committed by the figure authorized to prosecute and punish them, Jacobean revenge tragedy spoke to the cultural moment.

My discussion focuses on four plays—*The Maid's Tragedy, The Second Maiden's Tragedy, Valentinian,* and *The Duchess of Malfi*—which appeared during the years 1610–1613, a time when James's struggles with Parliament over absolute authority made tyranny an inflammatory subject. Chapters 2 and 3 discuss the explicitly male contest between tyrant and revenger. Chapter 2, "The Stage Tyrant and Jacobean Absolutism: In the Throne of God," examines the connection between the theory of absolutism and the representations of tyrants in revenge tragedy, exploring the way these plays translate political debate into sexual terms. The King of *The Maid's Tragedy,* the Emperor of *Valentinian,* and the Tyrant of *The Second Maiden's Tragedy* all declare their divine absolutism by appropriating another man's familial and sexual rights to a woman, thereby absorbing the domestic world into the theory and practice of statecraft. The tyrant sits in the throne of God as if it were his, inscribing the text of his divinity on the bodies of women.

The male characters who not only refuse but return his assault—Maximus and Melantius—are discussed in the third chapter, "The Revenger as Rival Author."[22] Like the tyrant, the revenger accepts the orthodox view that sex and gender are continuous and that maleness is authorizing; in his struggle against the tyrant, he too leaps from a limited, externally granted authority to a godlike freedom from limitation. Because both adhere to a concept of maleness that requires them to declare victory by unmanning and feminizing an opponent, the revenger's triumph does not constitute change but rather reiterates the sexual binarism that initiated the conflict. The failure of both tyrant and revenger to achieve the absolute dominance each seeks suggests that male conflict rewrites itself endlessly in violence and destruction.

Chapter 4, "Androgynous Heroes: Kneeling Soldiers and Swooning Kings," focuses on Affranius and Govianus, those men who do not accept the imprisoningly misogynistic terms of the tyrant's and revenger's definition of maleness. They take their lead from two of the powerful women indigenous to the genre— Eudoxa and the Lady—and move with them into an androgyny that allows them to embrace in themselves attributes constructed as female and to respect in women attributes constructed as male. These figures break the self-perpetuating cycle of endless, futile male rivalry, and their plays close in a promise of social regeneration. The peaceful future of the state indeed rests on men and women breaking through the cultural barriers erected between the sexes.

Chapter 5, "'I am not to be altered': The Authority of Women," concentrates on the plays' heroines, concluding the argument that, under the pressure of tyranny, gender can and must be unlinked from sex. By reintroducing into the political world the religious discourse that supersedes and empowers maleness, and by empowering themselves in and through that discourse, vowing obedience to divine law alone and to men only when they obey it, they contradict the presumption of male dominance and female subjection. The Lady, Lucina, and Eudoxa do not challenge male authority in principle, but they do assume the right to judge men's worthiness to command both the world and them. Like

Elizabeth, they apologize for being mere women, but they take pride in virtues they perceive as inherent in their sex.

Evadne, with her lust for dominance, complements the representation of these heroines by demonstrating the folly of aspiring to a delusionary absolutism that the plays construct repeatedly as both male and tyrannical and, in the process, rejecting the authority of her sex. Though superficially more revolutionary, Evadne is, in fact, trapped and helpless, a misogynist who, like the men who surround her, uses her body as property. She effects no change while her heroic counterparts, supported by the nostalgically glowing structure of female authority that Elizabeth had established, come to represent what should be and, when they find men courageous enough to forge alliances with them, what could be.

Chapter 6 is an exploration of tyrants, a revenger, and an androgynous couple in the years' most famous tragedy, *The Duchess of Malfi*. Although the play does not slip neatly into any category, its marriage of tyranny and sex and its challenge to normative gender systems place it within the genre of revenge. The Duchess and Antonio are destroyed, but the audience's sympathy remains firmly with them, approving their rightful seizure of law and religion from her tyrant brothers.

Gender in Jacobean revenge tragedy, then, is not a simple question of male executioners and female victims. In the plays' violent, sexually conflicted world, characters of both sexes are subjected to and rebel against unprincipled political authority. The revenger's overthrow of the tyrant, however, merely deepens the doubt cast on maleness as the natural and proper basis for authority. Like the posthumous Elizabeth, the heroines and the men who share their androgyny challenge the presumption of male authority. Given the flexible, unorthodox maleness of the players who wrote and acted these characters, it is not surprising to find their dramas populated by women and men who shatter the dogmas that imprison both sexes.

2

The Stage Tyrant and Jacobean Absolutism: In the Throne of God

While revenge tragedy became popular during the troubled latter years of Elizabeth's reign, its bloody heyday occurred during the reign of James I. Fredson Bowers remarks on the change from the "highly moral" Elizabethan plays, where violence was "a testing ground for the human spirit," to the sensational and gratuitous violence of the Jacobean, with its focus not on heroism but on villainy, horror, and love (1940, 154–56).

That the genre altered in the political climate of James's absolutism is strongly suggested by the Jacobean plays' habitual and steady portrayal of rulers as self-authorizing tyrants. We do not find any comparable number of tyrannical rulers occurring in dramas written during Elizabeth's last ten years (Turner 1989, 123). Early English drama in general responded to royal politics and, if in no other way than by censoring it, royal politics responded to the drama. Jacobean revenge tragedy, however, demonstrates a particular and consistent strategy for handling the political issue of absolute monarchy. It focuses on the political through the familial and sexual, translating a matter of state into a competition between men.[1]

To point to the connection between the clash of authorities occasioned by James's speeches and policies and the stage tyrants of revenge tragedy is to say neither that the plays were written in intentional and partisan response to the political debate, although that is possible, nor that the tyrants of revenge tragedy mirror James feature by feature.[2] What is evident is an intense topical interest in tyranny and its effects on subjects' personal and property rights, including and signifying the sexual rights of men. Henry Howard, Earl of Northampton, for example, distinguishes the royal monarch from the tyrannical and the lordly as one who leaves his free-born people "all liberties both of their person and goodes" (qtd. in Peck 1991, 157). Under Stuart monarchy, public discussion of tyranny was suppressed (Bushnell 1990, 72), but in drama, with its honorable tradition of ranting Herods, it was in full voice and view. Whether the players intended their dramas to participate actively in Jacobean politics is a matter of speculation,[3] but it is a certainty that they were plying their trade, capitalizing on the very heated debate of the moment to draw audiences into the playhouses.

Tyranny is a central issue in the trio of revenge tragedies—*The Maid's Tragedy, The Second Maiden's Tragedy,* and *Valentinian*—that appeared at the end of James's first decade of rule, when his financial struggles with Parliament prompted him to emphasize (from his subjects' point of view, to exaggerate) his claim to divine authorization. The King, Valentinian, and the Tyrant, in the genre's hyperbolic mode, distort James's philosophy and policies, having their way not only in the state but in other men's families. In representing their extension of authority as sexually illicit, revenge tragedy criminalizes absolutism, thereby making its premise—the absolute right of the monarch to command and the absolute duty of the subject to obey—relative and conditional. Such a reconfiguration of terms allows damnable regicide and just execution to inhabit the same dramatic landscape. Overtly, the plays support the taboo against killing a king, but regicides like Maximus and Evadne are not punished solely or explicitly for that offense, and Melantius is not punished at all. In revenge tragedy, regicide is not the ultimate crime.

On the English Throne

While his sexual behavior problematized the analogy between royal authority and maleness, James relied on it as the basis for his right to rule. It constituted, for him, a seamless cloth of entitlement. Indeed, absolutist theory answered in advance any objection to the king's performance of the analogy by insisting on the separability of the king's two bodies, his divinely derived authority as male monarch superseding, even absorbing, his fallibility as a mortal man. With not uncommon political irony, however, the theory designed to quell opposition served to create and strengthen it. Radical Protestant groups affirmed the separability of man and monarch while denying James's absolutist premise. By refusing to work through the royal intermediary and bringing God directly into the political discourse, anti-royalists would claim an authority that allowed them to disobey a king and, within a generation of James's determined argument for absolutism, to behead one. They would, however, maintain the analogy between authority and maleness in the private, familial world, and not always to the king's benefit.

In *Basilikon Doron*, the treatise written for his son and heir apparent, James sets forth the absolutist position. He argues that the king, who derives from God, is answerable only to God; that he is the author of law and, therefore, above it; and that, while a good king will obey his country's laws, he is under no compunction to do so. The king, then, has unlimited jurisdiction over his subjects, while only God has jurisdiction over him. According to this theory, a subject is prohibited not only from attempting to overthrow his monarch but also from disobeying him, even, we infer, in issues involving conflicting male rights. If James was, in Shuger's words, "God, pontiff, father" (1990, 156)—even if a nurturing and not a despotic father—then all authority was vested in him, including the authority granted to fathers and husbands within the family.

Despite James's distinction between a good king, who rules in the interest of his people, and a tyrant, who rules from self-interest, the similarity between the two absolute monarchs was both striking and alarming. James routinely tempered his comparisons of kings to God by declaring that the just king governs according to the will of God. In "A Speach in the Starre-Chamber," delivered in 1616, he asserts: "Kings sit in the Throne of GOD, and they themselues are called Gods," but he adds, "And therefore all good Kings in their gouernment, must imitate God and his Christ, in being just and righteous" (James I 1918, 26). His repeated and tactless insistence on his royal prerogatives, however, seemed to confirm suspicion that he had tyrannical inclinations. In a famous speech before Parliament in 1610, he rose to inspired rhetorical heights in his paean to kingship: "The State of MONARCHIE is the supremest thing vpon earth: For Kings are not onely GODS Lieutenants vpon earth, and sit vpon GODS throne, but euen by GOD himselfe they are called Gods" (1918, 307). His ultimate intent in the speech may have been to "adapt his theory to the English situation" by stressing his belief in common law (Christianson 1991, 76–77), and he did frequently deny any intention of depriving his subjects of their native rights and liberties, but such arrogation of divine authority seemed ominous, especially when linked to metaphoric indicators like James's comparison of his suffering to Christ's (Ashton 1969, 144). Gods, after all, do not need to debase themselves before human parliaments.

If an absolute monarch empowers himself by declaring he is God's fellow divinity, those who oppose him empower themselves by affirming God as the only absolute authority, thus constructing themselves as the king's spiritual equals. Such opposition to royalist claims had been emerging in Renaissance Europe during the previous century, largely in response to the religious struggles between Catholic monarchs and Protestant subjects. When religious conscience was at stake, a subject's proper response to a prince no longer had to be unquestioning obedience. The Huguenot Duplessis-Mornay argued that a king who violates God's commands must be opposed, and while he conservatively placed that responsibility only in the hands of the magisterial class, George Buchanan, James's own tutor, held the more radical position that any subject could rise against a tyrannical prince (Pinciss and Lockyer 1989, 132). Opponents of royal absolutism also used divine law to deny the king's right to intervene in the government of the family, constructed as an autonomous little state. "Puritan writing," Tennenhouse observes, "represented the family as a fiefdom within the state over which the monarch had little or no authority" (1986, 172). The "godly household might withdraw into itself rather than associate with sin" (Amussen 1985, 203).

The more James asserted his unlimited and irrevocable authority, the more voluble became the voices for restricting and putting conditions on his rule. He had, in fact, created and empowered an opposing set of rights based on authorities his assertion of divinity had usurped. The political and religious arguments for resistance to tyranny rested on the right of the subject, male or female, to obey God and conscience and of the right of the male subject to govern his family without permission or interference from the king. By separating the source of a monarch's authority from its enactment, absolutist theory created a space in which others could authorize themselves. They could claim to speak for a God whose presence was separate from the king's, whose intent was readable by subject as well as monarch, and who supported a traditionally constructed understanding of maleness to boot.

On the English Stage

Revenge tragedy reflects a full range of variations on royalist and anti-royalist positions. As ideology becomes theater, it is expressed more in the concrete language of gesture, ceremony, and action than in political abstractions. While the drama borrows the language of absolutist debate from treatises for its forensic scenes, its heavier debt is to the physical language of signifiers—the bodily postures that enact ideological postures—that it adapts from the theater of state. The king stands while the subject kneels; speaks while the subject remains silent or speaks only at his request; allows or debars the subject access to his person; controls his subject's ability to marry and procreate and even to live as a free man.

When, for example, the roles of king and subject were reversed, Charles I's accusers used the physically controlling—and, in the cultural context, feminizing—public signifiers he had formerly employed against them to demonstrate their authority over him. They locked him in their prison, forced him to hear their voices in the charges against him, condemned him to death, and, finally, brought him to his knees on the scaffold of his execution. During his humiliations, Charles maintained his dignity and manhood by protesting that his submission was not to them but only to God, thereby replicating the self-authorizing claim to enact God's will that his judges had made when they were subjects and, often, prisoners of the crown.

In such deeply ingrained gestures of dominance and submission, the bedrock of analogy between the political and the sexual has great residual power. The male subject, in a smoothly functioning political hierarchy, must at some time forego the display of male gender and play the woman's part. Yet the rationale that underwrites the hierarchy, the rituals that perpetuate it, and, above all, the exclusion of women from it, all maintain and valorize the maleness of subjected men. When, however, the relationship between men in superior and inferior positions in the hierarchy is no longer based on such a mutually honored set of signs, the affirming bond between them becomes rivalry, the gestures of fealty female and feminizing. The tyrant's power over his male subjects relies, in fact, on their mutual misogyny in understanding signifiers of femaleness as degrading to men.

The tyrants of *The Maid's Tragedy*, *Valentinian*, and *The Second Maiden's Tragedy*, evocatively named King, Emperor Valentinian, and Tyrant, are images not of James himself but of the ruler his opponents feared he might become. They embrace without qualification the absolutist position that separates the source of their authority from their enactment of it; James had theorized—although in his critics' eyes failed to practice—the good king's imitation of "God and his Christ." The theatrical tyrants rule not for God, but as God, a categoric leap conflating political authority

and maleness, its traditional basis and signifier, thereby rewriting
the definition of both. Their sexuality, therefore, can depart, as
did James's, from the cultural standard, which in the plays is
embodied by their rivals and represented as military and familial.[4]
As divine authorization slides into divinity, authority becomes
authorship, a megalomaniacal flight into autogeny and parthenogenesis that appropriates the biology and gender of both sexes.
The tyrant has authored himself, and he has the right to author
his subjects: they become, in Valentinian's word, his "creatures."

In revenge tragedy, those creatures are forced to assume the
shape of the tyrant's sexual fantasies. Women are not allowed
autonomy; they are passive matter he shapes, like a Baconian
scientist, to his will. Adopting the most conservative and misogynistic of his culture's attitudes, he uses the female body as his
text. Women must indeed be chaste, silent, and obedient, but to
him alone. Men, therefore, must be his cuckolds and panders,
roles that validate his sexual dominance by denying theirs. The
tyrant erases the cultural signifiers of their maleness, which have
as their locus the private world of the family and extend outward
to the public arena. In the early Jacobean *Revenger's Tragedy*, for
example, the Duke unmans two generations of one family, dis-
gracing and exiling father and sons. As self-proclaimed head of
state and family, the revenge tyrant marries mothers, seduces
sisters, and rapes wives, in the process infantilizing sons, undermining brothers, and, most publicly shameful, cuckolding husbands. The horned figure is no longer a man but a beast, forced
to display the sign that represents both his own forfeited and
displaced potency and the cuckolder's sexual dominance.[5]
Through the agency of a woman theoretically subject to him, he
is made subject to another man.

In plays like *The Maid's Tragedy* and *Valentinian*, the tyrant inten-
sifies the sexual degradation by maneuvering his rival into the
role of pander, thereby forcing him to collude in his own cuckolding. Amintor is married to Evadne in order to go between her
and the King; Maximus, forced to gamble and lose his ring to
Valentinian, is made the Emperor's instrument in luring Lucina
to the court and her rape. Pandering, as Govianus sternly informs
the Lady's father in *The Second Maiden's Tragedy*, is an "unmanly
sin" (2.1.29); "'tis not man's work" (3.1.3–4). A scene from *The
Revenger's Tragedy* suggests the explanation for Govianus's rebuke.
As Lussurioso hands over money to seal his bargain with Vindice
disguised as the pander Piato, he announces, "And thus I enter
thee" (1.3.85). In both physical unions identified with that allu-

sion—demonic possession and sexual penetration—Lussurioso's line identifies the pander as female to his male. When the tyrant forces the role of pander of an unwilling rival like Amintor or Maximus, his sexual domination is a form of rape.

Pandering, then, is not merely unmanly but feminizing. When the tyrant forces a man to cede the signifiers of his maleness and assume those of femaleness—in Stallybras's succinct formulation, the enclosed body, the closed mouth, and the locked house (1986, 127)—he has successfully authored himself as sole male by authoring other men as women. The tyrant controls and encloses his rival's body sexually by denying him access to his wife or betrothed, in the case of Vindice's Duke by murdering Gloriana when she refuses to submit to him.

The tyrant also controls his rival's other phallic signifier, the tongue. The rival is disallowed presence and voice in the political world of men, permitted to appear in court only on the tyrant's command, to remain there only as long as he adopts public postures of submission, and to speak only if his speech is ventriloquized. Often, in addition to enclosing his body and closing his mouth, the tyrant completes the feminization of his rival by driving him out of the male world altogether into banishment or prison, the locked house to which the tyrant alone holds the key. The rival has no active recourse for his sexual subjection except revenge.

The stage tyrant's flamboyant violations concretize in extreme form the contemporary fear that an absolute ruler could invade the family and seize his subject's right to govern as absolute monarch there. Given the connection between a man's commanding position in the family and his social validation as male, any usurpation of that position is a claim to absolute ownership of male gender. Not only can the king assert his right to transgress the boundaries of the family, he can also declare those boundaries illegitimate, substituting state for family and monarch for father and husband.

The Breath of Kings

The degree of personal injury inflicted by the tyrants of these three plays on their rivals depends on a number of variables: the extent of the male subject's belief in divine right and, therefore, in his forced passivity before the injury; the relationship between the woman who has been the instrument of his cuckolding and the tyrant; and, most important, the violence of his reaction to an injury he interprets, correctly, as an attack on his maleness. When tyrant and rival agree on the misogynistic terms of their culture's gender binary, and when the rival will not accept the authority that denies him permission to respond to the tyrant's assault, the play ends in the bloodbath of regicide and revenge that is the genre's hallmark.

Even before the King's entrance, the rhetoric of *The Maid's Tragedy* constructs him as an absolute monarch in the style of James. "The breath of kings is like the breath of gods" (1.1.15),[6] announces Lysippus, a simile the King transforms into equation. His courtiers also ignore "like" and obey his commands even when they contradict other claims on them. When Melantius rebukes his brother for disobeying his order to follow him to the wars, Diphilus responds, "my excuse / Is my king's strict command" (1.1.31–32). Amintor does not marry the woman he has promised because "the King forbade it" (1.1.138). Neither Diphilus nor Amintor are troubled by their transgressions: Diphilus cheerfully welcomes his brother to court; Amintor is pleased to marry the beautiful Evadne. Although he will at first take responsibility for jilting Aspatia—"he [the King] / Has not my will in keeping"—he shakes off his guilt only four lines later: "I only brake a promise, / And 'twas the King that forced me" (2.1.130–31, 135–36), he says, brushing aside a premonitory frisson. The King has successfully directed obedience to him alone.

When his claim to that unquestioned obedience challenges the chain of family command, however, the King becomes a rival to the men of his realm. His countermanding Melantius's command to Diphilus clearly usurps the elder brother's rights, preventing him from initiating Diphilus into the family's tradition of military service to the state. The military tradition loosens the personal bonds of loyalty between monarch and subject, allowing a man to commit his loyalty and obedience to the idea of a country rather than to the monarch who represents, and claims to be, that country. Instead of allowing Melantius to shape Diphilus in the family tradition as a soldier, the King authors the younger man as a courtier. In refusing Aspatia's and Amintor's betrothal, he invades another family, there interfering with Calianax's paternal right to arrange his daughter's marriage. Even the foolish, bullying old sycophant whom Evadne's soldierly brother Melantius calls "unmanly" (1.2.63) and "womanish" (70) questions the king's right to that interference: "The King may do this, and he may not do it; / My child is wronged, disgraced" (2.2.83–84).

The King's liaison with Evadne makes the invasive pattern explicitly sexual as he seizes from brother and then husband their right to command her obedience, her tongue, and her body. The King has emptied the rival roles of brother, husband, and father of their authority and absorbed them into his monarchy. Evadne serves as the King's surrogate in the sexual contest between him and Amintor, an empowering role she is initially pleased to perform. Because the King has cloaked her in his own authority, he has made her as autonomous, as culturally male, as he to all men except, he believes, to him.

Amintor's wedding night is not his sexual initiation into manhood, but rather a vying with Evadne for authority in a marriage that is, he will learn, an extension of the state. He reads Evadne's reluctance to come to bed as a bride's modesty and refuses at first to understand her scornful "A maidenhead, Amintor, / At my years!" (2.1.194–95): either she jests or she raves (168, 229; 195). No less than his ability to live as male in his society is at stake, and he alternates between begging and menacing her to act the role of wife: he appeals to the coy (159, 213), mild (168), "sweet" (181) woman she is supposed to be; he rages and vows to "scorn [Hymen's] laws" (219) and turn from marriage and legitimate children to rape and adoption. Finally, he threatens violence. Because he is a man, he is able to force her, and because he is a husband, he is entitled to force her:

> I'll drag thee to my bed, and make thy tongue
> Undo this wicked oath, or on thy flesh
> I'll print a thousand wounds to let out life.
>
> (2.1.277–79)

Evadne, however, cuts the sinews of his strength by appealing to the superior male authority of the King. Within the state, he learns, he is the King's subject; within the family, Evadne's.

The full extent of their reversal of gender is evident in the ensuing scene with the King. Amintor has asked Evadne not to "let the King / Know I conceive he wrongs me" (339–40) because only her silence protects him from the impossible choice of having either to defend his honor as a man or to admit that he has been rendered powerless to defend it. Endangered by the King's jealous accusations that she has allowed Amintor to cuckold *him*, Evadne snatches away the last thread of Amintor's protection. She not only breaks her promise of silence—"Fear not, I will do this" (356), she has reassured him—but also demands that he confess to the King that they have not consummated their marriage. The woman whose tongue should be his to command commands his, and he is forced to abase himself verbally before the man who has sexually humiliated him. To that, Amintor gives a name:

> Y'are a tyrant, and not so much to wrong
> An honest man thus, as to take a pride
> In talking with him of it.
>
> (3.1.222–24)

The tyrant King, with Evadne's assistance, has both unmanned and feminized Amintor—"the harem master teasing his eunuch" (Squier 1986, 97). Together, they have enclosed his body by disallowing his marriage to Aspatia and denying him sexual access to his lawful wife. Now they have closed his mouth by making any public revelation a confession of his shame while forcing him to hear the king speak of his cuckolding. They have, moreover, assigned him the empty role of husband to which he must frame his speech, a ventriloquism that is an even greater violation than forced silence. It is an impossible conflict: maintaining silence and pretending joy in his marriage protects him from exposure as a cuckold, but it simultaneously makes him a woman not only to his sovereign but to his wife as well.

Because Amintor believes unswervingly in the religious grounds for a subject's submission to his sovereign, he believes himself powerless to take revenge for his injury:

> I fear not swords, for, as you are mere man,
> I dare as easily kill you for this deed
> As you dare think to do it: but there is
> Divinity about you, that strikes dead
> My rising passions. As you are my king,
> I fall before you and present my sword
> To cut mine own flesh if it be your will.
>
> (3.1.236–42)

In Amintor's acceptance of the argument that divides man from king, he can at least mitigate his shame by constructing it as the proper obedience of a subject: the King's rights as sovereign supersede his rights as husband. Amintor's presentation of his sword makes the sexual negotiation of their positions clear: if the King so wills, he may confiscate Amintor's phallic authority and use it against him. In the same gesture, however, Amintor maintains a semblance of male control and dignity by kneeling not to the "mere man" but to the divinity he represents.

The King's offer to bribe Amintor to be his pander, however, shatters that fragile dignity, and Amintor is brought back to the point of violence from which he had retreated:

> A bawd! Hold, hold my breast! A bitter curse
> Seize me if I forget not all respects
> That are religious, on another word
> Sounded like that, and through a sea of sins
> Will wade to my revenge . . . .
>
> (3.1.270–74)

To submit to the King on religious principle allows Amintor to continue to see himself as a man; to be asked to pander his wife for reward, however, is a crime against his manhood so serious that Amintor, in that moment, dismisses religious considerations and considers revenge.

The King exits before any violence can occur, but he and Evadne have made it impossible for Amintor to function as male in the public world, and the young man's subsequent behavior disintegrates into an irrationality that verges on hysteria, a woman's ailment: he weeps, he mopes, he laughs. His conduct draws the attention and sympathy of Melantius, whose repeated protestations of love succeed in freeing Amintor's tongue, but confession does not restore him to maleness. While Melantius weeps with and for him, the older man at last tells him to "cast a manly look upon my face" (3.2.196). He humors Amintor and attempts to lock him away from harm as if he were a weak, helpless dependent—as if he were his wife.

Amintor never recovers male gender, even in death. Aspatia, cross-dressed in the disguise of her brother, insults and kicks him into a duel. She dies as she planned, consummating their aborted marriage with Amintor's sword; again, he is the agent of another man-woman's will. Taunted into defending his soldier's honor, he finds that he has succeeded only in violating it. Only by turning his sword against himself does he regain a semblance of autonomous control over that signifier of his manhood. It will be the brother Melantius, not the cuckolded husband Amintor, who becomes the tyrant's revenging rival because, unlike Amintor, Melantius will neither acknowledge the divine right of a king who violates his manhood nor allow a woman to use that authority to supplant his.

Beaumont and Fletcher's *The Maid's Tragedy,* and the genre to which it belongs, tests the doctrine of divine right by exaggerating absolutism into tyranny and placing the state in direct conflict with the family.[7] To stage the overthrow of a king, revenge tragedy criminalizes absolutism and then shapes it to the genre's insistence on punishment for transgression. Political oppression is reconfigured as sexual assault, and the tyrannical monarch pays with his life for violating not the political but the sexual rights of his subjects. While the treatment of regicide in *The Maid's Tragedy* is "evasive" (Craik 1988, 12)—the killer commits suicide over love rather than from guilt, and the crime's plotter goes unpunished by the state—we are left with the feeling, as Finkelpearl states, that "the king, for the devastation of private lives by public power, deserves to be expunged" (1990, 206). When we add the construction of Evadne's stabbing of the king as an act of passion (Bushnell 1990, 169), we find the culture's sexual discourse, with its emphasis on gendered roles within the family, supplanting the political discourse. A king who violates the sanctity of a subject's family and body can be killed with impunity.

Raping the Soldier

In *Valentinian* as well as in *The Maid's Tragedy,* political absolutism is translated into sexual criminality. Situated in Rome, the setting regularly used to reflect Jacobean England,[8] *Valentinian* conflates the cuckolded husband Amintor and the soldier revenger Melantius in the single figure of Maximus. The rivalry between Maximus, who, like Melantius, locates male gender in a family tradition of military service, and the Emperor Valentinian, who claims sovereign authority against that tradition, is again simultaneously political and sexual, with absolutism once more represented as a tyrannical invasion of the family.

Cuckolding Maximus is richly satisfying for Valentinian. Not only does it satisfy his considerable lust for Lucina—he enjoys the rape and informs her he is "the same man still, / Were it to doe again"; "Ye are so excellent, and made to ravish" (3.1.100–101, 103)[9]—but it also forces her warrior husband to acknowledge powerlessness—impotence—before his monarch. The rape announces publicly that Valentinian's predatory and uncontrolled sexuality, an aspect of his self-authored divinity, supersedes the Roman military and patrician construction of male gender.

Valentinian's enactment of maleness, like James's, runs contrary to cultural tradition. The soldierly Pontius, Aecius reports, has seditiously preached that it was dishonorable for soldiers "to serve a Prince so full of woman" (2.3.27). Seduction is the only war in which that Prince excels; he is general and master strategist of his army of bawds and panders. Nor is his lust restricted to women: Maximus will later allude darkly to the tricks of the Emperor's eunuchs and black-eyed boys. Valentinian, however, in his godlike conjunction of political and sexual authority, sweeps aside Pontius's view of what constitutes a man. In terms of absolutist theory, Valentinian is his own standard, above tradition as well as law.

The doctrine of absolutism is argued even more prominently and heatedly in *Valentinian* than in *The Maid's Tragedy*. Prompted by defection among Roman colony nations and unrest in the army, Aecius and Maximus confront the question, using both the abstract terms of absolutist discourse and the specific case of the Emperor Valentinian to position themselves. The immitigable authority of the Prince is forcefully defended by Aecius, who categorically denies a subject's right to overthrow him under any circumstances:

> We are but subjects *Maximus;* obedience
> To what is done, and griefe for what is ill done,
> Is all we can call ours: the hearts of Princes
> Are like the Temples of the gods; pure incense,
> Untill unhallowed hands defile those offrings,
> Burnes ever there; we must not put 'em out,
> Because the Priests that touch those sweetes, are wicked . . . .
> (1.3.17–23)

Like Amintor, Aecius justifies behavior he would otherwise eschew as unmanly. His position, like James's, is rooted in the conflation of divine and human law. Only God, and the Prince in his name, can make law; subjects are bound to obey the laws of both. Whether the wicked Priests Aecius refers to are sycophants or Princes themselves is ambiguous, but the argument remains the same. A subject "dare not," "cannot" (24) put out the fire in that sacred temple. The Prince's two bodies are separable, and the subject obeys the sanctified body politic, no matter what.

Ignoring Aecius's analogical grounds for obedience in the rule of "Gods and Angels" (28), Maximus secularizes the debate, arguing instead from the traditions of the Roman state as they move from generation to generation, from father to son. Three times he invokes patrilinear descent: "Or are we now no more the sons of *Romanes*"; "And to what end, are we the sonnes of Fathers / Famous, and fast to *Rome?*"; "Why are we seeds of these then, to shake hands / With Bawdes and base Informers . . ." (38, 48–49, 53–54). Maximus replaces the hierarchy that places Valentinian above him, as Melantius does, with one based on filial loyalty to father and state. Rome is not its Emperor but its patrician family, the rival male hierarchy in which Maximus is Valentinian's superior.

The events of the play move general and soldier to the extremes of their positions. In the ensuing scene, Aecius attributes his military prowess as a soldier to Valentinian's authorship: "all that goodness / Is but your Graces creature" (120–21). Echoing Amintor's gesture, he will later turn his sword against himself rather than against God's deputy. Maximus, on the other hand, extricates himself from the hierarchy Aecius defends to authorize himself as his Prince's judge and rival author.

The "ought to be" god Valentinian recognizes Maximus as the man he must defeat and humiliate, beginning, like the King, by invading his rival's family and shattering its illusion of autonomy. He is offended, he tells Lucina, that her "daring husband" has "kept an Offring from the Empire / Too holy for his Altars" (3.1.112–14). The terms of Lucina's pleading only incite and excite him more: "Consider what I am, and whose" (2.6.10), she begs:

> His fame and family have growne together
> And spred together like two sayling Cedars,
> Over the *Roman* Diadem; ô let not,
> (As ye have any flesh that's humane in you)
> The having of a modest wife decline him,
> Let not my vertue be the wedge to break him. . . .
>
> (24–29)

In presenting Maximus as a rival and spreading male authority and reminding Valentinian of the position of Maximus's family "over" Rome, she merely extends his anticipation of pleasure from the sexual to the political. Moreover, in her appeal for Valentinian to show humanity, in her hope that he is "too neere the nature of the Gods, / To wrong the weakest of all creatures: Women" (33–34), she boldly presumes an authority that exists before and beyond his.

Valentinian delights not only in the rape but in his correction of her "neere": "Justice shall never heare ye, I am Justice" (3.1.34). Rather than deify his humanity by mirroring divinity, he humanizes his borrowed divinity by having the gods excuse criminal acts. They are extensions of his will, not he of theirs: "For as they make me most, they meane me happiest, / Which I had never bin without this pleasure" (130–31). A mortal man's fame and family mean nothing to him: "Your husband cannot help ye, nor the Souldier, / Your husband is my creature, they my weapons, / And only where I bid 'em, strike; I feed 'em . . ." (126–28). What she believes is hers and separate from the state, "Your husband," is his and a subject of the state, "my creature." Maximus, Valentinian declares, has no autonomous authority; like Aecius, he is a creature authored and used by his Emperor, an instrument and puppet without a will of his own.

In the tyrant's vein, Valentinian declares victory over his rival by unmanning and feminizing him. Lucina's rape and subsequent suicide deny Maximus the right to function as male within his family. Moreover, Valentinian has sexually violated him by making him the unwitting pander to his own cuckolding: "T'has pleasd the Emperor, my Noble master, / For all my services, and dangers for him, / To make me mine owne Pandar" (164–66), Maximus remarks with bitter irony. Valentinian now governs his body, his physical space, and his tongue, and, like Amintor, he finds that last appropriation especially humiliating: "It was my wife the Emperor abus'd thus; / And I must say, I am glad I had her for him; / Must I not my *Aecius?*" (287–89). He is, perforce, chaste, silent, and obedient.

In the scenes following his discovery of Lucina's rape, Maximus ignores the injury to her and broods over his own, exploring the meaning of his obliteration as a man: he has no home; no friends (he believes Aecius is mad to keep him company); no right to wear a sword—he is "a fellow / My own Sword would forsake, not tyed unto me." He corrects his initial assessment of his new state: "A Pandar is a Prince, to what I am falne; / By heaven I dare do nothing" (294–95; 96–97). Ranging freely and seemingly randomly across the analogous hierarchies of his world, he redefines himself according to the nonmale categories to which not only Valentinian but he himself assigns him. He is "a branded slave," "a child" (298, 302). He cannot rejoin the army, he says, because his fellow soldiers, by implication still men, will cut his throat: "I am an Enemy, a wicked one, / Worse than the foes of *Rome*, I am a Coward, / A Cuckold, and a Coward, that's two causes / Why every one should beat me" (3.3.82–85). Pander, slave, child, enemy of Rome, coward, cuckold: all share the female side of the cultural binary that identifies mastery with maleness.

Unlike Govianus, Maximus has no inclinations toward androgyny. He believes in the rightness of that binary: everyone
"should" beat him.

As he and Valentinian have constructed it, his position is intolerable. Unable to accept Aecius's justification of unmanly inaction
as honorable piety, he will not be the passive receptacle of an
injury he dare not return. Maximus may profess Amintor's belief
in divine right—"Should I now see the Emperor i'th heat on't, /
I should not chide him for't: an awe runs through me" (3.1.317–
18)—but Aecius accurately perceives his insincerity. Even before
Valentinian gave him reason, the patrician and soldierly Maximus
questioned the Emperor's right to author Rome and everyone
in it. Given provocation, Maximus, like Melantius rather than
Amintor, will reject submissive obedience to a criminal monarch
and, regendering himself as male, become the play's revenger.

His revenge, however, transforms Valentinian—"I am mortall"
(5.2.140), he will announce—even as it unmans and feminizes
him. The Emperor is amazed that he is human and not divine, a
part and not the whole—"O flatterd foole, / See what thy god-
heads come to" (28–29). He rages—threatening, for example, to
have his doctors "flead, and dride" (54)—but, like Doctor Faustus,
he also begs for mountains to hide him (94). Confessing his
crimes, despising and denying the gods, asking for their forgiveness if they exist, Valentinian concludes his final speech pleading
for an hour or any time it will take to "make a soule in" (136).
The revenger Maximus will not have even that luxury.

The Unmanned Tyrant

While there is a difference in degree between the "weak sensu-
alist" king and the "Neronic" Valentinian (Finkelpearl 1990, 213),
both *The Maid's Tragedy* and *Valentinian* explore absolute monarchy that has become tyranny. The main plot of *The Second
Maiden's Tragedy*, even in its censored form—i.e., without the references made to the Tyrant's absolute power, to corruption and
luxury at court, and to the king's right to take the Lady as "for-
feit" (Heinemann 1980, 47)—shares the genre's fascination with
the sexual criminality of tyranny. In the figure of the Tyrant, we
have another self-proclaimed god whose crimes include intended
rape and, what is merely a hint in *Valentinian*, necrophilia.

Although a usurper, the Tyrant shares his fellows' assumptions
of a godlike authority that claims sexual omnipotence as its natu-

ral extension. He takes command of state and stage with a deictic "Thus high" and, from the platform he has ascended, looks down on his subjects, in particular on the defeated Govianus:

> Thus high, my lords, your powers and constant loves
> Hath fixed our glories like unmovèd stars
> That know not what it is to fall or err.
> We're now the kingdom's love; and he that was
> Flattered awhile so stands before us now
> Readier for doom than dignity.
>
> (1.1.1–6)[10]

While he cannot claim divine right, which belongs *a priori* to Govianus—"God's agent"—he nonetheless declares his "glories" as fixed as the unfalling and infallible stars. Like Valentinian, he has appropriated heaven and made it synonymous with his will.

Both the political and the sexual aspects of that appropriation are present in his use of the word *love*, which occurs twice in the first four lines. The Tyrant first places it in a political context: the "constant loves" of his lords, which, added to their powers, glorified him. Next, however, he speaks of the "kingdom's love" that is now his to command, a claim that ambiguously covers the political and the sexual. The Tyrant is the victor in what he constructs as a contest for love—of the lords and country and, we hear moments later, of the Lady. From his elevated position, he declares his desire for her specifically in terms of Govianus's presumption in rivaling his claim: "There was but one / In whom my heart took pleasure (amongst women), / One in the whole creation, and in her / You dared to be my rival!" (1.1.10–13). Like the jealous King and the possessive Valentinian, the Tyrant must be sole owner of the woman he desires.

Like his fellow tyrants, the Tyrant of *The Second Maiden's Tragedy* presumes himself a god, but, unlike them, his efforts to demonstrate his divinity are instant and repeated failures. That his supremacy is tied to his maleness is evident, first, in his assumption that only a man can rival him and, second, in his enlisting the patriarchy—his lords and the Lady's father—in his struggle to defeat Govianus and win the Lady. Unlike the King and Valentinian, he does not have to invade and seize family authority because the ambitious Helvetius willingly cedes it. Moreover, Govianus concurs in the misogynistic assumption that women will follow power; he fails to credit the Lady with an autonomous will, believing she will leave him for the man who now controls the state.

When the Tyrant orders the Lady brought onstage, his intent is to use the public arena he now commands to claim her for himself and, equally, to refute Govianus's prior claim. The man who "dared to be my rival" (13) must be stripped of all signs of authority. The Tyrant's aim is to stage the Lady's validation of his victory, to torment Govianus with the sight of the woman he has lost, and then to banish him. Such a scene would unman Govianus thoroughly and publicly by depriving him not only of sovereign rule but also of sexual and familial rights in marriage. Forced into passivity, bearing witness to his betrothed's sexual betrayal, he would become the chaste, silent, obedient cuckold, the feminized male who signifies the Tyrant's absoluteness. With the Lady's surprising refusal to be the text of the Tyrant's authority, however, the Tyrant finds it is he who is unmanned, and not by a male rival but by the Lady he assumed he would possess by right: "I am he that's banished; / The king walks yonder, chose by her affection" (1.1.145–46). She has authored the scene and not he.

Because his attempts to cuckold Govianus are ineffectual, the Tyrant, like Valentinian, turns to the assistance of a pander, here the self-appointed Helvetius, whose position in the new state is clearly dependent upon his daughter: "Happier than a king / And far above him, for she kneels to thee / Whom we have kneeled to" (1.1.16–18). When the Lady refuses to be the medium of her father's vicarious absolutism, Helvetius prods the Tyrant "to force her to you / And pluck her from [Govianus's] arms" (188–89). Like Maximus, he has empowering sexual fantasies. He promises the Tyrant that "if [your content] be locked / In any blood of mine; the key's your own; / You shall command the wards" (241–43). By proposing his daughter's rape, he participates in it as the rapist. By declaring the Lady "blood of mine," he also participates, although less directly than Maximus, as the raped: if the Tyrant's pleasure can indeed be taken in "any blood of mine," Helvetius can substitute for her. This pander's "unmanly" trade involves both sodomy and incest.

The Tyrant's imprisoning Govianus with the Lady also problematizes his rival's gender. Govianus, head of a household that is another's space, is both male and female. As a man, he defends his seemingly autonomous domestic world with gun and sword, firing a pistol shot over Helvetius's head and stabbing Sophonirus to death. When, however, Sophonirus, before dying, informs him that they are surrounded by the Tyrant's men, Govianus's seeming mastery shatters. He is both locked into women's space and locked out of man's space, deprived of access to other men and to male authority. The increasing uncertainty of his gender is furthered by the Lady herself, who tells him that he must kill her if he is a man and berates him when he hesitates. Govianus is forced to confess his fear that he will be unable to kill her well (3.3.125), a prediction that proves accurate when he swoons in the attempt.

Govianus's apparent feminization, however, leads to the androgynous reversal of gender roles that allows the Lady to take up Govianus's sword and, acting according to her own will, remove herself from their contest. The Tyrant's apparent victory, on the other hand, isolates him in an increasingly deranged and violent maleness. His attempt to break down the walls of her tomb and seize the lifeless matter interred there is a kind of rape, as his soldiers' *double entendres* make clear: "This is ten thousand times worse than ent'ring upon a breach," one remarks (4.3.56). The Tyrant must explain away the Lady's demonstration of will and courage. Where, he wonders, did she get

> such boldness from the rest
> Of all thy timorous sex, to do a deed here
> Upon thyself, would plunge the world's best soldier
> And make him twice bethink him, and again,
> And yet give over?
>
> (4.3.106–10)

If to be female is to be a mindless, soulless body, to be male is to be necrophiliac: "I'll clasp the body for the spirit that dwelt in't . . . . / Thou art mine now, spite of destruction / And Govianus, and I will possess thee" (111–14). At last, he can shape her to the contours of his obsession, dressing her, speaking with her, ventriloquizing her responses. With the Lady unable to speak the shattering "I," she is at last his "most silent mistress," not Govianus's and certainly not her own.

The effects of the Lady's autonomous actions cannot, however, be denied. By admitting that she could use a little color, the Tyrant unwittingly reintroduces his rival into the perfect world of his creation. The terms of their rivalry have changed since their last encounter: Govianus no longer dismisses the authority of the Lady, instead fashioning his art to reflect her will, which she fashioned as a reflection of God's will. Because Govianus has learned to reject the construction of maleness as always and solely ordering and authoring, he escapes the revenger's contagious illusion of divinity and the punishment for it, both of which over-take Maximus. In accepting the androgyny occasioned by his forced reversal of gender with the Lady, he also escapes the re-venger's misogyny.

His and the Lady's firm rejection of the Tyrant's understanding of love as political and sexual possession changes its definition within the play. By the time of the Tyrant's death, his divinely constructed absolutism has lost the love of lords and country, whose fealty has reverted to Govianus. There is no suggestion that Govianus be punished for killing the Tyrant, although he is willing to die. Instead, reinstated as monarch, he acknowledges the Lady's authorial power to shape them all, ordering her body placed on the throne—"crown her our queen" (5.2.200)—and de-claring that he will rule in the light of her "constancy," which "strikes so much firmness in us" (202).

Misogyny returns, like a reflex reaction, in Govianus's last lines of the play with his wish that all ladies might "be borne so honest to their tombs" (212). His judgment against women, however, is not even fully supported by the play's subplot, where the "at least partly sympathetic" Wife (Ingram 1987, 154) falls into an infidelity engineered by her jealous tyrant husband.[11] Revenge tragedies may insistently, even obsessively, express misogyny, but they do not represent it as an appropriate attitude toward women. It is the despised, criminalized tyrant who stubbornly insists on authoring the women of his world as whores or corpses, the men as cuckolds and panders or revengers, and all as idolators of his false divinity.

In his denial of their rights, the tyrant gifts his subjects with the power to overthrow him. Commenting on *The Maid's Tragedy*, Lee Bliss puts the matter succinctly: "In splitting his two bodies and allowing the private man's lust to subvert the royal figure's responsibilities, the king has forced his subjects to reevaluate not merely their duty to him but the whole system of values and beliefs he theoretically embodies" (1987, 94). The impiety of the tyrant's claim loosens the constraints that compel his subjects' obedience not only to him, but also by extension to the essentialist standards of the culture that he cites as authorization. It allows characters like Govianus and the Lady to experience an androg-yny that undermines the analogy between maleness and dominance.

3

The Revenger as Rival Author

As a strategy of statecraft, the division of the king into two bodies is intended to silence opposition. Absolutist theory acknowledges the fallibility of the natural body in order to dismiss it as irrelevant; subjects owe obedience to the political body. In Jacobean revenge tragedy, that paradox of union by separation becomes what the chary English feared in their monarch: royal caprice justified on the grounds of divine right. The theatrical tyrant's fantasy of total presence, however, creates an absence that others will fill, as it did for the radical Protestants of James's rule. Men can claim authorization for rebellion because, in denying their rights and violating their maleness, the tyrant also violates the rules of law, tradition, and, above all, God. Women too are freed from obligatory obedience to the patriarchy because its head no longer represents the principles that support either him or patriarchy itself. The tyrant, then, rather than silencing opposition, gives it voice by undermining the integrity of the structure that authorizes him.

In the theater of revenge tragedy, his opponent is the genre's eponymous revenger. The tyrant destroys a predictable and orderly male hierarchy, absorbing the political and sexual rights of other men into himself; the revenger extricates himself from the constraints of submission to declare himself the tyrant's equal and, ultimately, superior. Opponents of the philosophy of divine right found grounds for disobedience in religion, with that zone of freedom extended into the family and its tradition of independent male governance. The revenger, shaped to a genre that insistently constructs the political as the sexual, emerges from the domestic world. Yet his rivalry with the tyrant is predicated on their shared belief in the analogy between gender and authority. Although they disagree on what constitutes maleness, they concur on male dominance as natural and proper. The revenger ostensibly seeks the justice no longer provided by the rule of law, but the impetus and defense for his revolt reside in the tyrant's assault on him as a man.

To function as male within a patriarchal society, as we have seen demonstrated in the plays, means to maintain a potentially precarious balance between command and obedience. Authorization to command requires, in a binary scheme, a woman's obligation to obey: a man is, first, not a woman and, to use Maximus's "wild" extensions of that category, not a child, slave, pander, cuckold, or coward. Maleness, however, also involves the social connections that embrace a man's service to other men. As long as the hierarchy of the social structure is clearly defined, with one male role superseding another according to cultural precept and example; as long as that hierarchy is understood as a male province, with women excluded by definition; and as long as a man retains his own sphere of authority, his maleness is unthreatened by obedience to another man. Indeed, it is enhanced if the superior is a male icon: soldiers boast of the generals they serve under.

Even when that superior is not a "man's man," however, obedience to him is not ignominious if it can be construed as submission to the will of God or as duty to the society that affirms the subjected man as otherwise in command. Amintor attempts to rescue his dignity on those grounds; Aecius clings to them even in death. When, however, the superior collapses the authority spread along the hierarchical chain into his person and disallows other men's authority, especially when he is emphatically not the culture's male ideal, service to him is intolerable, unmanly. The higher the subjected male in the social hierarchy, the more explosive in its consequences is the violation of his manhood and, for the tyrant, the more politically and sexually irresistible.

The criminal assault committed by a theoretically unassailable head of state produces conflicting responses in his victim-subject: retaliation on the one hand, submission on the other. He heeds the first imperative because to follow the second is to embrace the virtue of patient passivity rather than the virtù of heroic action, to choose the moral authority of Patient Griselda, which, in his terms, is to collaborate in his own feminization. If he will not accept the victim's role, and if he cannot transcend his imprisoning understanding of gender, the revenger must reconstruct his maleness so that it no longer ties him to family and community. To oppose the tyrant, he must become like the tyrant, which means freeing himself from the network of relationships that once

supported his maleness and now deny it. Like his rival, the revenger must become autogenous.

Lacking the dubious sanction of political absolutism, he finds
the grounds and method for self-creation in the theater. Like playwright and actor, the revenger fashions himself as his own character, adopting a disguise that will allow him safe entry into the
tyrant's world. Disguise is, of course, one of the genre's conventions, the revenger's assumption of a protective mask. It is also,
however, his first step in fashioning himself as the tyrant's equal.
In creating a disguise, the revenger acquires two bodies: his authored self, ephemeral and dispensable; and his authoring self,
godlike in its self-creation. Disguise, he finds, allows him to fashion others as well as himself: he can set scenes, prompt action,
write dialogue, and stage everything from impromptu sketches
to formal masques.[1] Most important, he can snatch control of the
text from the tyrant. Like him, he is now author of his world's
law and, therefore, above and outside it.

If we discern the English fears of James's absolutist principles
in the plays' tyrants, we also hear echoes of the contemporary
polemic on theater in the revenger's seizure of authorship. Subversive in his orthodoxy, the revenger practices the art of his creators to author a world and kill a king. The genre's coupling of
transgression and playing confirms the general fears of theatricality emanating from both royal censors and Christian moralists:
suspicions that players seize the power of illusion illicitly and use
it irresponsibly. Because theater represents its dramatic offerings
as self-enclosed and discrete, it constitutes a dangerously self-
fashioned authority competing with already divided and competing official authorities.[2]

In a world where the ties of analogy are coming undone, the
players can readily be seen as presumptuous, dangerous pretend-
ers to the voices of God and king. Within the theater, they function as gods and challenge the claim of monarchy to sole earthly
possession of God's authoring power. In that realm, external authorities are dramatic characters, their words and commands
playwrights' lines and actors' gestures. If monarchs use theatrical
strategies to represent and reify their political authority, players,
in representing political strategies theatrically, demonstrate an authority over monarchs.

Outside the theater, of course, the players are servants and
subjects who cannot entirely control what they author. They must
face possible objections from official censors and self-appointed
guardians of the public good, weighing them against public taste

and company profits. The doubleness of their position accounts, in part, for the simultaneously radical and cautious representation of public authorities in revenge tragedy. Monarchy becomes tyranny, and tyrants are killed, but the subjects who respond by becoming players and revengers do not, despite the plays' failure to condemn them explicitly for regicide, walk offstage in triumph. Ultimately, both figures are brought to ruin: the tyrant's claim that nothing comes between him and God is disproved by the revenger; the revenger's heady victory, even in the case of Melantius, is called into doubt by its aftermath.

In *The Maid's Tragedy*, where the discourse shifts from politics to love and guilt becomes grief, the players' denial of the revenger's authority, and their own, is evasive and ambiguous. In plays that end in the conventional masque, however, like the early Jacobean *Revenger's Tragedy*, the revenger visibly and invidiously performs a player's function only to have his control of the events within the play revealed as a delusion. The players, in effect, disclaim authority over the political world outside the theater when they deny the revenger the authority granted him over the political world inside it. Meanwhile, however, they have authored the king who claims he is his world's sole author as a tyrant.

In the moments of intense metadrama that frequently accompany closure in revenge tragedy, the players often enlist in their defense the figure recognized as definitive outside the play: the thundering, omen-sending Author whose play encloses all others. Like their radical Protestant enemies, they can justify their assumption of an authority equivalent to a monarch's by deferring to God's. The revenger and the tyrant, the subject and the king, and the players who are the point of convergence between the worlds inside and outside the theater—all are merely creatures posturing as creators, and the authority they erroneously took to be their natural right is rescinded in their exposure.

The revenger denies the tyrant's authority; the players deny his; God denies theirs. The players, while exposing as false all claims to absoluteness except God's, including their own, simultaneously reinscribe their authority by ceding to God the theatrical voice that supersedes theirs. Yet God is a figure within the play. The specter of the theater as an unpredictable, independent, dangerous social force is raised in the moment of its denial.

The revenger, onto whom the players can deflect criticism of their own dangerous theatricality, is an easy sacrifice. Created in their image, he can be punished in their stead, in part because the tragedies ultimately reveal that he has fashioned himself in

the image of his rival. Initially, he functions as the tyrant's opposite, his sense of identity derived from the familial and communal
roles that empower him: husband, brother, soldier, friend. His
authority as a man is defined by what he understands as a network of mutually reinforcing bonds that confer responsibilities as
well as rights. Such a construction of maleness, especially when
the revenger's network includes the military, threatens and is
threatened by the tyrant's restriction of political and sexual authority to himself.

The differences between the two men, however, prove less powerful than the sexual ideology they share. The revenger's final
resemblance to the tyrant, his use of the theater to match the
tyrant's use of the state, is founded on a necessary initial likeness:
their belief in an indissoluble, unquestioned tie between authority
and maleness; their understanding of the political as sexual and
the sexual as political; the exclusion and appropriation of the female in their rivalry; their fear of being gendered female; their
use of that fear as a weapon against each other.

Melantius and Maximus are, with natural variations, revengers
of a classic type, while Govianus, more intent on saving the
Lady's body from further desecration than on exacting revenge,
differs from them. Accepting female gender in himself and male
gender in her—despite or, more accurately, because of his struggles over what constitutes manhood—frees him from the imprisoning and ultimately fatal terms of male rivalry. When a man
maintains his connection to a woman despite the threat to his
manhood and learns from her to reject the identification of
women with weakness, the tyrant has no weapon against him.

The revenger, however, because he believes that his maleness
confers automatic authority over women, is vulnerable to the tyrant's assault on his gender and to the virulent misogyny it precipitates. Because women are, he believes, prone to error, they
require men's protection and control. When the tyrant takes from
him his ability to perform his male function, the revenger must
choose between accepting his unmanning or dissociating himself
from women. Under that pressure, his unexamined, institutionalized sense of male superiority becomes hostile recoil from the
female. The revenger chooses to save his manhood, which means
severing the connections that once validated it. The woman he
has known intimately as wife or mother or sister is now the undifferentiated Other, relegated to the category *woman*. He can con-
sole himself by concluding that she was *a priori* weak and

lascivious, always a potential victim and betrayer, a ready-to-hand tool of tyranny against him.

Disentangling himself from his compromising attachment to a woman means the revenger can free himself from the sexual humiliation of what has happened to her and exchange the inhibiting social virtues he once espoused for the tyrant's ruthless singleness. Respect and trust turn to contempt and suspicion; union is replaced by separation, mutuality by solitariness, community by isolation. To ally himself with a woman is to remind himself of their shared powerlessness and of his invalidated sexual authority. Like his creation of a second body, misogyny puts the revenger on an equal footing with the tyrant. Autogeny, in fact, begins with misogyny, the necessary extirpation of women from the procreative act, and it manifests itself in misogyny, the use of women to signify and validate maleness. The revenger will demonstrate his victory over the tyrant in kind, unmanning and feminizing the man who unmanned and feminized him.

Unlike their Jacobean inheritors, Elizabethan revengers respond to attacks on their maleness without assuming women are to blame. Hieronimo is unmanned by the seizure of his public authority and the denial of access to the king, but his outsider's position is not identified with femaleness, nor does he hold women responsible for it. He takes Bel-Imperia as his trusted assistant, and he applauds the part she writes for herself in his revenge play. Hamlet, on the cusp of the Elizabethan and Jacobean worlds, does blame women for his ills, but the play gives no indication of a misogynistic bent in him before Gertrude's "o'er-hasty marriage." His rights as an adult male heir are under attack—he is forced back into the dependent roles of son and courtier; Claudius assails his grief as "unmanly" (1.2.94); he is sentenced to the "prison" Denmark—and for that he blames mother and women's frailty. Yet Hamlet stops short of the Jacobean revenger's gratuitous violence against women: he speaks daggers but uses none. On the Stuart side of the royal divide, we find Vindice's ingrained misogyny; his prurient quickness to test the virtue of his sister and mother; his assault on Gratiana, dagger pressed to her breast; his unreflective, intoxicated rush to theatrical power; his failure to relinquish it with the Duke's death.

The Jacobean revenger emerges from a highly specific ideological climate where issues of gender and authority are complicated by the unpopular rule of a misogynist king who does not figure maleness as it is traditionally defined and by a corollary nostalgia for a queen who fashioned herself as politically male. The result is a remarkably multivalent drama. The revenger sees women as corruptible and contaminating, but the plays' heroines are morally compelling. The revenger is given motive, if not unequivocal justification, for the great taboo of Stuart kingship—regicide—in the tyrant's collapse of sexual and political hierarchies into himself, but in seizing control of play and state, he replicates the tyrant's action. He represents his society's traditional, hierarchical definition of maleness. Yet in growing to resemble the tyrant the English feared James might become, the revenger violates the communal terms of that maleness and—abandoning the roles of soldier, brother, and friend to author himself—forces other men as well as women to play a culturally female role. The Jacobean revenger is a hero, but he is an increasingly suspect one, and the assumptions about gender and politics that he shares with his rival—and with the English king—are insistently challenged by the plays that contain him.

The Soldier Maximus: "Above the fate of women, / And made more perfect far"

Maximus begins his revenger's career assuming the cultural rights and responsibilities accorded a patrician male and soldier. In his aristocratic family, he wields an authority as inviolable as Valentinian's; in the Roman army, although he serves under Aecius, Maximus occupies a position of high command. Family and army, however, exist within the political state governed by Valentinian, who has separated his Rome from both those structures, isolating and empowering his emperorship at their expense. The political, the familial, and the military have ceased to form a mutually supportive network, and the noble Maximus is reduced to the status of subject—under Valentinian's leveling of the hierarchy, little more than a slave.

Such extreme positions of authority and submission in Maximus's social roles make his place as a man in his society volatilely discontinuous. At first, he attempts to consolidate his position by appealing to a definition of maleness that, like Aecius's, is predicated on service to Rome: the aristocratic scion and soldier invokes his authority for the common good. His rebellion against Valentinian, however, involves the separation of his maleness from the social order in whose name he rebels. Maximus is not Valentinian's creature, but neither will he be Lucina's or Aecius's.

Misogynistic and "wild," he becomes his own author, a player whose two bodies elevate him to an emperor's divinity.

Maximus enters his play in heated debate with Aecius over absolutism. Presenting himself as spokesman for the traditionally linked Roman values of patriarchy and war, which he assumes Aecius shares, and against the luxury and pacifism of Valentinian, whom Aecius supports, Maximus presents his case in the question-and-answer mode of a sacred catechism:

> . . . wherefore
> And to what end, are we the sonnes of Fathers
> Famous, and fast to *Rome?* Why are their vertues
> Stampt in the dangers of a thousand Battailes,
> For goodnesse sake? their honors, time out daring?
> I thinke for our example.
>
> (1.3.47–52)

The bond of martial tradition passed from generation to generation of aristocratic men defines Maximus's understanding of the family and gives authority to his rebellion against the emperor he constructs as an outsider. It also establishes him and not Valentinian as the rightful heir to Rome.

For a Roman—or contemporary English—traditionalist, the military world is the arena where manhood is tested and validated. With the noble Aecius in charge, the army hierarchy affirms its members as men, yet because Aecius willingly submits himself and, therefore, his soldiers to the superior command of the emperor, the "great Souldier" of the *dramatis personae* cannot avoid the knowledge that serving him also means serving Valentinian. According to his own stated standards of virtue, Maximus must obey Aecius as his worthy superior and, at the same time, challenge Valentinian as Rome's enemy.

To resolve his conflict, Maximus must persuade Aecius to deny Valentinian unquestioning loyalty. The idealized portrait of virtuous fathers setting examples for virtuous sons is designed, in part, to gain Aecius's support. Equally forensic are Maximus's catechistic and rhetorical questions, all of which presume shared cultural response: "Why is this Emperor, this man we honor, / This God that ought to be—" he asks (41–42). As Maximus shapes his argument, Valentinian is no more than an "ought to be" god and, therefore, not owed obedience; he is instead "this man," given divine status by the honor "we" pay him. In Maximus's "Good, give me leave, why is this Author of us—" (43), he proceeds to undeify, neuter, and dehumanize Valentinian.

Maximus's emerging rebellion is based on his denial of the absolutist premise that the right to rule is separate from the character of the ruler. He insists on merit as the proper basis of command, an argument that in its extreme makes all obedience voluntary. For him, obedience is owed only to the man who exemplifies the Roman code of male conduct for which he, explicitly rivaling Valentinian, speaks as interpreter and judge. While claiming to speak for Rome, however, Maximus in fact asserts the primacy of his own judgment; while claiming to represent the principles of Roman hierarchy, he removes himself from the hierarchy itself.

Aecius, who voices the absolutist position with fervor and frequency, understands male gender entirely in terms of that hierarchy. A man is part of a social continuum, not a separable entity: personal judgment—or injury—is irrelevant to the debt he owes the political body. Based on the obedience of an individual man to something larger than himself, Aecius's unswerving obedience to Valentinian is his patriotic support for a structure of command that keeps chaos safely outside Rome. To be a man is to put common good above self-interest, to serve Rome in all capacities, not merely as a warrior. Aecius will later instruct Pontius that he cannot claim to govern Rome unless he can govern himself (4.4.143–45), that he must possess a mind that is "sweet in peace, as rough in dangers" (152). He does not equate those "sweet" peacetime virtues with being female, nor does he find obedience to a man above him, even a weak and corrupt one, feminizing. Unlike Maximus, he has no difficulty squaring his sense of manliness with kneeling before Valentinian and announcing himself as "your Graces creature" (1.3.121).

For Maximus, however, that posture of submission is unmanly. Implicit in his insistent interrogation of Aecius is the determination to rebel against Valentinian and, therefore, either to sway his general or, failing that, to find grounds that make him unworthy of loyalty. When Aecius impulsively tries to execute the seditious Pontius, Maximus springs to judgment and, using the same standard he applies to Valentinian, finds his mentor lacking. "Are yee a man?" (2.3.9), he demands, the accusation dangerously naked under Maximus's habitual interrogatory mode. Through Rome's humiliating losses and defections, only personal respect for his general has kept Maximus a loyal subordinate to Valentinian. In the moment's heat, however, he subdues Aecius physically and attacks his manhood verbally. In this scene he stops short of rejecting Aecius's authority, but Maximus has already replaced it, and the principle of common good, with his own.

Even before Lucina's rape, then, Maximus demonstrates the revenger's resemblance to the tyrant he opposes. With Aecius situated uneasily between them as the voice of self-government and social harmony, Maximus and Valentinian occupy the extreme positions on the male spectrum—Maximus a harsh, soldierly aggressor and Valentinian a sensual, courtly predator. Both, however, define maleness as synonymous with themselves, and both accept without question the link between it and dominance. In their belief that they are Rome, they place themselves above Rome and its communal interests. Absolute maleness makes them beasts or gods, a condition of human isolation and estrangement whose verbal signifier in the play is wildness. Like the genre's conventional madness, wildness liberates a man from civil and religious laws and customs.[3]

Within those social edifices, women theoretically occupy positions inferior to men's; in fact, however, women perpetuate them and give them meaning. Wives and daughters bear witness to the success of their husbands' and fathers' military campaigns; their obedience defines and validates male freedom and command; their chastity insures the legitimate perpetuation of patrician blood lines. To insure social stability, a man must defend and control them. If, however, he is wild—unfettered by a wife or sister and, therefore, free from the larger structure that holds him responsible for keeping her true and safe—female weakness cannot unman him in his own eyes or in other men's. If the tyrant is wild by definition, the revenger grows wild. Driven by his perception of women's betrayal, he severs his ties to them and denies their role as validators of manhood and agents of procreation. Like the tyrant, he will not need a woman in order to be a man or to create life.

In *Valentinian*, wildness is first attributed to the emperor. Maximus dubs him "this wild man" in the first act (1.3.2); Aecius reiterates the term when he argues that Lucina, alive, may "draw from that wild man a sweet repentance" (3.1.210). When, however, Maximus presses the defiant question "Why are we thus, or how become thus wretched?" (1.3.36), Aecius responds, "You'l fall againe into your fit" (37), linking Maximus's incipient disobedience to the violent paroxysm that makes a man unable or unwilling to govern himself. Maximus's early and recurring "fit" establishes prior kinship with the lawless emperor, and when Lucina presents Maximus with his ring, his already weakened ties to law and custom break. In that signifier, he confronts his failure as a man within his society. He could not protect Lucina from Valentinian, and she did not (when he is interpreting the event generously, could not) protect herself.

Abandoning the heterosexual bond of marriage for the homosocial bond of friendship, he orders Lucina away and turns to Aecius: "I have my feares Aecius: / Oh, my best friend, I am ruind" (3.1.155–56). Lucina remains on stage, but Maximus cuts her out of the scene. Better that she "seeke heaven, / And there by *Cassiopeia* shine in glory, / We are too base and dirty to preserve thee" (190–92). He wraps his own sense of shame and unworthiness in that generic and ambiguous but clearly male "we," and, in his sweeping condemnation, both cloaks his specific failure to protect her and identifies himself and Aecius with her "base and dirty" rapist.

To ease his pain, she must die:

> . . . since it was not youth, but malice did it,
> And not her own, nor mine, but both our losses,
> Nor staies it there, but that our names must find it,
> Even those to come; and when they read, she livd,
> Must they not aske how often she was ravishd,
> And make a doubt she lov'd that more then Wedlock?
> Therefore she must not live.
>
> (3.1.239–45)

As the male *we* shifts to a distant, future *they*, Maximus discards his marriage's *our* for *she* and *her*, the separated and discarded third-person feminine.

Embedded in Maximus's argument for Lucina's suicide is an emerging sexual obsession that, with her death, grows unchecked into misogyny. His already lurking distrust of women is apparent in the rapidity with which "they" ask "how often she was ravishd," and it takes little time after raising the question for Maximus to merge Lucina and Eudoxa into an empowering fantasy of revenge: "Ile make as bold with his wife, if I can" (3.1.327). Reduced to interchangeable signifiers in the war between men, women are stereotypes of female sexuality, the wife he cryptically states was "too chast" to him (183) "a whore now, / A kind of kicker out of sheetes" (340–41). If Lucina and Eudoxa blur into the pejorative category of unchaste vessels, then he and the Emperor are also one: he is no longer Valentinian's cuckold and pander but the Emperor himself and, again, Lucina's rapist. Maximus's imagination insistently empowers him, putting him back in control, as he is even when he sardonically considers the possibility that Lucina did it only for his advancement: "Wilt not become me bravely?" (352).

When Maximus wishes that Valentinian had raped him, fantasizing becoming not the Emperor but Lucina, he erases women even as agents in his struggle. The dream allows him to transform the culturally female position forced on him into a literal appropriation of femaleness. If he rather than Lucina is raped, he does not have to face his inability to protect her, nor is he forced to imagine her with Valentinian. Moreover, the constraints on his ability to retaliate are removed, and his revenge can be immediate and direct: "I would have payd him, / I would have taught him such a trick, his Eunuches / Nor all his black-eyd boyes dreamt of yet" (3.3.118–20). For Valentinian's making him a cuckold and pander, Maximus will castrate him. By substituting himself for Lucina with Valentinian, he can substitute himself for Valentinian with the husband Maximus and become the ultimate and only male.

It is with a certain relieved willingness, then, that he monumentalizes Lucina by consigning her to the "Time, Story" that will "stand to eternitie" (3.1.271, 274).[4] He is now free both to apotheosize her virtues and fantasize her vices. He has split the complex, living woman into the twin figures of saint and seductress, images of Otherness he can imprison within himself and subject to his will.

Misogyny allows Maximus to withdraw from the heterosexual union designated by a double-gendered and, therefore, threateningly androgynous *we* into the exclusively male, homosocial *we*. To rival Valentinian completely, however, he must also, like him, separate himself from that homosocial *we*, that powerful, exclusively male community that he believes reads his wife's rape as his ruin and, as represented by Aecius, also tells him he must do nothing about it. Separation from that male community frees him entirely from law and custom. Despite Maximus's rebellious "fit" against Valentinian, he had remained within the confines of the Roman patriarchy with Aecius, whose right to author him he acknowledges and resists. With Lucina dead, only Aecius has the potential ability to hold him to obedience.

Indeed, Aecius insistently and repeatedly calls on that powerful male bond, "do ye love me?" (311), to control the wilding Maximus. He seeks to prevent Maximus's flight from community, neither trusting him alone in his pillaged house nor accepting his statement that he is not dangerous (316). While convinced by

Maximus's behavior that he is "craz'd a little" (333), Aecius also wonders whether the madness is genuine: "Do's he but seeme so, / Or is he made [mad] indeed?" (357–58). He doubts too the sincerity of Maximus's protestations of loyalty to Valentinian: "This is a maske to cozen me" (322).

To become author of himself, Maximus must seize control of the text, which means isolating himself from those who purport to author it and replacing them. Aecius's authoring of him as an obedient servant to Valentinian must now confront its complicity in Valentinian's authoring of him as a cuckold. To be either his general's or the Emperor's creature, Maximus must consent to become tame, castrated, female. Since his foster father's counsel unmans him as much as Valentinian's assault; since Aecius has placed his authority over Maximus between Maximus and Valentinian; and since Maximus cannot confront that authority directly, Aecius, like Lucina, must be—in Maximus's usual evasive style— "not living."

As equivocation and duplicity develop into plotting and acting, Maximus moves into the liminal space between play and audience, liberating himself from the conventions of dramatic dialogue that constrain other characters. The linguistic theatrical habits that mark his character change from the catechistic, rhetorical question to the soliloquy and aside. Between visits by Aecius, Maximus is a man fashioning himself anew, searching among the discourses that shape his relationships for one that will allow him to perform his new self. Beginning his soliloquy with its end— "he [Aecius] must die" (3.3.1)—Maximus devotes himself to rationalizing his intent. At first, Aecius is "friend," "soule," "perfectnesse" (2, 4). To challenge that model of Roman manhood directly is unthinkable, yet "like a Sea / He bares his high command, twixt me and vengeance" (10–11), cutting off all attempts to "make a question of [Valentinian's] ill" (15). He must, therefore, take "that pretious life I love most" (8); "*Aecius* dies, / Or I have lost my selfe" (17).

He cannot, however, immediately confront the murderous act that will end Aecius's authorship of "my selfe." Instead, he recasts the problem as a conflict between love and friendship, between the loyalties one owes a woman and a man. With the problem thus posed, the solution is deceptively simple:

> . . . let her perish.
> A freind is more then all the world, then honor;

> She is a woman and her losse the lesse,
> And with her go my greifs . . . .
>
> (34–37)

Yet if he avows male love, Maximus is a man in Aecius's eyes but not in his own.

To be free of Aecius, he must return Lucina to the argument, establishing her in a discourse where a woman is superior to a man. Her death gives her a distinct advantage over Aecius: like Vindice's Gloriana, she cannot intrude herself into his narrative. Maximus is her author and ventriloquist; he controls her meaning so that it supports his, and no Valentinian can take that control from him. The issue, he decides, is not, after all, whether love for a woman is of lesser consequence than friendship for a man; rather, it is the fact that an incomparable and universally worshipped virtue has been destroyed.

At last, Aecius's death has become "necessity" (64): "he shall dye, / I have found a way to do it, and a safe one, / It shall be honor to him too" (67–69). Although troubled with conscience, wishing he were himself dead (70–72), Maximus has successfully become author of "my selfe" and the narrative that supports it. He is no longer Aecius's creature; Aecius is his. He has translated both the marital *we* and the homosocial *we* to his *I*. Doubt and regret will recur, but Maximus next faces Aecius as playwright and actor, exaggerating his wildness into the feigned, theatrical madness of the revenger: "That that leads mad men, / A strong Imagination, made me wander" (73–74); sometimes, he tells Aecius, he has "a buzzing in [his] brains" (77).

Maximus is the tyrant's equal, the detached author of himself and of his world, "a stranger" not only to Aecius but "every one" (128, 129). Like Valentinian, he behaves like a god, appropriating others' lives and meanings and exercising absolute power. He plants the letter that will lead to the order for Aecius's execution and stands aloof from the action—"I am least in rumour, / And so Ile keep my selfe" (4.2.3–4). Gone is any concern that Aecius's role in the revenge "be honor to him too" (3.3.69): "If he be lost / He is my Martyr" (4.2.5–6). His friend is no longer an autonomous being; he has been absorbed into the religion of Maximus's *my*. Smarmy protestations of loyalty to Aecius become, after the scene is played, an invisible, godlike control:

> Goe worthy innocent, and make the number
> Of *Cesars* sinnes so great, heaven may want mercy:

Ile hover herabout to know what passes:
And if he be so divelish to destroy thee,
In thy bloud shall begin his Tragedy.

(4.2.67–71)

As the playwright of Valentinian's "Tragedy," Maximus commands the sacrificial "innocent" who must unwittingly obey and then hovers to watch his plot unfold. He has acquired the tyrant's habit of assigning his desires to heaven and the consequences of their fulfillment to others.

Entering unseen after Aecius's death, Maximus uses his disguise as a grieving friend to prompt Phidias and Aretus into taking revenge. In an aside, he asks the gods to forgive him, but to these pawns he feigns the bonds of male comradeship only to dupe them. He reshapes his fellow characters to suit the tragedy he is writing: Lucina is his saint, Aecius his martyr, Phidias and Aretus his agents. He has replicated the absolute authority of Valentinian by claiming as his own the authority allowed him by the players. His ultimate moment of triumph—the act of revenge—he enacts through others.

From his player's vantage above and behind the play's action, Maximus writes the scenario for Valentinian's death at the hands of Roman soldiers whom he can trust to reduce Valentinian politically and sexually. The poison Aretus administers strips Valentinian of authority and maleness, rendering him chaste, silent, and obedient to Aretus, and to Maximus behind him. Valentinian enters "*sick in a Chaire, with* Eudoxa, *the Empresse, and* Physitians, *and Attendants*" (5.2.12). When we see him for the first time as husband, he is emphatically unable to function as a man in that role. Lust, even mobility, is gone. He is equally impotent as Emperor. Although he can still speak, he cannot command. The chilly waters of the Danube and Volga will not flow through his body to cool it; his physician countermands his desire to drink, "You must not Sir" (35); his murderer cannot be tortured to death on his order because Aretus has preempted him. In death, Valentinian must face the folly of his divine dream of absoluteness: "I am mortall" (140).

Revenge was to have meant Maximus's, not Valentinian's, return to humanity: he would retreat from his solitary, self-authoring repudiation of his humanity, pay his debts to those he had used, and, in death, become part of his community again. As he begins to assess the consequences of his action, however, he remains alone:

> Gods, what a sluce of blood have I let open!
> My happy ends are come to birth, he's dead,
> And I reveng'd; the Empires all a fire,
> And desolation everywhere inhabits:
> And shall I live that am the author of it,
> To know *Rome* from the awe o'th world, the pitty?
>
> (5.3.1–6)

His early judgment of Valentinian—"Why is this Author of us"
(1.3.43)—echoes in his acknowledgment that he, as author, has
spread the wildness until it becomes the wildfire Aretus caught
and spread to Rome. Like Rome, his friends are "gone before too
of my sending" (7): Aecius's and Lucina's virtues, that were to
be the "lines to lead me to *Elizium*" (19), cannot be equaled on
earth. Maximus sees clearly the ashy remains of all that had once
defined him as a man—state, profession, family, friendship.

Again using rhetorical questions to persuade, he attempts to
move himself to honorable suicide. He knows he will be condemned: no man, knowing of his acts, can love him (14); his way
to justice was "crooked" (16). But he is not persuaded. As he calls
on Aecius and his "honored Lady" (17) to lead him to Elysium—
"I would not leave your freindship unrewarded; / First smile upon
the sacrifice I have sent ye, / Then see me comming boldly . . ."
(21–23)—he stops short and, midline, changes course: "stay, I am
foolish, / Somewhat too suddaine to mine own destruction, / This
great end of my vengeance may grow greater" (23–25). For the
self-authored man to follow Lucina and Aecius in the name of
friendship, reward, sacrifice, and boldness is to re-empower their
authorship of him.

Before "stay," Maximus's soliloquizing *I* speaks for a social self.
The *I* that insistently follows, however, speaks for the "stranger"
Maximus. No other figures intrude:

> Why may not I be *Caesar*, yet no dying?
> Why should not I catch at it? . . .
> I will, I dare; my deare freinds pardon me,
> I am not fit to dye yet if not Caesar. . . .
>
> (26–27, 30–31)

With an official farewell to the friends he left long before, he
moves towards the imperial seat of Rome, irresistibly drawn into
a tyrant's divinity. Climactically, he rises to megalomaniacal
heights:

And I will forward, and as goodly Cedars
Rent from *Oeta* by a sweeping tempest
Jointed againe and made tall masts, defie
Those angry winds that split 'em, so will I
New peec'd againe, above the fate of women,
And made more perfect far . . .

(33–38)

The note of autogeny is struck: "above the fate of women," Maximus gives birth to himself as a phallic mast tall enough and
tough enough to defy fortune's angry winds. If he can make
himself a man without the imperfections attending female
agency, he cannot be unmanned. Nor, in his expanding *I*, was he
ever unmanned: "If I rise, / My wife was ravish'd well" (38–39).

Maximus's absolute *I* isolates him from human beings of both
genders. As Rome's new Emperor, he adopts the language of
Jacobean monarchy to senators and soldiers: "Ye are my children,
family, and friends / And ever so respected shall be" (5.4.57–58).
Alone in his assumed divinity, accustomed to writing the script
according to which he rules and others obey, Maximus acknowledges no human will or intelligence outside his. He has become
the tyrant who shapes women to his demeaning fantasies and
men to the feminizing authority of his maleness. He is, as a result,
blind to the emergence of Eudoxa and Affranius as rivals, and
especially to Eudoxa. Gone is his acknowledgment that a woman
had the strength and conviction to die rather than defile her
home. In place of admiration, Maximus has substituted a destructive disdain for women's intelligence and virtue. The price is his
failure to see that Eudoxa is merely feigning obedience, that she
is her own author and will become his.

The simultaneous emergence of Affranius in the fifth act mea-
sures the distance Maximus has traveled since he was Rome's
great soldier. Affranius is Maximus's immediate enemy, replacing
both him and the now dead Aecius and Pontius as spokesman
for the best values of Rome's military. Unlike Maximus's rebellion,
however, Affranius's signals genuine change. He does not repli-
cate Maximus's misogyny and wildness, nor does he engineer
Maximus's death; he honors and supports Eudoxa, using his
voice to force Rome to listen to hers. When the city chooses another emperor, it will be with the assistance of a man and woman
who act in respectful unison against the principles of male
absolutism.

In death as in life, Maximus replicates Valentinian and, like a replica, he proves less than the original. He lacks the divine authorization that made Aecius obey Valentinian no matter how tyrannical his reign had become, and, exposed as a liar and criminal, he loses the theatrical authorization on which he had presumed to build his divinity. That is repossessed by the players and given to Eudoxa, who, in avenging Maximus's victims rather than revenging herself, cancels the theater's implied challenge to monarchy. Poisoned by the Empress, replaced as exemplar of Roman manhood by Affranius, Maximus dies a mute, abrupt version of Valentinian's death.

"She says" / "trust me": Melantius and Masculine Love

The obvious revenger in *The Maid's Tragedy*, Amintor, cannot extricate his maleness from the tangle of culturally female roles—cuckold, pander, and subject—he is forced to play. While Amintor has the genre's conventional motive for revenge in the tyrant's intimate violation of his manhood, he does not follow the revenger's path because he is prevented by his belief in divine right monarchy: "but there is / Divinity about you, that strikes dead / My rising passions" (3.1.238–40). "But take heed: / There's not the least limb growing to a king / But carries thunder in't" (4.2.324–26). His manhood, therefore, is not his own but the King's. It is as if revenge in *Valentinian* had fallen to Aecius.

The revenger's career belongs instead to Melantius, whose male rights as a brother, like Amintor's as a husband and Calianax's as a father, have been usurped by the King. Unlike them, however, Melantius rejects the political theory that allows such a usurpation. As Rhodes's great soldier, Melantius never doubts his own sexual and political authority. Like Maximus, he defines his authority as a man in terms of the interpenetrating and reinforcing hierarchies of family and army, which for him take precedence over political authority. He serves the state rather than the King. As a man, he presumes himself the monarch's equal; as a soldier, his superior. When Melantius understands the crime committed against him, his umbrage is at the King's audacity: "Where got he the spirit / To wrong me so?" (3.2.185–86). The effete head of state, who presides over a court life Melantius sees as female, somehow found the "spirit" to challenge the manly Melantius and the military family whose scion he is:

My worthy father's and my services
Are liberally rewarded. King, I thank thee;
For all my dangers and my wounds thou hast paid me
In mine own metal: these are soldiers' thanks.

(4.1.126–29)

The King's criminal incursions into his family have extended beyond a brother's obedience and a sister's body to Melantius himself, and Melantius never doubts his right to punish that crime.

As theatrical revengers, Melantius and Maximus are, in fact, constructed in similar ways. Their unshakable belief in the inviolability of their rights as men means that they suspect and fear women, whose presumed weakness makes them vulnerable to the attack of other men. Both, therefore, reject threatening female ties: Maximus severs his intimate connection to Lucina; Melantius has no intimate ties to women to sever. Denying the procreative authority of the female, both author themselves, using the strategies of the theater to create a second body and control the play's events. Moreover, both use that theatrical authority to effect their revenge through surrogates.

Yet at closure, Melantius is the focus of what sympathy the tragedy generates in the audience while Maximus, having rejected all ties to the human community, becomes the despised and alienated monster he rivaled.[5] To account for that difference by pointing to Melantius's technical innocence of regicide ignores his commanding the murder and engineering his survival following it. Rather, he remains affectively connected to the audience because, after the success of his plot, he returns to human relationship.

Unlike Maximus, Melantius remains a man's man: soldier, brother, and friend. His self-assigned role in the regicidal plot is military—to seize and hold the fort. He does not stab the unarmed King in his bed, nor does he, like Maximus, manipulate an unwitting surrogate: he directly commands his sister to kill the King and argues away her ideological objections. Melantius is fraternal with Diphilus as well, casting his brother in an honorable role in the revenge plot. Yet love for a friend holds the preeminent place in his construction of himself as a man, and in the final moments of the play, Melantius rejects all other ties to devote himself to the grief and loss occasioned by Amintor's death.

Melantius's code of manhood, which flowers in his love for Amintor, is based on military comradeship, the power—and eroticism—of its friendships in contrast with the debilitating love between men and women:[6] Melantius first "styled [him] man" (4.2.164), he tells us, when he was a boy fighting in his country's cause. For a man who defines his gender according to the purely male world of the army, the bond between men surpasses, supersedes, and absorbs all others. As Melantius will explain to his brother, Amintor was "my sister, father, brother, son, / All that I had" (5.3.265–66). For such a man, the dutiful nature of relationships in the family unit and the presence of women within it make familial love inferior to friendship.

Theoretically, Amintor's marriage to Evadne elevates him to the status of Melantius's brother, but Melantius will have none of it: "to me the name / Of brother is too distant: we are friends, / And that is nearer" (3.1.41–43). When Amintor's accusation of Evadne in the next scene presents him with the conflicting demands on his loyalty of family and friendship, Melantius struggles, but he chooses Amintor: "The name of friend is more than family / Or all the world besides" (3.2.167–68). In contrast to Aecius, who tells Maximus that "to dye, / Because I could not make you live, / were woman" (*Val.* 3.3.111–12), Melantius will attempt suicide in the face of Amintor's death.

In the terms of Melantius's military world, women's sole function is to perpetuate maleness. As long as their intimate contacts with men do no more than populate armies, whose soldiers live apart from their contaminating female origins, women can be tolerated, even honored. Melantius blesses Aspatia, whom he believes to be Amintor's bride, with the wish that she may "bring a race / Unto Amintor that may fill the world / Successively with soldiers!" (1.1.61–63). Otherwise and generally, however, Melantius sees femaleness pejoratively. In his confrontation with Evadne, he prays for the "weaknesses of nature / That make men women" (4.1.94–95) to forsake him. Court life is corrupt because it is female and feminizing: that world of music and dance where wars are "soft and silken" (1.1.41) threatens the "shrill" music that stirs his blood and makes him "dance with arms" (42, 43). A court denizen like the backbiting, cowardly Calianax is "unmanly" and "womanish" (1.2.63, 70). Pettiness, cowardice, spite, betrayal—for Melantius, these are *a priori* female traits.

His is a perfectly contained system of exclusion: he casts the ills and sins of humanity onto women, and he appropriates for men virtues like compassion and grace that are customarily attributed to women. For example, Melantius acknowledges tears as signifiers of femaleness—he tells Amintor, "Dry up thy watery eyes, / And cast a manly look upon my face"—but he "must weep" over Amintor's plight (3.2.195–96, 236). In fact, Melantius weeps repeatedly and copiously throughout the play. He has wept at their reunion, and he will weep at Amintor's death. When another man sheds tears—Lysippus in mourning for his brother—Melantius praises them as "lovely on thee" (5.2.37). For a man to weep is not a shamefully "unmanly" or "womanish" act but rather a masculinized, and so purified, form of female behavior. If men can weep for and with each other, if they can serve each other as mothers, lovers, and wives, then women, except for their brief role in procreation, become unnecessary.

Melantius's tears at his reunion with Amintor trigger such an explicitly competitive comparison: "credit me, young man, thy mother / Could do no more but weep for joy to see thee / After long absence" (1.1.126–28). Shortly thereafter, he repudiates his own female companion, who has a brief and nonspeaking role, in an implied comparison between man's and woman's love: "I have a mistress and she has a heart, / She says, but, trust me, it is stone, no better" (150–51): "She says" / "trust me." While Melantius will defend the lady's honor against Calianax's insults, he presumes her hard and deceitful. As mothers, women can do "no more" than men; as lovers, they do less.

With Evadne, Melantius's competition becomes most appropriative. When he hears of her intended marriage to Amintor, he tells her, "You looked with my eyes when you took that man" (1.2.114). Stealing her gaze so that her eyes, her choice, and her marriage are his—a substitution made all the easier for their being related by blood—Melantius denies Evadne a body or life separate from his. By substituting himself for the women in Amintor's life and dismissing the woman in his, Melantius paves the way for their collaboration in a strictly male androgyny that is akin to James's.

The moment of their union occurs in the scene where Amintor, after Melantius's prodding, finally reveals his secret humiliation and each in turn challenges the other to a duel. Responding to the affront to his family, Melantius draws his sword on Amintor, who draws his in response, then sheathes it when he accepts Amintor's word. Moments later, fearful that Melantius's revenge will shame him, Amintor draws his sword on Melantius, who draws in response, then sheathes it when Melantius, invoking "the name of friend" (3.2.231), sheathes his. The swordplay is indeed a dance with arms, a choreography of male love.

When phallic bravura concludes in a tearful reaffirmation of their bond, their expression of love shifts to terms culturally associated with the relationships of wife and husband, mother and child. Amintor leans against Melantius for support and "feel[s] a kind of ease" (250); Melantius cheers him: "Look up; we'll walk together; / Put thine arm here. All shall be well again" (252–53). Amintor's marriage to Evadne has failed him; his friendship with Melantius has not: "Thy love (O wretched I!), ay, thy love, Melantius— / Why, I have nothing else." "Be merry then," Melantius responds, ending the scene (254–55).

The discovery of Evadne's infidelity is, in fact, felicitous because it both validates Melantius's misogyny and removes her as medium and obstacle between him and Amintor. That does not mean, however, that he can leave her shocking affront to his authority unpunished. She has given the body that is his and Amintor's to a man he neither chose nor desired, allowing an uninvited fourth party into the union with Amintor she mediates. In Melantius's appropriation of Evadne, he became Amintor's wife and lover; in his loving union with Amintor, he became Evadne's husband and lover as well. A chaste and dutiful Evadne would keep her brother's misogyny in check and channel his love for Amintor into categories culturally broad enough to hold them. Her infidelity and defiance, however, unleash a violent, erotic rage. On the one hand, it is as if he has cuckolded Amintor; on the other, as if she has cuckolded him.[7] He must abandon his appropriative fantasy and see her again as outside of him, as object and not subject. She is not he after all, but rather a refractory inferior whom he must return to his control.

To the confrontation with his transgressive sister, he brings the full force of cultural, familial, and physical maleness in a sexually charged display of dominance that will succeed where Amintor's failed. Arguably, the assertion of authority, which overrides another's autonomy, always conceals a violent eroticism. In Melantius's case, sex and power are both present from the first moments of his encounter with Evadne. He opens their contest for authority and authorship by locking the door so that the female and feminized creatures of the court, "your gilded things, that dance / In visitation with their Milan skins" cannot intervene (4.1.10–11). Evadne is now locked out of her house and locked in his, and, as his contained property, she is subject to his erotic gaze:

> . . . thou art young and handsome,
> A lady of a sweet complexion
> And such a flowing carriage that it cannot
> Choose but inflame a kingdom.
>
> (18–21)

Melantius authors her femaleness according to his own and his culture's misogynistic discourse—hers is a dangerously inflammatory sexuality, a fire or disease that "cannot / Choose" but spread and infect an entire kingdom.

When Evadne resists that discourse, claiming not to understand him, Melantius responds with verbal and physical violence. He renames her—"foolish woman," "fool" (22, 26), "wretch" (45), and, here and throughout the scene, "whore" (51, 69, 95, 148). Against the dissonance of her female sex and male gender, he pits the consonance of his male sex and male gender. His accusation that her "lusts . . . would fill another woman, / Though she had twins within her" (31–32) categorizes Evadne as female in order to demonstrate that she is neither a woman nor a man. Women's bodies swell only in pregnancy, a definitively female event that, in the eyes of a man like Melantius, merely confirms men's natural superiority. Evadne is unpregnant but inflated, a condition that proves her body not only other than female but also competitively male.

Unable to reduce her to submission either by threatening or by seizing her, he invokes the hierarchical structure in which his male authority is rooted and calls upon the eponymous patriarch "whose child thou wert, / Whose honour thou hast murdered, whose grave opened" (86–87) and asks the gods "in their justice" (88) to raise him from the dead "to revenge this scandal" (90). Evadne's flippant response, "The gods are not of my mind: they had better / Let 'em lie sweet still in the earth; they'll stink here" (91–92), reveals to him the enormity of her crime. Her bold seizure of authority over her body is an assault on maleness itself.

Purifying himself by disavowing "all weaknesses of nature / That make men women" (94–95), Melantius draws his sword, forces her to the ground, and commands her to speak the name of her lover, "Or, by the dear soul of thy sleeping father, / This sword shall be thy lover" (96–97). The repeated invocation of their father becomes a brutal threat of incestuous rape and, in the threat of penetration by sword, sodomy. Standing over Evadne wielding the phallus of patriarchy, Melantius strikes the extreme posture of male dominance. He denies her the right to author either herself or the men around her—brother, father, husband; he denies women's right, despite their part in human procreation, to author men at all.

In their contest, the victory goes to Melantius because he controls the scene and play in which they perform. When Evadne bragged that she would not care if her faults were written on her forehead (28–29), she asserted her power to govern the discourse according to which her body is read. Melantius, however, had already written the scene in which they apparently vie for authorship, and he is careful to construct a plot that leaves her ignorant of what he knows—the identity of her lover. That authorial advantage is enforced on the bodily level by his physical strength and military training. Using the force Amintor had threatened but abandoned at the mention of his great rival, Melantius demonstrates that he can literally inscribe his meaning on her body:

> When I have kill'd thee . . .
> Nak'd as thou hast left thine honour will I leave thee,
> That on thy branded flesh the world may read
> Thy black shame and my justice. Wilt thou bend yet?
>
> (105–9)

To that definitive denial of her ability to write herself, Evadne responds with a simple "Yes" (110). Melantius has reasserted his authority as the male who writes her, and she capitulates, opening her closed mouth and, a final testament to his superiority, using her voice at his command to name the lover whose identity he already knows.

With Evadne reconstructed as female, Melantius turns to his rival. The King's crimes are great. He has seduced a sister and married her to Melantius's greatly loved friend; worse, he has allowed a woman the power to harm men. Absolutist dogma does not deter Melantius from his revenge because for him manhood and the traditions that underwrite its prerogatives precede and supersede his duty. His relationship to king and state is, like Maximus's, based on personal judgment: "where I find worth, / I love the keeper, till he let it go, / And then I follow it" (1.1.23–25). From that premise follows a political philosophy that ties love and obedience to his assessment of their recipient's worthiness. Like Maximus, Melantius serves himself even when he ostensibly serves the state and his community. Later, like England's radical Protestants, he will assert that his own conscience is above a monarch's reach, and he will place it above the gods' as well: "where I am clear / I will not take forgiveness of the gods, / Much less of you" (4.2.114–16).

With the female body his text, Melantius can rival the King by authoring himself without benefit of women's participation. His competitive elimination of the female through subjection and appropriation allows him, like Maximus, to become wild, in violation of nature: he has, in fact, told Amintor that "nothing is so wild as I thy friend / Till I have freed thee" (3.2.197-98). For both, revenge is an action predicated on jumping the wall of civilization and leaving behind the ties that force them to obey an unworthy monarch and to control and protect women who make them vulnerable to injury. With Amintor unfeignedly playing the revenger's conventional role of madman, Melantius's self-creation takes a different direction. The second body that will allow him to control the text as author and actor is not the wild man but a simplification and exaggeration of his former identity as the honest soldier. In disguise as his own hyperbole, Melantius can outplay the King for control of the play.

He writes his public court scene as he wrote the scene with Evadne: only he—and Diphilus, who remains silent—knows the full truth. Calianax, from whom Melantius has demanded the keys to the fort, mistakenly believes he is in author of the scene: "This fighting fool / Wants policy" (3.2.323–24). The King assumes he is author of all. With feigned *bonhomie*, he tests Calianax's story by chatting offhandedly about rebellion. The King believes that only he wears an impenetrable mask, that Melantius cannot possibly carry off a lie. Melantius, however, has already penetrated the King's disguise; doubled himself so that he is both inside and outside the action; seized the authorial function from the King; and written the scene, Calianax's role in it, and, without his knowledge, the King's. His demonstration of control is a theatrical *tour de force*. Before the court, the actor Melantius feigns innocence of the King's purpose while in asides the author Melantius presses the bedizened Calianax to turn over the fort. He raises and drops his mask with a turn of his head, and the King, who prides himself on remaining hidden while others reveal themselves, judges his pretense honest and Calianax's honesty either vengeful pretense or senile delusion.

From this scene to the play's end, Melantius's theatrical authority overwhelms and usurps the King's political and sexual authority on all levels. He has already arrogated the King's claim to divine right by becoming the voice not only of the patriarchy but also of the gods: invoking their justice in wishing his father back from the dead; proclaiming, in response to Evadne's demurral at the murder because "All the gods forbid it" (4.1.144), "No, all the gods require it: / They are dishonoured in him" (145–46). According to Melantius's construction of maleness, the courtly monarch was never his equal. Now he need not even establish his superiority by challenging the King in his person; the "dance of

arms" Melantius performs with Amintor is unsuited to this offense to manhood. To kill a dishonorable man, Melantius will use
the only creature beneath him—a dishonorable woman. As it has
with Maximus, being author of himself and of the play, not victory
in combat, has come to demonstrate his absolute maleness. Melantius can leave the murder in the hands of one of his surrogates.
With the taste for poetic justice he shares with his fellow revengers, he will use the very instrument the King had used against
him.

According to the principle of revenge, the tyrant must, before
death, experience the tyranny he has visited on others. His discovery that Evadne's presence in his quarters does not signify
submission to his sexual will, that neither her body nor tongue
respond to his command, unkings and unmans him at once. He
is merely a body awaiting her inscription. Feminizing him as Melantius had feminized her, she imprisons him in his own quarters,
forcing him to close his mouth and utter only what she ventrilo-
quizes: "Stir nothing but your tongue, and that for mercy / To
those above us" (5.1.86–87). He must hear her speak not the
sweet and gentle words he would write but her bitter and harsh
ones, and he must watch, from his constraint, her unrestrained
arms wield the knife against his body. Deprived of command,
motion, and volition, forced to obey Evadne and deliver the lines
she puts into his mouth, he feels the repeated stab wounds—
"love-tricks"—of a slow murder that is, in its violent penetration
of his now feminized body, a rape.

Through Evadne, Melantius wins a revenger's victory, inscribing his maleness on his rival by reducing him to a woman's victim. Necessary to that success, however, is his division into
character and player, a leap to authority that leaves Amintor behind. Once the self-proclaimed center of certainty in Amintor's
shattered world—"All shall be well again" (3.2.253)—Melantius
now speaks only of the King's crime against himself and his family: "I will wash the stain / That rests upon our house off with
his blood" (4.2.289–90). The agency of Evadne, the assistance of
Diphilus are folded into his encompassing *I*. Amintor's appearance on the scene reminds him of his other motive for revenge—
"Who can see him thus, / And not swear vengeance?" (294–95)—
but, like the King with his subjects' honor and manhood, Melantius appropriates Amintor's cause and his revenge.

In the asides and third-person references that mark his withdrawal from their union, Melantius even speaks of his loved friend
as a threat: "He'll overthrow / My whole design with madness"

(308–9). No more than the King and Evadne can Amintor be allowed to write himself. To neutralize that danger and quash any independent action on Amintor's part, Melantius uses his player's skills, disguising himself as a deferential and obedient subject:

> I dare as much as valour,
> But 'tis the King, the King, the King, Amintor,
> With whom thou fightest. (*Aside*) I know he's honest,
> And this will work with him.
>
> (310–13)

Melantius maintains control of the design, but the cost is estrangement from Amintor. Amintor is no longer the chosen partner in the dance of men but, as he is with the King, a feminized male, passive, helpless, silent, and obedient.

His duplicity estranges him from other men as well. Beneath the candid, soldierly model of maleness, Melantius betrays the revenger's tyrannical arrogance. With Diphilus, he affirms the common goal of bringing "our banished honours home" (5.2.3). For both Strato and Lysippus, he remains exemplary: "mighty-spirited and forward," "noble," "his mind . . . ever / As worthy as his hand," says Strato (16, 19, 20–21). Lysippus prays only that he has "not left [himself] and sought this safety / More out of fear than honour" (31–32). Melantius's justification for seizing the fort, however, is his assumed right to choose the man he serves:

> Thy brother,
> Whilst he was good, I called him King, and served him
> With that strong faith, that most unwearied valour,
> Pulled people from the farthest sun to seek him
> And buy his friendship. I was then his soldier.
> But since his hot pride drew him to disgrace me,
> . . . like myself
> Thus I have flung him off with my allegiance,
> And stand here mine own justice, to revenge
> What I have suffered in him, and this old man
> Wronged almost to lunacy.
>
> (39–44, 48–52)

The agency of Melantius's *I* dominates the speech: that *I* supplied the King with allies and friends; suffered when the king dishonored "my sister"; and even revenged Calianax's suffering—another and unlikely appropriation of the man he himself drove "almost to lunacy." In Melantius's exposition of the grounds for his rebellion, in his insistence on taking "mine own justice"— "like myself," he sweeps past his vow to Amintor and exposes him as the King's cuckold.

His motive, Melantius assures his audience, is not ambition (55), nor has he left himself and honor out of fear, as Lysippus suggested. He is happy to commit himself to the new King's service, he says, but he delivers himself back into servitude not in the language of subjection but of provision, ultimatum, and command:

> I do desire again
> To be a subject, so I may be free;
> If not, I know my strength, and will unbuild
> This goodly town; be speedy, and be wise,
> In a reply.
>
> (56–60)

Lysippus obeys him; as ordered, he speedily and wisely throws Melantius the blank on which he writes his own and his compatriots' pardons. Melantius's justice has prevailed, destroying one political order and erecting a new one that will, however, govern only so long as he deems it worthy. In Rhodes, absolute authority now clearly belongs to Melantius.

The price Melantius pays for political and sexual victory, however, is high. Like Maximus before he succumbs to ambition, Melantius believes that he can now put aside the player's authority and return to his former self, which he defines by his androgynous union with Amintor. When he descends from the upper stage, however, he discovers the gruesome finale of his plot. Ignoring the dead bodies of Evadne and the as-yet-unidentified Aspatia, he rushes to Amintor. Diphilus tries to turn his attention: "O brother, / Here lies your sister slain! You lose yourself / In sorrow there" (5.3.261–63).

Melantius, however, rejects his brother's familial definition of that self. His sister's death is merely "a thing to laugh at in respect of this: / Here was my sister, father, brother, son, / All that I had" (264–66). In denying family, Melantius also denies his revenge and its basis. At the heart of his statement of absolute value is the old invidious and appropriative comparison between men and women, but the Melantius who rediscovers "all" in Amintor has altered. He is no longer a brother or even a great soldier: Diphilus, a lesser man, disarms him. He is no longer the exemplar of all that is traditionally male or patriarchal: he ignores his brother's calling his attempt at suicide "unmanly" (278) and unbecoming their "strain" (279). For Melantius, the "dance with arms" is over, and what is left is a renewed love and an unbreakable pledge: "I vow, Amintor, I will never eat, / Or drink, or sleep, or have to do with that / That may preserve life: this I swear to keep" (288–90). In his pursuit of revenge, he betrayed "All that I had," but he will follow Amintor into a place where they may love without tyrants or female intermediaries, perfectly one and purely male.

Melantius's decision to forgo the ambition of tyrants and return to their love makes his end tragic as Maximus's is not, but he nonetheless follows the revenger's path: the autogenous self-creation of an omnipotent authorial body that replicates the tyrant's political body; the reduction in that expansion to a single, solitary, dominant male self. The revenger's career is a pathological retreat from the female, an attempt, like the tyrant he opposes, to control the sexual Other through strategies of domination and appropriation. Melantius, however, although he persists to the end in showing only contempt for women and extending his rejection of them to the family connections forged in and through their bodies, does not isolate himself from all humanity. With Amintor dead in his arms, he returns to the meaning from which he was diverted by a revenge that now seems paltry. The revenger Melantius triumphs over his tyrant rival and lives; the lover Melantius loses everything.

4

Androgynous Heroes: Kneeling Soldiers and Swooning Kings

The tyrant's and revenger's insistent connection of maleness and authority culminates in the tragedy of blood. In presuming women no more than male texts, both reduce their world to one gender and then, further, to one another. The result is mutual destruction: the tyrant at the revenger's hands and the revenger at his society's or his own; both, of course, at the players'. When Maximus defeats and replaces Valentinian and when Melantius, though submitting to the new king, defines his community as Amintor, they have reached the logical ends of male self-authoring and self-authorizing.

With Affranius in *Valentinian* and Govianus in *The Second Maiden's Tragedy*, we witness the development of a different definition of male gender. Neither is contained by the military and aristocratic traditions of the patriarchal family. While Affranius is a soldier, he chooses to exercise his authority politically; Govianus can use his sword like a soldier, but he is, first and in name, a ruler. Nor is familial authority wrested from them. They are not wounded by the sharp sexual edge of a wife's rape or a sister's infidelity to a loved friend. Eudoxa has no familial connection to Affranius, and the Lady chooses death over abduction and assault. Affranius and Govianus are, therefore, not driven to retreat from intimate connections—either to women or to men—into solitude and self-creation. Both characters assume a protective disguise—Affranius feigning loyalty to Maximus and Govianus posing as a portrait painter—but their creation of another self does not flower poisonously into delusions of divine autogeny and omnipotence, nor is it accompanied by misogyny. Like the revengers, these heroes initially accept unquestioningly the ingrained belief that women are weak, but they end by admiring the courage and resolve of specific women who, like them, are persons of principle and action in the midst of general corruption.

In their world, a woman can play an active, verbal, public role, and they can play the traditional woman's part. As a result of their extricating themselves, even if in a limited and local way, from the sexual binary and its presumptive hierarchy, their worlds expand rather than shrink, and their plays end in renewed social and political stability.

Questioning sexual difference in a society where institutional foundations rest on the theory of male superiority requires men to doubt and then relinquish grounds for entitlement. In Jacobean England, however, the retrospectively glorified reign of Elizabeth belied the presumption that men would inevitably suffer loss if they acknowledged authority in women. For more than four decades, men had knelt to female sovereignty and, in return, received title, honor, and wealth. The mutual benefit of the gender exchange, especially with submission to a queen made palatable by men's playing the conventionally acceptable—if seemingly contradictory—familial and Petrachan roles of husband and servant-lover, made androgyny less threatening. The memory of a female monarch who supported the authority of men, even as she asserted a female authority as its counterpart and balance, could exert a powerful subterranean force of tradition and certainty in a world where the definition of maleness had become slippery.

Men's acceptance of female gender in themselves, a necessary complement to the queen's royal maleness, could also be supported by religious doctrine and tradition. The Judeo-Christian God, as Kimbrough asserts, is both hermaphrodite and androgyne (1990, 15); the soul and mind of humankind, created in the divine image, without sex or gender. The New Testament offers instances of Christ's crossing the marked boundaries between women and men: despite warnings of scandal, he speaks to the Samaritan woman at the well; he befriends Mary and Martha and welcomes Mary as his student; he accepts Mary Magdalene as his follower. Moreover, Christians of both sexes, because they are admonished to adopt Christ's meekness, humility, and patient endurance, assume characteristics that early modern English society associated with women. Indeed, a long textual and iconographic tradition identified Christ's body as maternal and his suffering flesh as female (Bynum 1987, 261). In the course of practicing his religion, then, even the most aggressive and military of men would have to put aside his working definition of maleness to entertain and honor what he considered female qualities. While there is no evidence of that attitude toward sex and gender transferring readily into daily life, Christianity at least offered the possibility for men to consider women devoted to virtue and piety as their spiritual equals and, in some cases, betters.

For the players who inhabited not only the larger cultural world of early modern England but the world of literary tradition as well, there was strong precedent for a philogynous male androgyny. Sidney's *Arcadia* represents the noble, humanist man-of-arms Pyrocles transforming himself into the Amazon Zelmane to pursue an ennobling heterosexual love. Ultimately, his quest is successful while Amphialus, the rival who narrowly defines his manhood as aggressively military, dies by his own hand. Breton's "The Praise of Vertuous Ladies" offers an androgynous version of a humanity that includes men as well as women; Spenser's Adonis and Marlowe's Leander are male in sex but both male and female in gender. In the days of Queen Elizabeth, androgyny was good politics.

It was not under King James, however, where the ideology of sexual difference formed the basis of political authority. In Jacobean revenge tragedy, an alliance between women and men that recognizes inherent likeness and allows each to play the other's role is subversive. While the tyrant and revenger are problematic figures politically, the threat they pose to the state is mitigated by their adherence to the governing sexual ideology. With the exception of Maximus's reference to Valentinian's "black-eyd boyes," the theatrical tyrants are safely represented as unlike the enthroned monarch of England in their generic lust for women. They do, however, share with him the belief that manhood is defined by their embodiment of it and that their rights and claims supersede those of male heads of families. Melantius's absorption of the female into an apotheosized maleness and his consuming love for another man echo the sexual attitudes of the reigning monarch—a strong counterbalance to his culpability in engineering a successful regicide.

Affranius and Govianus, however, do not conform to the *de rigueur* misogyny of the times. In their support of divine right, they seem politically innocuous: Affranius, like Aecius, is loyal to Valentinian; Govianus, although overthrown by the Tyrant, is his country's rightful monarch. Yet in their public recognition of a woman's authority, in their willingness to hear and support rather than silence or ventriloquize female voices, they revert to the gender politics of the preceding monarchy and cast doubt on the premises and practices of male governance. These heroes' refusal

of the misogynist premise behind James's appropriative androgyny has, as its consequence, a veering away from the bloody
nihilism produced by the tyrant's and revenger's rivalry. *Valentinian* ends with Affranius preventing Eudoxa's slaughter, *The Second
Maiden's Tragedy* with Govianus triumphantly reclaiming his
throne with the spectral Lady and her physical remains at his
side. At closure, both plays promote the socially healing harmonies of men and women who function as one.

In a world where men have abandoned the connection between
principle and politics, women's firmness and courage in asserting
truth over expedience deny the tyrant authority over their lives
and, therefore, over men's lives as well. When men like Affranius
and Govianus stop defending the borders of maleness against
incursions from the female and share leadership with women,
the power of tyranny is broken.

"It was more / Than I was able to perform myself": Men Allied with Women

Affranius, the "eminent Captaine" of the cast of characters,
emerges from the carnage perpetrated by the man he calls "Lord
Maximus" (5.4.34) to resolve the conflicting principles for which
his fellow soldier and Aecius had stood. Like Maximus, he is
Rome's warrior ideal; like Aecius, he obeys those above him in
the hierarchy. Finally, however, he is like neither. He does not
support the principle of divine right when Maximus claims it,
nor does he replace the state with himself. In his willingness to
recognize virtue in Eudoxa—a woman who has murdered a man
who is also her husband and a crowned monarch—and to share
his public authority with her, Affranius offers a healing androgyny. Absent from the murderous political and sexual climate of
Valentinian's first four acts, he enters in the final act to join Eudoxa
in bringing peace to a Rome ravaged by aggression.

Affranius is constructed as a classically male figure. Soldierly,
controlled, taciturn, he is a marked contrast not only to the de-
luded, amoral Maximus, who was once Rome's model of manhood, but also to the three scurrying, babbling senators who
enter with him. Like Aecius, Affranius understands manhood as
serving the state. To quiet the rebellious army, the senators make
rash promises they cannot and, undoubtedly, do not intend to
keep—of veto power; of corn, wine, oil, new garments, new arms;
of equal portions of the provinces (5.4.9–16)—and ask him to

convey them. Affranius obeys. With a simple, dignified "I shall do it" (17), he exits, leaving the senators alone on stage to reveal a cowardly desperation that demonstrates their unfitness to rule. Affranius reappears moments later to announce "A Cesar" and to add three terse, pregnant lines—"Lord *Maximus* is with the Souldier, / And all the Camp rings, *Cesar, Cesar, Cesar:* / He forcd the Empresse with him for more honour" (34–36). The political leaders of Rome choose to ignore his implication; they are busy looking after their interests —property, wives, daughters. Affranius alone considers the damage to a larger community, represented here by Eudoxa and later, when he speaks in soliloquy, by Rome.

Like Aecius, Affranius serves men who are unworthy of their superior position because he believes in hierarchy itself. He declares his loyalty to the principles of absolutism manifest in Valentinian (64) and, again like Aecius, he concerns himself with the health of the state he serves, looking beyond his military position toward Rome's governance in peace as well as war: "Oh turning people! / Oh people excellent in war, and governd; / In peace more raging then the furious North . . ." (40–42). Affranius's connection to Aecius and Rome extends to his mention of Eudoxa, with whom Aecius is also linked: Valentinian first establishes a relationship between his wife and the great general—"My Empresse sweares thou art a lusty Souldier, / A good one I beleeve thee" (1.3.119–20)—and Eudoxa reinforces their connection in her later eulogy of Aecius. In Affranius, the values for which Aecius stood and which, the general had argued, define true manhood return stronger than ever, and they include a concept of community and state that embraces both sexes.

Initially, Affranius seems to resemble Maximus even more closely. He enters the stage after Maximus's autogenous rebirth "above the fate of women" to claim the soliloquizing liminal space between play and audience that Maximus had abandoned only moments before. Both men respond to the betrayal of those they serve by isolating themselves from their fellow characters. Assessing his position in a hostile world, Affranius, like Maximus, authors a second self by separating *I* from the duplicitous player who will pretend loyalty to the new regime:

> I must give way,
> Although I neither love nor hop'd this *Cesar,*
> Or like a rotten bridge that dares a current
> When he is sweld and high, crack and farwell.
>
> (5.4.44–47)

For Affranius, however, disguise does not slide into a pseudo-divinity of appropriation and exploitation. He holds fast to the manly ethos of service.

His view of the family, the intermediary world between the self and the state peopled by both men and women, also indicates his difference from Maximus. Maximus invoked the Roman family to justify rebellion, his idealized, self-serving portrait of a patriarchy where honorable sons follow the example of honorable fathers belied by the civil war he forced on Rome. For Affranius, who confronts the "sluce of blood" Maximus "let open" (5.3.1), the male-dominated rhetoric of patriarchy has already been emptied of meaning:

> Well froward *Rome,* thou wilt grow weak with changing
> And die without an Heire, that lov'st to breed
> Sonnes for the killing hate of sons: for me,
> I only live to find an enemy.
>
> (69–72)

Affranius's vision of the Roman patriarchy is not fraternal but fratricidal, not a continuum of fathers and sons but a slaughterhouse that leaves no inheritors. He has witnessed the destructive inward turn of male aggression in civil wars that arise from and perpetuate relentless, debilitating change. The future, he predicts, will leave Rome weak and sterile—unmanly. Affranius, however, will focus his own aggression carefully on an enemy he "only live[s] to find." He does not specify the target—"an enemy" can be either within or outside Rome—but he does not choose to perpetuate the random killing. He will stop the unchecked flow of Roman blood by relinking male aggression to the political and social order he willingly serves.

Affranius's vision of Rome does not include daughters as heirs; he does not doubt that society should be governed by men. Nonetheless, because his definition of maleness includes not only dominance and aggression but human generation, his perspective embraces social functions socially assigned to both men and women. That openness and flexibility allow him to recognize his complement in Eudoxa, a woman who, like him, does not define her gender narrowly. Maximus began his flight from human society by severing his intimate ties to Lucina, then to Aecius, and, finally, to Rome. Affranius will reunite the severed parts, and he will begin with the broken tie between men and women.

In the woman who has identified and killed the enemy of Rome he lived to find, Affranius recognizes and embraces his natural ally. Literally separating himself from the army, he positions himself between Eudoxa and the wild mob, who would cut her into a thousand pieces, seizing the public space that is his by virtue of his sex in order to give Eudoxa voice and space. At this point, her authority is borrowed from his. His healing gesture is based on the presumption of male superiority. Like Maximus, he believes that his role as a man is to protect women who, presumed weak, are subjects not for swords but pity, occasions for men's compassion and mercy. Yet when Eudoxa uses her own voice in the space provided by his and presents her case against Maximus eloquently and forcefully, he reconsiders the terms of their alliance. He has foreseen Rome's men becoming weak with change; now he sees a Roman woman with the strength to act their role:

> What lesse could nature doe, what lesse had we done,
> Had we knowne this before? *Romans*, she is righteous;
> And such a peece of justice, heaven must smile on:
> Bend all your swords on me, if this displease ye,
> For I must kneele, and on this vertuous hand
> Seale my new joy and thankes,—thou hast done truly.
>
> (5.8.109–14)

Not only is Eudoxa not his or any man's inferior; she is "righteous," "a peece of justice," "vertuous"—Astraea returned to earth. Affranius had begun his address to the assembly by asking them to hear Eudoxa as his substitute; now he offers himself to them as hers, bidding them turn their swords from her to him if his kneeling before her and kissing her hand displease them.

His signifiers of loving obedience and respect do not culminate in Rome's granting her political authority—there is no cry for Eudoxa to become the next caesar. Affranius has invoked the mythic female figures of justice and righteousness from Elizabeth's empowering pantheon without connecting them to a political order. Sempronius quickly whisks Eudoxa away from the world of state power by completing her apotheosis—she is now a saint (115)—and then exhorting the assembly to "pray before we choose, then plant a *Cesar* / Above the reach of envie, blood, and murder" (118–19). As saintly intercessor, she can reunite the realms of divine and political election, her function to reinscribe divinely ordained absolutism.

Nonetheless, Affranius's kneeling before Eudoxa, the manly soldier willingly ceding authority to active virtue figured as fe-

male, visually echoes Elizabeth's rule and the relationship between gender and authority she established. In Eudoxa, Affranius
finds not only a political ally but a principle that transcends and
should inform the political. As his ally, he defends her, but as the
woman who has reconnected a heavenly ideal to the human
world, he bows to her. The presumption of essential difference
between the sexes is superseded by the theoretically genderless
but, within the play, female authority of virtue.

Affranius's maleness does not depend for definition on the control and suppression of the female. He is, therefore, able to recognize in the woman he had assumed a passive victim of events an
active arm of justice. Their alliance does not cast doubt on his
manhood; it validates it. Separately, he and Eudoxa are only partially effective as forgers of a new Rome. She is willing to die for
the murder she understands as just; he is willing to devote his
life to finding and fighting an enemy. Their androgynous union
restores them to meaningful life within the larger community to
which they offer the gift of stability.

"Our Virtuous King"

In *The Second Maiden's Tragedy*, political alliance shifts to the
intimate ground of the family. Like Affranius, whose relationship
to Eudoxa progresses from protective paternalism to respectful
partnership, Govianus evolves beyond the traditional constructions of sex and gender. As a man, he is compromised. His function, he believes, is to shield the Lady from harm, yet he is unable
to prevent her assault except by killing her. The only way out
of the paralyzing crisis created by conflicting demands on his
maleness, he discovers, is to refuse its terms. Fainting, Govianus
plays the woman's part, escaping the revenger's fate by experienc-
ing the reversal and, therefore, interchangeability of male and
female gender.

Like Affranius, Govianus initially accepts the male-female binary and its corollary assumptions about women's inherent weakness. An active, if shallow, misogyny allies him to the Tyrant—
both believe the Lady will alter with alteration—and marks him
as a prospective revenger. As a malcontent, moreover, Govianus
plays the theatrical type often conflated, as it is in Hamlet and
Vindice, with that stock figure. He fleers at the "ponderous nobility" (79) created under the new regime and waits for the Lady to

break faith with him. If Govianus's country and nobles have betrayed him, surely a woman will prove fickle:

> O, she's a woman, and her eye will stand
> Upon advancement, never weary yonder;
> But when she turns her head by chance and sees
> The fortunes that are my companions,
> She'll snatch her eyes off, and repent the looking.
>
> (1.1.63–67)

Anti-feminist clichés about women's ambition and materialism flood Govianus's self-pitying reflections on the loss that "sits closer to my heart / Than that of kingdom or the whorish pomp / Of this world's titles" (1.1.59–61). The Tyrant, of course, concurs: "'Tis well advised," he responds, rushing to banish Govianus and summon the Lady to "afflict [his] soul" (1.1.104). The rivals tacitly agree that the woman whom both desire is a lesser form of life, no more than a pawn in their struggle for authority.

In refusing that construction, the Lady replaces the exclusionary male discourse of sex and politics with one whose power is situated in divine law and, therefore, in her as its spokesperson. In *Valentinian*, Affranius uses his voice to give Eudoxa audience; here, the Lady authorizes herself in order to grant authority to Govianus. Her assumption of male voice does not deny her biological sex or negate her faith in an authority that is female any more than it shakes Govianus's belief in his natural superiority as a man. Indeed, her use of authority to re-empower his confirms that premise. It also enables Govianus to cast aside the rote misogyny that ties him to the Tyrant and ally himself with her. With the Lady as its representative, femaleness is neither threatening nor pejorative. He does not need to abandon the man's part; he simply transfers the site of his monarchy from state to family, reconstructing his gender exclusively through and in his relationship to her. Although he exits the public world that had formerly defined him as a man to enter the confinement he declares "Love's best freedom" (211)—it is, in fact, policed private space—Govianus does not consider himself unmanned or feminized. In their new domicile, he will be head, arm, and voice of their unofficial family: its monarch, soldier, and minister.

His presumption of absolute authority, however, is immediately challenged by the invasion of panders, men who have abandoned the independent authority of their gender to play the female role to political power. The first is Helvetius, who intends to use his paternal sway to make the Lady serve the state as he does. She is site and prize in the war over who commands within the male hierarchy, a war with implications extending as far as a subject's right to overthrow a crowned monarch. Govianus, in order to maintain his kingly position within the family, must delimit Helvetius's authority and subordinate it to his own. He begins with a soldierly demonstration of physical power: he fires over Helvetius's head, missing, Govianus explains, only because Helvetius is the Lady's father. With that statement, Govianus proclaims Helvetius's rights as proceeding neither from himself as patriarch nor from the tyrant he serves but from the Lady. With Helvetius subordinated to her and she to Govianus, the respective positions of the two men are established.

Having used a soldier's arm to make good his authority, Govianus then adopts a ministerial role, demanding that the "ancient sinner" (2.1.113) examine his conscience. With the Lady standing by in silent affirmation, he lectures Helvetius on his "unmanly sin" of "panderism" (129, 127). For Govianus, manhood is linked to virtue, and both are tied to "business" or "work," a concept of labor that insists on consonance between worldly activity and salvation. "Follow thine own business" (144), he instructs Helvetius, and Helvetius does by kneeling to him: "Be you my king and master still" (2.1.162). Govianus has doubled the number of his subjects.

Gender follows sex in his paradigmatic domain: Helvetius dedicates himself to the business of fealty; the Lady passively, silently obeys Govianus. Govianus is her voice; he speaks for her when Helvetius asks her pardon: "Mine shall bring hers" (167). Yet while she and Helvetius may support Govianus's sense of control within his prison, the Tyrant holds sway over the world that contains it. In the inevitable clash between the rival monarchs, Govianus and the Lady will both be driven from the essentialist positions to which they cling and, in the process, break the theoretical continuum of sex and gender.

The second pander forces that change. Like Helvetius, Sophonirus defies Govianus's authority and role as the Lady's spokesman by approaching her directly. Govianus's first response to the news is flat denial: "he will not dare / To come about such business; 'tis not man's work. / Art sure he desired conference with thy lady? (3.1.2–4). Govianus insists the servant is mistaken: "'tis with me, certain" (5):

> There's no man is so dull but he will weigh
> The work he undertakes, and set about it

E'en in the best sobriety of his judgment,
With all his senses watchful.

(8–11)

Yet Sophonirus's actions cannot be read in any other way. For the venal old courtier, manliness is as his monarch defines it, and Govianus must see his constructed paradigm of domesticity as a prison in which both he and the Lady are physically helpless. Their enclosed space is circled by the Tyrant's men, who have instructions to take the Lady by force if necessary.

As the awareness of his failure to protect her from the Tyrant grows, Govianus becomes increasingly "wild." The servant he commands to ask again with whom Sophonirus wishes conference speaks in an aside of his "strange humour, we must know things twice" (7). The Lady is shocked when he suddenly stabs the "panderous lord": "Las, what have you done, my lord?" (26, 28), a question he fobs off with a flippant, "Why, sent a bawd / Home to his lodging; nothing else, sweetheart" (28–29). Denial alternates with acknowledgment of their situation's hopelessness: "And no plank to save us!" (53). His control of himself and others deteriorates into sudden bursts of uncontrollable anger. He calls Sophonirus a liar for reporting the Tyrant's men waiting for report of his success, then snaps at either him or the Lady (it is not clear which): "'Tis boldly done to trouble me / When I've such business to dispatch" (44–45). He sharply rebukes the servant who tells him, because he has commanded the telling, of the men surrounding the house: "I think thou'st never done; thou lov'st to talk on't. / 'Tis fine discourse. Prithee find other business" (59–60).

Govianus's anxious harping on business, his metonym for manliness, is reinforced by the Lady's accusatory participation in the metaphor: "Have you leisure to stand idle?" (63), she demands. He should, she insists, be busy killing her. When he, like Maximus, becomes tangled in his dependency on a woman whom he supposedly owns but whose body and fate he cannot control, she pulls him back roughly to the situation at hand: "Come on, sir! / Fall to your business; lay your hands about you" (67–68). She accurately predicts the revenger's future for him if she is "lost the cruel'st way"; he will "curse / That love that sent forth pity to my life" (78–79). By demanding that he prove himself a man and protect her by killing her, however, she has set two cultural imperatives of manhood in conflict. A true man protects the woman he loves; he does not murder her. Yet refusing her is equally unmanly: it denies her wishes, it proves he is unable to defend her, and it places her in the Tyrant's hands.

Govianus's helplessness and her demand permanently disrupt his sense of himself. He simply no longer knows how to behave; nothing is automatically, clearly man's business. He ponders suicide: "O, fie! / And leave her here alone? That were unmanly" (118–19). Yet while he rejects that act, he has been rendered incapable of any other. He is as physically passive and compromised—as "female" against the Tyrant's forces—as the Lady. Admitting self-doubt, he becomes vulnerable to her as well:

> 'Tis the hard'st work that ever man was put to.
> I know not which way to begin to come to't.
> Believe me, I shall never kill thee well;
> I shall but shame myself. It were but folly,
> Dear soul, to boast of more than I can perform.
> I shall not have the power to do thee right in't.
>
> (122–27)

In exposing his fear that he will prove unable to do what she has declared his work, Govianus confesses to the greater fear he will fail her as a man. Unable to determine the proper business for his sword and therefore to use it, he finds himself impotent in the two areas conflated in that signifier—sexual union and soldierly aggression. The Lady's passive acceptance of death and her vow to speak no more do not restore him. He is immobilized: he runs at her with his sword and swoons. Passive rather than active, fainting rather than killing, Govianus becomes female in their union.

When he awakens to find that the Lady has, in turn, played the man's part, he at first indicts himself:

> Was I so hard to thee? So respectless of thee,
> To put all this to thee? Why, it was more
> Than I was able to perform myself
> With all the courage that I could take to me.
> It tired me; I was fain to fall, and rest.
> And hast thou, valiant woman, overcome
> Thy honour's enemies with thine own white hand,
> Where virgin-victory sits, all without help?
>
> (170–77)

The moment of self-recrimination is brief; his attention moves instantly from his inadequacy to her courage. Unlike the revenger, who recoils from the female he fears he has become and recommits himself to male contest, Govianus neglects his apparent failure in order to admire and revere the Lady's "virgin victory." He was too "tired"—a self-ironizing euphemism for his faint—to perform his duty but, like Affranius finding his enemy dead at Eudoxa's hands, he is delighted rather than horrified to learn she did not need him; she was capable of performing the act she had assigned to him. In his discovery that he was not alone, the revenger's wildness is tamed.

This liberating androgynous moment does not mean that Govianus entirely abandons his traditional definition of maleness as conferring authority and demanding work. He continues his battle against the Tyrant after the Lady's death by setting Sophonirus's body against the door for the Tyrant's men to kill again. He relishes his pretense of unmanly submission to their demand for the Lady—"Take her, then" (205)—as if he were indeed, the "honest subject" praised by the Second Fellow who would "do the like myself to serve my prince" (206, 207). He is not, after all, a hapless subject. He is what her suicide has made him: a king: "Now I praise / Her resolution; 'tis a triumph to me / When I see those about her" (212–14). Nor does the Lady's example move Govianus to revise his views on women's virtues in general. He maintains his early misogyny in his invidious remarks to the Tyrant's ruffians about how few of their ladies would believe the Lady would die for honor.

In transforming his victimage into victory, the Lady has again gifted him with the opportunity to deny their reversal of gender. He can reduce her silenced voice to his text, as Maximus does with the monumentalized Lucina and, forgetting his indecision and passivity, appropriate her suicide as his triumph, her virtue as an offering to his worthiness. He does not. Even before the Lady's visitation, Govianus acknowledges her agency in his victory over the Tyrant. Not only did her "resolution" effect his "triumph," but it was she who taught him how to read her suicide: "she told me / Her everlasting sleep would bring me joy, / Yet I was still unwilling to believe her" (232–34). She remains his androgynous complement: the woman he has taken as wife, the author of their text. He will kiss her to commemorate their love, and he will entomb her "by my father's side" (252), a decision he feels compelled to defend: "Without offence in kindred there I'll place thee, / With one I loved the dearest next to thee" (253–54). Her authority and courage have opened not only him but patriarchy itself to femaleness.

The tomb, like Govianus's prison, is female space—the cold, silent, faithful womb of humanity's second birth. He willingly followed the Lady into their locked house; now he joins her in death's enclosure. In both instances, he rejects the male ideal that prides itself on freedom from the female. As soon as he entered the tomb, he says, "a tear"—an explicitly female and obedient tear—"Ran swiftly from me, to express her duty" (4.4.2–3):

> Chamber of peace,
> Where wounded virtue sleeps locked from the world,
> I bring to be acquainted with thy silence
> Sorrows that love no noise; they dwell all inward,
> Where truth and love in every man should dwell.
>
> (5–9)

Govianus joins the Lady on her terms. To her silence, he brings his sorrows, uniting with her as supplicant and partner. She is again his guide, and he willingly seeks an inwardness that is biologically, socially, and culturally associated with women. In direct contrast is the Tyrant's entrance to the tomb—his comparison of the marble's tears and his own "slow springs" (4.3.11), his violent assault on the stones with axes, his possession of her body by force.

The androgynous union of Govianus and the Lady is, however, cut short by the Tyrant's actions, which force the Lady to return from the dead to prompt him to further work. Govianus accepts the task—"I must dispatch this business upon earth / Before I take that journey" (4.4.85–86)—but his connection to the Lady undermines his ability to complete it. Once more, she asks him to perform an act that will take her from him, and he procrastinates, preferring her ghostly visitations to conducting her "business." His inability to do man's work, however, here and earlier, is also his strength. The revenger remains trapped in an ever-narrowing definition of maleness from which Govianus, with the Lady as guide, frees himself. While he must destroy the Tyrant to prevent the Lady's body from abuse, he, unlike the revenger, feels no compulsion to visit upon him the indignities to male gender that the Tyrant had intended for him. He adopts a disguise to effect his plan, but he does not use it to seize control of the play's action or to author himself as the Tyrant's master.

The similarities between Govianus and the Tyrant suggest the relationship between revenger and tyrant. Both choose the pleasure of the Lady's company over her wishes, a weakness Govianus overcomes. Both place love above country, and both kiss and crown the Lady's corpse (Bushnell 1990, 155). Yet Govianus's emergence from his early essentialism into androgyny differentiates him markedly from the Tyrant in their final scenes. While the Tyrant delights in the lifeless obedience of his "most silent mistress," Govianus revels in the Lady's voice and command. The Tyrant's thwarted physical lust becomes necrophilia; Govianus's love emerges as the desire to be one with the Lady's spirit. The rivals' final contest, therefore, is not waged for absolute political and sexual authority, as it is with the revenger and tyrant. Govianus does not desire the throne, and the Lady's irrevocable and eternal love is his.

Nor does victory proceed from his wresting theatrical control over the play's events from the Tyrant in order to shape them to his own desires. The Tyrant, in hiring an artist to create the appearance of life on the Lady's bloodless cheeks, proceeds on the belief that he can shape the world to his will, that he can, through art, reverse, violate, and diminish what exists in nature. He separates it from the continuum of physical and spiritual life in the same way that he separates his authority in the world from the divine authority on which it is based. He prefers a manageable facsimile of life to life itself:

> Let but thy art hide death upon her face,
> That now looks fearfully on us, and but strive
> To give our eye delight in that pale part
> Which draws so many pities from these springs.
> (5.2.81–84)

While he acknowledges that art cannot "renew heat / Within her bosom" (96), he vows "By art [to] force beauty on yon lady's face" (110).

Govianus, on the other hand, shakes at the impiety of even feigning obedience to the Tyrant's will, but he proceeds with "such unhallowed business" (92) because, he says, "revenge calls for't, and it must go forward. / 'Tis time the spirit of my love took rest" (93–94). For Govianus, revenge is not sexual retaliation but rather, in his usual definition of maleness, "business," a task to perform. Moreover, his art as a painter is itself enclosed within his art as a player: like his authors, he consciously adopts a role. In classic revenge tragedy, the revenger punishes the tyrant for abusing the authorial position granted him by God; the players, in turn, punish the revenger for abusing the authorial power granted him by them. Govianus, however, is not a revenger or, in fact, an avenger. He kills the Tyrant neither to regain the throne nor to punish him for the Lady's death but because it is the only way to dispossess him of the Lady's body. As a painter, Govianus does not vie with the authorities of nature and heaven nor, as a player, with the authorities of state and religion. Although he embraces the suspect androgyny of his player-authors, he can be crowned with impunity. His ability to reconnect the theatrical to the divine and, ultimately, the political extricates him from the revenger's fate and releases his play from the conventions of tragic closure.

The Tyrant's end, by contrast, does follow convention. While Govianus is not motivated by the need to unman and feminize his rival, the Tyrant, like his fellow tyrants in the genre, is nonetheless stripped definitively of sexual and political authority. We see him, like them, struggling ineffectually against the increasing inability of his tongue to command his world. He is shocked when the Lady's spirit appears, unsolicited, before him: "I called not thee, thou enemy to firmness, / Mortality's earthquake!" (153–54). Unlike Vindice's Gloriana, she actively participates in her enemy's demise, functioning with Govianus to destroy the Tyrant's illusion of sexual control by pronouncing Govianus again her "truest love" (163).

The Tyrant dies, rendered chaste by the chaste woman he had desired, silenced by the paint he had ordered to correct her pallor, and obedient to the poison's passage through his body. It is he who is dominated, forced to face the total collapse of his usurped authority and maleness. The last command of his life is transformed to its opposite: Memphonius responds to his order to lay hands upon Govianus by responding "your will shall be obeyed" (172) and crowning him. In his final moments, the Tyrant loses state, Lady, and command to the man who has rejected their rivalry, hearing thunderous shouts of "Live Govianus long our virtuous king!" (178). In following the Lady's path, Govianus has won claim to the virtue she has represented from the play's opening scene.

Like Affranius with Eudoxa, Govianus locates in the Lady the informing principles of political life. Before reinterring her body, he orders it crowned "in memory / Of her admirèd mistress" (196–97), at which point her ethereal body enters to accompany it. In closure, female virtue is again separate from worldly power: like Eudoxa, the Lady is accorded the respect, and even the ceremony, due a queen without becoming her country's ruler. Her crowning, however, takes the authority of women a temporal step backward and a political step forward. Her throned presence conjures up an image of the dead Elizabeth she has resembled, from her title and virgin status to her iconic presence in black and pearls, as she presides in spirit over a purified royal court. Govianus will be the physical manifestation of their androgynous unit, a male figure enacting the harmonies of male and female, spirit and flesh as "our virtuous king" (5.2.178). In Jacobean England, even a hint of female rule is radical.

Male androgyny in this play is not, as it is for Maximus and Melantius, a hostile appropriation of the female for the greater glory of maleness. Govianus and the Lady affirm the biological difference between men and women, but they also dismantle the connection of biology to gender and level the hierarchy implicit in the binary. Determination and action are traditionally coded male, indecision and fainting female, but here sex and gender are reversed, which casts doubt on the coding itself. The Lady, from her name and its Elizabethan echoes to her protestations about her sex, is insistently a woman, Govianus equally insistently a man. They are not represented as those cultural *bêtes noires*, the effeminate man and the shrewish virago, the exempla of a topsy-turvy world where people become their sexual opposites. Instead, they are presented sympathetically as figures who do not ignore the sex of their bodies even though they are forced to reject its accompanying behavior. It is possible to read the woman who uses a sword and the man who faints as no more than cultural exceptions to the rule that sex and gender are naturally linked, but their presence denies, at the very least, the universality of the rule. In reminding an audience of the honored exception of Elizabeth, the exceptional Lady even suggests the shallowness and folly of that rule.

Valentinian and *The Second Maiden's Tragedy* avert revenge tragedy's bloody ending, the unions of Affranius and Eudoxa and of Govianus and the Lady instead a matrix for cleansing and healing. Both men avoid replicating the tyrant they oppose by rejecting the terms of his rivalry, refuting the seemingly natural polarity between male authority and female submission to support and even to obey the authority of women. Eudoxa and the Lady disobey corrupt authority, act on principle, and control their own bodies, exhibiting a heroism that allows Affranius and Govianous to accept and honor what is explicitly female. They are able, therefore, to eschew the tyrant's and revenger's hypertropically male, self-deifying presumption that all authority can and should be collapsed into himself. Acknowledging a woman's authority and benefiting from her actions, changing under her influence rather than appropriating her, they bring an androgynous humanity into harmony with the androgynous authority that created it.

5

"I Am Not to Be Altered": The Authority of Women

To locate the cause of Jacobean revenge tragedy's glaring and often violent misogyny in the cultural habit of viewing women as inferior and dangerous is to focus too narrowly on the relationship between men and women. In *The Second Maiden's Tragedy*, *Valentinian*, and *The Maid's Tragedy*, the long tradition of misogyny is shaped by the struggle between men over what constitutes maleness and who wields authority, a battle fought over and through a woman's body. For the rivals, the contest is a political-erotic triangle in which only they are granted will and agency.[1]

If that triangle obeyed the geometric laws of its male members, revenge tragedy would indeed be a misogynistic genre. That it does not in either *The Second Maiden's Tragedy* or *Valentinian* is directly attributable to the refusal of the plays' heroines to play their assigned role. Political tyranny liberates women from sexual tyranny: when men create a gap in the hierarchical structure by usurping the divinity that empowers them, women can fill the gap by authorizing themselves in the name of that divinity, a holy ventriloquism that breaks the obligation of obedience to men. They become, as their culture defines gender, androgynous, female in form and male in function.

The androgyny of Eudoxa and the Lady, and of their male counterparts Affranius and Govianus, does not, as we have seen, represent a neoplatonic, otherworldly transcendence of the sexual binary. It does not deny biological difference or reject as ideal the continuity of sex and gender, nor does it directly challenge men's "natural" authority or erase cultural misogyny. It does, however, break the link between sex and gender, allowing men and women alike to behave in ways associated with each other's sex. Women assume the prerogative of voice to disobey sanctioned but tyrannical male authority, and men, who are equally subject to that tyr-

104

anny, not only value them for that rebellion but follow their lead, in the process adopting postures of obedience before them and behaving in ways presumed female. By late twentieth-century standards, the androgyny presented in these plays is certainly limited—it is not an all-embracing theoretical rewriting of cultural beliefs—but it is significant nonetheless because it breaks the social molds that are supposed to shape humans according to the sex they were born.

Because revenge tragedy relies heavily on essentialist assumptions for its conflicts and plots, it is predictably also the genre that deconstructs those assumptions. In these plays, virtuous women begin the process, refusing their passive roles as trophies and changing the terms of the political debate. Because they redefine female gender, men have the opportunity to redefine male gender. Affranius and Govianus embrace a definition of maleness that involves more and other than being not a woman, more, too, than the exclusionary male life of combat and honor defined by loyalty to kin and, by extension, state. To be a man means to participate in a political world that values the common good. Women are not shut out and away; in the search for justice, they are allies, not enemies. At closure, it is men who govern the salvaged state, but it is women who have created the opportunity for its restoration.

In the small time and little room of the playhouse, final authority is theatrical, and it belongs to the figure granted control of the play's text. The stage tyrant's claim to that authority derives from his role as absolute monarch: in his political body, he writes himself and his play, theoretically in the name of God, and commands character-subjects to act it out. The revenger counters by splitting into two bodies—his disguise and its author—wresting control of the plot from the tyrant and manipulating his fellow characters into acting out his play. The virtuous heroine, however, challenges both tyrant and revenger by insisting on the primacy of divine authorship. In opposition to the tyrant's and revenger's atemporal political and theatrical bodies, she invokes the eternal soul, the second body believed common to all humankind regardless of rank or gender. Because the laws that govern that ethereal body take precedence over all others and because men have failed to obey them, she can, within the context of their failure, refuse her presumed inferiority. Constructing herself as God's agent, she creates her own agency. Unlike the tyrant and revenger, she bridges the gap between theatrical and extratheatrical authority by locating the discourse above both, empowering herself as God's ghostwriter to deny all other texts.

Although the heroine is a dramatic figure who situates herself above and outside the dramatic debate, a voice "not to be altered" that challenges both state and theater, she is nonetheless, like the tyrant and revenger, a creation of the players. In Jacobean England the bond between female characters and the men who authored and acted them was tangled and intimate. Even more than most men, players were forced onto common ground with women, forced to hear the pejorative comparisons radical Protestants insistently drew between them as painters and deceivers; as occasions of sin that had to be controlled in the interests of social order; most strikingly, as cross-dressers. Both were permanently liminal. Like women in pointed doublets and broad-brimmed hats, players donned the clothing and impersonated the behavior of the other sex, a glaring and obvious violation of the theoretically approved relationship between sex and gender and between maleness and authority. Not only did their plays dramatize problems with the theoretical structure of sex and gender in Jacobean England, they themselves were site and example of those problems.[2] Inherently if no doubt often unintentionally subversive figures, players challenged the basis for authority by pretending—in their accusers' eyes, like women—to be what they were not. They could even use the carnival tradition of men's donning female masks to voice unpopular or unsanctioned views. Like women and as women, players were an unruly, perverse, and potentially dangerous group.

Given the hostility behind the comparisons, it is not surprising to find misogyny a strong element in the drama, especially when it was likely to find favor among audiences royal and common. The roots of misogyny ran deep in the antifeminist institutions of early modern England, and the gender politics of King James nourished it. Indeed, the notorious violence of revenge tragedy is lavished generously on women. Mothers and sisters are regularly revealed as sirens and whores, weak and cunning creatures who advance their interests and their authors' plots by betraying men for sex, security, or whim.

Yet revenge tragedy represents misogyny as a destructive force, as a predictable but dangerously narrowed male response to the common ground of subjection that men occupied with women. Certainly, a man forced by another man into a woman's role is apt, as a cultural reflex, to reaffirm the sexual difference that makes him, in theory, superior to her. In revenge tragedy, the tyrant presumes and reinforces contempt for women by feminizing other men in order to control and humiliate them. The revenger's misogyny, a predisposition carried in the cultural bloodstream, is released as a wild, destructive energy by the tyrant's sexual assault. When a man does not check that reflex, his only movement toward androgyny is, as it is with Melantius, an appropriation of the female, a neutralizing of the Other by absorbing it into the male self. When it is a woman who absorbs and enacts that cultural misogyny, as Evadne does, she too values what is male and devalues anything identified with women.

The intimate connection between players and women, however, produces an antidote to misogyny in the genre's powerful heroines, who, like the men who speak their lines, are perforce androgynous and whose majesty recalls another powerful, androgynous, and, in the world of King James, subversive woman. Early in James's reign, although not before yearning for male authority had become disenchantment with its fact, a skull named Gloriana, the martyred virgin of *The Revenger's Tragedy*, bears theatrical witness to nostalgia for the dead queen who personified virtue. Jacobean women, if we can judge by Esther Sowernam's praise of Elizabeth as the "mirror of the world" (Henderson and McManus 1985, 231), by Aemilia Lanyer's wishful reference to Elizabeth as the "*Phoenix* of her age" in "To the Lady *Elizabeths* Grace" (1993, 1.4), and by the ladies of Queen Anne's court, many from the Sidney-Essex group (Barroll 1991, 8–9), found inspiration in her memory. Men like "Tom Tell-Troath," as well as Queen Anna's male courtiers, were also drawn to the comforting political and sexual certainties embodied by a tightfisted, pro-Protestant, anti-Spanish warrior queen.

When, like Astraea, Elizabeth left the corrupt earth for the heavens, the link she had made between female virtue and the governing politics of England was broken. The mythic echo of that connection, however, not only remained but strengthened, especially in comparison to James's all-too-public separation of his natural and political bodies. With Elizabeth dead and her myth alive, the connection between virtue and authority was free to extend to other women. In revenge tragedy, where resentment at current injustice is inseparable from nostalgia for an idealized past, Jacobean playwrights could tap the memory of commerce between the human and the divine to which Elizabeth had given female form. Like the apotheosized queen, idealized heroines could speak publicly for principles that the tyrants of their plays—who, within the dramatic context, resemble her successor king—refused to honor. In their heroic defiance of tyranny and injustice, such women are represented as the only remaining connection between divine law and the human world, a last hope in a society of corrupt men and, therefore, a foundation for social rebirth.

The virtuous heroines of revenge tragedy are only superficially manifestations of the "inlaw" principle (French 1983, 24). While most support male authority, often vociferously, it is they who determine what men are to be obeyed. Like Elizabeth's virginity, their sexual purity frees them from male dominance; it does not subject them to it. Like Elizabeth, too, they are emphatically women, but they are also emphatically not victims. They will not submit to an authority they do not accept by giving themselves sexually to a tyrant or even by silently obeying him. Instead, invoking divine authority, they unlock the doors of their private worlds and step into political space; they open their mouths in public; they give or withhold their own bodies. These figures all disobey some form of culturally accepted male authority, if not the public patriarchy of a tyrannical monarch, then the private patriarchy of a father, brother, or husband, and they publicly and articulately verbalize the reasons for their disobedience.[3]

The heroines' willingness to make themselves an active connection between the human and the divine serves to justify their textual control. Playwrights do not grant female characters the political authority Elizabeth wielded as queen of England, but they do grant them the ability to wrest that authority from a tyrannical monarch. Moreover, as public voices of virtue, they highlight the spiritual emptiness of male political authority. When a female character assumes the divine voice a tyrant has usurped, and when she affirms connection between the immanent and the transcendent, she problematizes the link between men and authority and, as a result, undermines the male order even as she overtly defends it. When women who cannot and will not fit neatly into the culture's mold for female behavior are linked to men capable of learning to question their own, even if the experience for both is selective and, ultimately, supportive of male authority, the play ends in comedy's promise of life and union rather than in sexual isolation and tragedy. Eudoxa and the Lady are affirmed at play's end despite their transgressive postures and actions. When there is a hero who is open to the usually forced experience of female subjection and who, instead of rivaling the tyrant in maleness, accepts both his femaleness and the heroine's maleness, the plays offer hope for a politically positive future.

A Most Unsilent Mistress: The Lady of *The Second Maiden's Tragedy*

"I am not to be altered" (1.1.123): no mindless object or removed third person, the Lady is a force capable of dismantling the political-erotic triangle formed by suitors—and a father—who consider her no more than a prize of battle. Because her *I*, unlike the Tyrant's, represents a community of virtue of which she is part and embodiment, she can defy the Tyrant's political and Helvetius's familial authority and name her own monarch and husband, imparting her authority to him by that process. She never denies the theoretical right of men to command women but, rather, fills the absence created by tyrannical men. Like the author of *Haec Vir*, the Lady presents herself as a woman forced to behave like a man because, after all, someone has to.

Her language and behavior nonetheless defy the cultural code that declares women virtuous only when they are docile. Virtue, as she defines it, is not merely obedience to the social and political laws that men design and enforce but fidelity to the laws that encompass men's right to govern. By embodying and giving voice to the divine will, she is able to affirm the principle of male rule even as she breaks free of it. Although she views her public authority as a temporary state, to be abandoned for wifely submission to the man she chooses as her husband, she discovers that she cannot retreat into the gender role she has repeatedly violated. Both before and after death, the Lady will, of necessity, play both the man's and the woman's part, leading Govianus into a collaborative androgyny.

The Lady's first challenge is to the Tyrant. Presuming on her role as subject and woman, he believes he can author her as his obedient goddess, a willing object who will accept the authority he has disingenuously given her to enhance his own. With her appearance in black and her declaration that she is not to be altered, the Lady immediately shatters that fantasy. Her *I* negates his right to author her: she affirms what she is not, and she positions herself as an agent by transforming an active construction in which she is the object into a passive one in which she is the subject. Moreover, in negating the passive—"not to be altered"—she negates passivity itself. She will not be the Tyrant's

Petrarchan Lady, shaping herself to his desire and validating his dominance over Govianus. She will not accept the debasing elevation that deprives her of will and reconstitutes her as malleable, alterable, and obedient.

In response to the Tyrant's incredulous "How!" the Lady makes a second and unnegated declaration: "I have a mind / That must be shifted ere I cast off these [garments]" (123–24). Her assertion that she possesses the faculty that neither the Tyrant nor Govianus have granted her is followed by another passive construction, this one with her mind the subject that "must be shifted" before she changes signifiers. The active subject that alone is capable of altering her, a force beyond him and beyond her as well, is unnamed but implied. Identified with the eye of goodness and contrasted with the "eye of glory" (128), that force, working through the Lady's mind, dictates her choice of dress, speech, and behavior. To please that eye, she wears black to express grief over Govianus's usurpation, uses her voice to confirm and explain her actions, and identifies the true king by moving to Govianus and kissing him when her father commands her to "entreat the king" (163).

The Tyrant has not merely lost control over her; he has lost control to her. Given his linkage of absolute authority with absolute maleness, her rejection of him as a lover is also a rejection of his assumptions about the nature and privilege of monarchy. The scene he has written as his triumph the Lady rewrites as his defeat:

> I am he that's banished;
> The king walks yonder, chose by her affection,
> Which is the surer side, for where she goes
> Her eye removes the court.
>
> (145–48)

The magnetic force of her eye, she has made clear, is not her own. Her ability to wrest control of his text and draw the court from him is a consequence of her virtue and, equally, of his blind disregard for it. Not only has the Tyrant presumed on mindless female ambition but, more important, he has attempted to collapse earthly and heavenly authorities into himself. His narcissistic presence creates the gap between the human and the divine that allows the Lady—and ultimately the state with her—to slip from his grasp.

She moves into the space he has tried to empty of God and then occupy as god, recentering the scene on the spiritual authority now figured in her. As she changes the discourse from the political and sexual to the spiritual, she becomes the voice of a law more compelling than any human construct, and, as a result, she is able to evade the tradition of female submission that theoretically applies when the patriarchy is functioning in consonance with divine will. The Tyrant's authorship of the Lady as Petrarchan mistress and the culture's authorship of the Lady as submissive woman give way to the sacred authorship whose voice and presence is the Lady's and, therefore, to her authorship of herself in that image. In one blow, she kicks over the Petrarchan pedestal and escapes the prison of patriarchal and political control.

The Lady's ability to break the connection between maleness and authority by affirming it revives the sexual and political strategies of Elizabeth I: both accept limitation to free themselves from greater limitation. Needing, like Elizabeth, to evade the terms of a male discourse that would render her powerless, the Lady assumes the carefully constructed androgyny of her royal predecessor: without denying femaleness, she rejects silence and submission and adopts a public, commanding voice. Unthreateningly androgynous, she can affect the political world from which she is theoretically excluded, and she does precisely that, to the surprise not only of the Tyrant but of her father and Govianus as well.

In the theatrical style of Elizabeth, she creates her onstage presence as the eternal manifest in the temporal, the harmonious point of convergence between intent and appearance, truth and manifestation, heaven and earth, the divine will and the human mind and body. The nameless title she is given grants her the Marian and aristocratic authority over the supernatural and natural realms that Elizabeth made one with her political body, and her outspoken claims to individual conscience echo the historical moment when the English queen spoke as defender of Protestantism in Europe.

In the iconographic tradition that Elizabeth foregrounded to support her monarchy, the play explicitly refers to Virtue and virtues as female. The Tyrant personifies as "herself" and "She" the virtue that has power to take command of his subjects:

> I beshrew that virtue
> That busied herself with him [Helvetius]! She might have found

Some other work; the man was fit for me
Before she spoiled him!

(2.3.55–58)

Helvetius, in turn, acknowledges that his new master is female: "truth," he declares, is "the gentlewoman I now serve" (91). The accidental feminization of virtues like truth does not mean that women are considered truthful (Warner 1985, xix), nor does it give women political power, but it does connect them to the extrapolitical realm that, theoretically, shapes the political. By fashioning herself according to those gendered virtues, the Lady restructures the discourse and effects a transfer of power from the play's men to herself, obeying her presumed masters in principle even as she disobeys them in practice.

The Lady succeeded in engaging and defeating the Tyrant while upholding the concept of royal authority; she also flouts her father while claiming to bow before paternal authority. When Helvetius commands her to "entreat the king," she tells him she will do "more for you, sir; y'are my father. / I'll kiss him too" (1.1.65–65). Her literal obedience to his command is, in fact, a corrective mimeticism: she is following the command he should have intended, she explains—"I happened righter than you thought I had" (167). She then turns from Helvetius to Govianus: "It is the mind that sets his master forth" (178). In the connection the Lady draws between mind and mastery, she again subverts the gendered structure she claims to support.

It is her second public claim, here implied rather that stated, to possess the human faculty that grants its owner independent agency and, therefore, cultural maleness. With her use of the masculine pronoun to refer to the mind—"his master"—her stance becomes explicitly androgynous. She may not be able to claim the heart and stomach of a king, but she can claim the mind of a man. Even more striking is the implication that she, and not the biological men whose minds have shifted, is truly male. That declaration of androgyny makes her obedience to all men, including Govianus, conditional. Her assumed freedom to accept or deny a man's claims to absolute authority over her sets conditions on men's general claims to absolute authority over women as well.

At her next meeting with her father, the Lady again employs the strategy of indicating her desire to obey while withholding obedience, kneeling in acknowledgment that she owes him "a reverence, / A debt which both begins and ends with life" (2.1.56–

57). But just as a subject is not necessarily bound by obedience to a tyrant, so a woman is not bound to a man when his commands violate sacred beliefs or trespass on another man's rights. Duty could, she informs him in the conditional, be transformed into something more—"Yet could you be more precious than a father, / Which, next a husband, is the richest treasure / Mortality can show us" (59–61)—if, she continues, he will pardon her from hearing him. Even before the climactic *if*, she has let him know that she, not he, determines whom to obey, that her reverence is based on his position and not his merit, and that, her fulsome praise notwithstanding, a father is less than a husband.

When Helvetius persists in commanding her body's uses for his political ends—he magnanimously allows her the choice of husband as long as he is allowed to choose her "friend"—her resourceful expedient is to cancel his authority over her by denying his paternity: if he doesn't behave like a father, then he is not her father. Insisting, as always, on the union of body, mind, and spirit, she concludes that the wicked being before her must be

> . . . some spirit
> Of evil-wishing that has for a time
> Hired his voice of him, to beguile me that way,
> Presuming on his power and my obedience. . . .
>
> (102–5)

In persistently disobeying Helvetius even as she affirms lawful patriarchal authority, she empties her father's role of its authority and, like a playwright, sets the stage for Govianus to fill the vacancy.

All unfolds as she authors it. With a warning shot and sharp rebuke, Govianus steps into the role she has prepared for him to play, bringing Helvetius to his knees before them. When Govianus instructs the Lady to grant Helvetius's request for forgiveness, she obeys: there is no conflict between Govianus's judgment and her own. Helvetius has at last behaved like a father and earned her respect; therefore, she will restore him to paternity with its privileges: "Now, sir, I honour you for your goodness chiefly. / Y'are my most worthy father; you speak like him. / The first voice was not his" (168–70). By setting conditions for her obedience, the Lady does with both Helvetius and Govianus what the Tyrant could not do with her: she retains authority over those she raises above her.

The Lady's love and allegiance belong to Govianus because he meets standards of virtue external to them both. They serve the same principles, and so she willingly accepts the hierarchy of marriage and her subjected position in it. He will be the voice and agent of their family unit, and she will bequeath him the mantle of public rebellion, becoming the protected rather than the protector, the authored and not the author. Yet she and not he has been the agent of action in their relationship: she recognizes him as worthy; she claims him as her husband. Even marital submission to his authority, therefore, does not erase her own. When, with the Tyrant's men surrounding them, she watches him grow wild and faces his inability to protect her from abduction and rape, she must again begin to take command even as she insists on her helplessness as a woman. If he kills her as she demands, he will remain her protector and a man, and she will die a woman in her own eyes.

Yet the more she insists on feminizing herself by masculinizing him, the more her stated gender separates from her enacted gender. Using the imperative and echoing Govianus's use of business and work as metonyms for ideal manliness, she orders him to play the man: "Come on, sir! / Fall to your business; lay your hands about you. / Do not think scorn to work" (3.3.67–69). She defines his proper role by comparing his inaction to that of a sea captain who tosses his treasure into the sea rather than let pirates seize it: "Be not less man than he," she prods. "Thou art master yet, / And all's at thy disposing" (72–74).

The aggressiveness of her challenges—"Be not less man than he"—and her unrestrained anger at his passivity—"Sir, you do nothing; there's no valour in you. / Y'are the worst friend to a lady in affliction / That ever love made his companion" (87–89)— sound less like the helpless woman or neuter treasure than, like Volumnia in the eyes of the tribunes, "mankind." The Lady is no longer the silent, obedient prop of his manhood; he has abandoned the male role to her, and she reviles him for it: "I speak thy part, / Dull and forgetful man, and all to help thee!" (92–93). Although she ends her tirade by returning to her image of a helpless woman "borne with violence to the tyrant's bed" and "forced unto the lust of all his days" (95, 96), she has presented herself as a goading, male challenger and, briefly, that transformation moves him to obey her by raising his sword against her.

Aborting his attempt in order to pray, the Lady authors herself as the perfect woman in death, rising from her knees to announce, "I have prepared myself for rest and silence / And took my leave of words"; "look not for more speech" (133–34, 138). Govianus, however, who could take arms against a male rival, cannot kill his Lady. His swoon, a usurpation of the female, denies her the chaste, silent, and obedient end she desires. When she discovers his unconscious body and takes him for dead, she is enraged:

> O thou poor-spirited man!
> He's gone before me. Did I trust to thee,
> And hast thou served me so? Left all the work
> Upon my hand, and stole away so smoothly?
> There was not equal suffering shown in this;
> And yet I cannot blame thee. Every man
> Would seek his rest. Eternal peace sleep with thee!
>
> (150–56)

The Lady's closing wish for his eternal peace does not lessen her sense of betrayal or the harshness with which she judges him. Her efforts to construct him as a man who would meet her standards of maleness, paradoxically by obeying her, and allow her to be a woman as she has defined femaleness, paradoxically by commanding him, have failed, and she is forced again to occupy space vacated by a man.

She breaks her "rest and silence" to address and take up Govianus's sword. The man she sought and found in Govianus did not save her; she must be her own savior. With the signifier of his maleness in hand, she prepares to play the man's part:

> Thou art my servant now; come, thou hast lost
> A fearful master, but art now preferred
> Unto the service of a resolute lady,
> One that knows how to employ thee, and scorns death
> As much as great men fear it.
>
> (157–61)

Using all the gender-coded vocabulary of their world, the Lady embraces her role and denounces his: she is the "master" who knows how to "employ" that sword, he the "fearful" man who left his business to her. Female weakness she attributes to Govianus, male resoluteness to herself. Angry, defiant, and proud, she becomes the better man, indeed the only man, by taking her own life.

For the Lady, death is the sole avenue of escape from imprisonment and repeated rape. In abandoning her reliance on Govianus to complete her, she becomes androgynously complete in herself: a warrior woman, a victorious virgin. Like Elizabeth, whose mythos relied on those heroic figures, she disconnects biological maleness from action and courage and biological femaleness from passivity and cowardice, and, in the process, she liberates not only herself but Govianus as well. Had she refused to fulfill her own command, both would have become victims. As in the first act, the Lady is the salvation of Govianus's manhood and the agent of his triumph. She leaves the world with scarcely a good word for him or any man in it, but she maintains her fidelity to the principle that recognized him as her master.

Neither her victory nor her solitary androgyny is final, however. While physical death is not important to the Lady, who views her body as the ephemeral text of her mind's inscription, it does allow the Tyrant to make her an unwilling performer in his perverse theater of love. He is as determined to separate her body from her mind and spirit as she is intent on maintaining the proper connection between mortal and immortal parts. Because death makes it impossible for her to take direct action against him, the Lady must seek Govianus's help in preventing the Tyrant from seizing her body for his uses. Her posthumous continuation of the struggle with sexual and political tyranny also allows her and Govianus to resolve the lingering issues of gender raised by her suicide.

Their final collaboration involves an understanding of gender contrary to the marital ideal of a man and woman, essentially different, uniting to form a whole neither sex is capable of separately. The Lady, female in form and lovingly deferential toward Govianus, speaks with a commanding voice, wears a regal costume, and wields an absolute authority. Govianus must love her and obey her, and he must be master of the events that will effect their will. Both must abandon the binary and, therefore, hierarchical terms of mastery and servitude, action and passivity, author and authored to become one another's subjects as they are subjects of the principles that bind them to each other.

As Govianus completes his work by poisoning the Tyrant, the Lady appears, unbidden by either man. For Govianus, her presence is a joy, her liberty unthreatening. For the Tyrant, however, she is alien and terrifying, like Freud's uncanny rising from the recurrence of what was repressed: "I called not thee, thou enemy to firmness,/ Mortality's earthquake!" (5.2.153–54). Correcting the Tyrant's separation of the body he believes he owns from the autonomous mind and spirit, her ghost, *"in the same form as the [body of the] Lady is dressed in the chair"* (152), joins that mute, costumed body. She and no other controls her representation, and she will repossess the color he has usurped and invest it with her meaning. Visually double—a still, seated dummy and a speaking, moving character—she figures both the unity of spirit and flesh, emphasized by the black garb of both forms, and their separation, emphasized by their position on stage side by side. In that visual comparison, the superiority of the active, commanding woman to the obedient, passive, silent body that even a tyrant can possess and dominate is demonstrably clear.

The androgynous partnership of the Lady and Govianus allows each figure autonomy and mastery. The Lady's spirit, unforced and unbidden, returns to attend her body and bless Govianus's reinvestment as monarch. Their union is at once a blurring of distinction and a healing of division—flesh and spirit, state and heaven—and a return to separate roles. The Lady reiterates her pronouncements in the first court scene by recognizing and authorizing Govianus as master—"My truest love, / Live ever honoured here, and blessed above" (163–64)—acknowledging the separation of the two realms and authoring their reunion through him. Under her otherworldly authorship, he assumes worldly authority over the state. At closure, she remains enthroned on stage, spirit and body, an active participant in their play's triumphant, comic finale.

The Lady, whose victimization ostensibly occupies the affective center of the tragedy, rewrites revenge tragedy as comedy. Her defiance of tyranny results in a redefinition of gender that allows sexual likeness and difference for women and men alike. Maleness is no longer the possession and mastery of the female body but an obedience to the same principles a woman obeys. Femaleness is not a mindless, corpselike obedience to all men; to be a woman is to possess a mind that judges a man's worthiness to assume authority. Because androgyny does not erase sexual difference, the position of women is, in fact, paradoxically strengthened. The Lady's defiant speech and brave actions do not erase her femaleness; men who adopt her principled and heroic stance against tyranny can, therefore, follow her without the risk of becoming unmanly.

"The tongues of Angels cannot alter me": The Heroines of *Valentinian*

In *Valentinian* as well as in *The Second Maiden's Tragedy*, androgyny replaces the competitive misogyny of male rivals. Like the

Lady, Lucina and Eudoxa initiate the movement away from a strict interpretation of gender and force the text to a new generic shape. Like the Lady, too, both are authorized by the allusive presence of Elizabeth as well as by the absence of responsible male governance. Lucina's name and her association with chastity are connected not only to her Lucretian literary predecessors (Pearse 1973, 9–99, 151–57) but also to the Virgin Queen. Eudoxa, a twice unhusbanded empress who admires and is admired by her courtier soldier Aecius and who acts effectively on the stage of empire, echoes the actively political Elizabeth in taking arms against tyranny and setting Rome to rights.

The Lady's triumphant struggle to author herself and determine her meaning is divided between *Valentinian*'s two heroines: Lucina chooses and wills her own death, thereby indicting Valentinian's tyranny; Eudoxa plots and executes the tyrant Maximus's murder before accepting Affranius's partnership in the creation of a new political state. Like the Lady, they refuse to be written as prizes of conquest. Instead of mutely signifying men's authority in politics and sex, they assume male voice and occupy male space, empowering themselves in the name of God.

It is easy to read Lucina as just another victim of male power,[4] her suicidal chastity a self-deluded adherence to a standard established by men in the interests of men, her outspoken dedication to physical purity the ventriloquism of male players. In the context of Jacobean nostalgia for a female monarch, however, Lucina's insistence on her right to control her body recalls the mythos supporting Elizabeth's authority as a woman. Like Elizabeth's public virginity, Lucina's chastity is an apparent acquiescence to male control that, in fact, places her outside it.

Aecius explicitly invokes the rationale behind the Cult of Elizabeth when he attempts to dissuade Lucina from suicide. He asks rhetorically whether "the eternall Gods" should "desire to perish, / Because we daily violate their truths, / Which is the chastitie of heaven" (3.1.225–27). While Aecius's conclusion—that the gods do not choose to die because humans violate their chastity—confuses the mortal with the immortal, his analogy nonetheless establishes the sameness of Lucina's and the gods' resistance to alteration. In explicitly linking her chastity to the gods' truth, Aecius grants her the power to manifest the divine will and, therefore, to occupy the space vacated by an emperor who is his own god.

Chastity, although a bodily state, is the enactment and reification of virtue, a link between earth and heaven, a mediator between timeless law and the temporal human community whose continuity resides in the family. For Lucina as for Maximus, family takes precedence over state. When Lucina attacks the bawds' attempt to seduce her, she speaks of her chastity as a force that connects her to abstract goodness on the one hand and to the concrete world of mothers, fathers, and ancestors on the other. Virtuous women merit respect; it is women like the bawds who allow men to "defame our Sex" (1.2.45). She would doubt herself, she tells them, "But that I had a Mother, and a woman / Whose ever living fame turnes all it touches / Into the good it self is" (109–11). The virtuous woman's "ever-living fame" bridges the eternal and the evanescent, her chastity an extraordinary generative and transformative force that resides in femaleness.[5]

Empowered by the authority of her own merit and her mother's as well, Lucina can reject Ardelia's declaration that "to the Emperour / She is a kind of nothing but her service, / Which she is bound to offer" (90–92). As Lucina practices it, chastity is a religion that liberates her from obedience to other imperatives. Categorically, Lucina rejects all an Emperor can offer her, including honorific titles like mother and queen, culminating her refutation by replacing his euphemistic inscriptions with the accurate one: the woman who accepts his offer is a "Whore." Lucina already has all she would seek: "a Noble husband, / (Pray tell him that too) yet a noble name, / A Noble Family, and last a Conscience" (160–62). The nobility she takes as hers derives from others, which is part of its power, but her conscience, like the Lady's mind, is her own, and she speaks that conscience and the text that authorizes it with an articulateness even her tormenters admire.

For such a woman, neither jewels nor the social and political influence that enables a woman to function as a man in the public world, a temptation Evadne will find irresistible, has persuasive force. Her virtue is her authority, and it is specifically female. When she refuses what Valentinian commands, she also refuses what it signifies: a male principle of dominance that is divisive and combative, that privileges men over women, that proceeds to narrow the field of men through aggression, and that understands truth as a prize of conquest rather than as a function of mind or conscience. The chaste woman accepts sexual difference, paradoxically in order to connect herself to others and serve as a link between realms and states of being. That fluidity, notwithstanding the rigid code of physical control at its heart, allows her to become androgynous with greater ease than a man who, caught in the increasingly desperate pattern of separation and domination, cannot assume the woman's part without seeing himself as a loser and victim.

Lucina's belief in herself as embodiment of her own—and the gods'—truth is as tempting and threatening to Valentinian as the Lady's is to the Tyrant. Her assumed right to refuse him strikes at the heart of absolutism. Repeatedly, his agents attempt to wrench her words and actions to their meaning. The bawds read her angry frowns as the potential coquetry of a royal mistress (134–38). The panders' songs deny women the right, desire, and ability to withhold themselves sexually: they are either fruit begging to be plucked or powerless before "mighty love" (2.1.26), the "fierceness of the Boy" (37) who can circumvent the will of "Ladies that despise" (25)—Calisto, Ledo, Danae. When Lucina refuses the offered jewels with "The Gods shall kill me first," they counter with "Ther's better dying / I'th Emperors arms" (90–91). Their strategy is to silence her by redefining her words so that her meaning is contaminated even as she speaks them.

A critical term in the textual struggle is *Lord,* that title of respect owed to heavenly, political, and familial rulers, theoretically without conflict. When the eunuch Lycias, the perfect emblem of Valentinian's feminized court of men, brings her the summons to court, ostensibly from Maximus, he asks, "Madam, what answer to your Lord?" She responds, "Pray tell him, / I am subject to his will" (2.2.41–42). Lucina accepts subjection first to the gods whose truth she shares, then to her husband, and last to the Emperor. She obeys those lower in the hierarchy only when they accord with those above them, which places Valentinian in an inferior position to Maximus and both in an inferior position to the gods and, therefore, to her. For Valentinian to prevail, he must become her Lord, absolute over her, her husband, and her gods.

When Lucina arrives in court, it is Maximus to whom she refers repeatedly as her Lord (2.4.40; 2.5.45, 49, 78, 84, 120). While seemingly acquiescing to her wishes, the bawds and panders use the honorific ambiguously, Chilas telling Lucina he is guiding her "to your Lord" (2.4.44); Proculus assuring her he is bringing "Your much lov'd Lord unto you" (2.5.99); and Phorba offering to "lead ye to him [Lucina's "my Lord"], hee's i'th Gallery" (122). Valentinian's appearance makes the verbal substitution of masters literal, and when Lucina does not relent, when she begs him to "Consider what I am, and whose" (2.6.10) and refers to Maximus before Valentinian as "My deer Lord" (2.6.19), Valentinian responds with the ambiguous double referent for the last time—

"Ile lead ye to your Lord, and give ye to him" (38)—before using physical force in an attempt to transfer the title to himself.

The strategy of linguistic usurpation continues even after his theft of her chastity, with Valentinian taking from her the words she uses to reach beyond his power: to her "Ile cry for justice," he replies, "I am justice" (3.1.33–34). Later in the scene, her gods become his "God of love," whom Valentinian imagines would have raped her first had he seen her (107–8), and he, godlike, "far above the faults I doe" (119).

Nonetheless, he does not succeed in replacing Lucina's husband with himself or her discourse with his own. He does not convince her that he, and not the gods, is truth. Moreover, she exposes his separation of what "should be" his title, "sacred *Cesar,*" and the accompanying honor "sent to you, / And from the gods themselves" from his use of that gift "to ravish women" (78, 77, 85–86). Rather than silencing her, he has given her voice by making the gap between his sacred title and his criminal act unbridgeable. He does not write her. Because her meaning is the gods', she writes him; because her curses are the gods' curses, they are his: "Behold [these ruines] and curse thy selfe" (41). She commands him to kill her, and when he does not obey, she foretells the aftermath of his crime. Because her body is linked to other texts, the "sacrilegious razing of this Temple" will have consequence:

> . . . the Gods will find thee,
> (That's all my refuge now) for they are righteous,
> Vengeance and horror circle thee; the Empire,
> In which thou liv'st a strong continued surfeit,
> Like poyson will disgorge thee, good men raze thee
> For ever being read again but vicious,
> Women, and fearefull Maids, make vows against thee:
> Thy own slaves, if they heare of this, shall hate thee;
> And those thou hast corrupted, first fall from thee;
> And if thou let'st me live, the Souldier,
> Tyrde with thy Tyrannies, break through obedience,
> And shake his strong Steele at thee.
>
> (41–52)

From his tyrannical defiance of heaven will come vengeance: the end of his empire, with its men, women, and maids; its slaves; its soldiers all turning against him. The sin of rape—of the Sabine women, of Lucrece—is now his alone: "where there has a chast wife been abusde, / Let it be thine, the shame thine, thine the slaughter, / And last, for ever thine the feard example" (92–94). Hers is an absoluteness that overmatches Valentinian's.

In the text her voice articulates, the word for herself is "whore," not "friend" (2.6.11, 12) or "a better woman" (3.1.97). Her "whore," however, is by no means the equivalent of Maximus's "kicker out of sheetes" (341). Lucina, like the Lady, understands her body as a tool and signifier of a greater truth, part of a continuum of life that is one with mind and spirit. Sexual violation for her means separation from the principles she has connected for her community and that connect her to her community:

> Gods, what a wretched thing has this man made me?
> For I am now no wife for *Maximus*,
> No company for women that are vertuous,
> No familie I now can claime, nor Country,
> Nor name, but *Cesars* Whore. . . .
>
> (73–77)

She enumerates and negates the meanings she once embodied as Lucina, the links she forged in herself with others: husband, virtuous women, family, country. Those inscriptions have been overwritten by "*Cesars* Whore" because his act separates her from what her chastity once united. Alone on stage after Valentinian's departure, she finds no earthly place for herself to reside. Reiterating her list of connections—to her house, her husband, her family, her neighbors and their children—she finds them all lost. With "no God but power, / Nor vertue now alive that cares for us" (145–46), she chooses, like Astraea, to depart for the heavens.

Lucina commits herself to death before Maximus chooses it for her. Her dedication to chastity is, in fact, precedent to and separate from her marital relationship with him. Although Aecius wishes that her thoughts "were rather alterd" (198), he cannot persuade her to reject suicide as a fitting response to violation, nor would Maximus have succeeded had he tried:

> The tongues of Angels cannot alter me;
> For could the world again restore my credit,
> As fair and absolute as first I bred it,
> That world I should not trust agen.
>
> (247–50)

Remaining alive would not profit Valentinian or the empire, she argues, which will by her life "get nothing but my story, / Which whilst I breath must be but his abuses" (251–52). Only by dying

will she be able to author herself again as the virtue she represents. Unlike the Lady, she is not forced to employ a man's
weapon to separate her body from her spirit; her mind proves
instrument enough. Her maids report that death comes at her
summons as she enters the home of Maximus's family, the private
world that political authority has invaded and sullied. She simply
discards the body that rape brutally severed from the world it
once connected.

As Maximus and Aecius watch her leave the stage, they consign
her spirit to the heavens, where justice still lives, and vow to erect
on earth a tomb that, Maximus declares, will eternalize her
meaning:

> All that is chast, upon thy Tomb shal flourish,
> All living Epitaphs be thine; Time, Story,
> And what is left behind to peice our lives,
> Shall be no more abus'd with tales and trifles,
> But full of thee, stand to eternitie.
>
> (270–74)

His inscription of Lucina as the eternal epitome of chastity, however, as a woman like her mother, whose "ever living fame" will
survive in epitaph and story, quickly becomes as self-interested
as Valentinian's "friend" and "better woman." Once she is dead,
she will again become his alone, as mute and docile a validator
of his desires as the Lady's body in the Tyrant's shrine. She will
bear the meaning he chooses—she is his motive for revenge, a
tool of his ambition.

As Maximus transmogrifies into Valentinian, however, he becomes not Lucina's master but her rival. The crowned Caesar is
the political connection between states of being, the embodiment
of the divine invested in the human. The words of Rome's salute,
"Stand to eternity" (5.8.27), reiterating those he used to apotheosize Lucina, merely reinforce the rivalry between their now competing authorities. It is a contest Lucina, the image of a virtue
greater than herself, will win. Despite Maximus's attempt to
usurp her meaning, she does, indeed, stand to eternity while he
is toppled from that elevation within a few brief moments as
Caesar. Like Valentinian, Maximus has cursed himself.

That Lucina's heroism is balanced and, arguably, contained in
the play by a *de rigueur* misogyny is predictable. Like the Lady,
she is seen as the sole embodiment of chastity, a standard used to
find other women wanting. She is unique and more than human,

Phoenix (1.1.82, 3.1.195) and goddess (1.2.34). While the bawds acknowledge virtue only hypothetically—"if there can be vertue, if that name / Be any thing but name and emptie title" (1.1.68–69)—they see that Lucina has "a God of vertue in her" (73). Lucina herself is cognizant of her status as the sole living embodiment of virtue when she asks Valentinian, "Where shall poore vertue live, now I am falne?" (3.1.95). After her death that seemingly rhetorical question is answered by another woman, the Empress who rises to champion Lucina's chastity and heaven's truth.[6]

Eudoxa, like Lucina, sees beyond the baubles and blandishments of the physical world to obey the dictates of conscience against ambition or greed. She contrasts with Lucina, however, in her courtly experience with men and in her public position as Empress of Rome. If the chaste Lucina occupies a comfortable niche in the iconography of the Virgin Queen, Eudoxa slips more readily into the image of the female regnant who addressed Parliaments, flirted with courtiers and ambassadors, went to war, and defeated enemies foreign and domestic. It is she who is the play's final author: of herself; of Lucina, Aecius, and Maximus; and, in collaboration with Affranius, of Rome.

Eudoxa first appears at her dying husband's side, where, as his loyal wife, she questions the doctors about their course of treatment and lovingly counsels Valentinian to patience. After his death, however, she demonstrates the ability to act on her own according to principles that are, like Lucina's, separate from her husband's. She is first mentioned in connection with Aecius, Rome's although not Valentinian's *beau ideal*. When Aecius responds to Valentinian's "Art thou in love *Aecius* yet?" (1.3.115) by protesting himself "too course for Ladies," fearing his embraces "would break their tender bodies," (1.3.115,117), Valentinian quickly reassures him:

> Never feare it,
> They are stronger than ye think, they'le hold the hammer.
> My Empresse sweares thou art a lusty Souldier,
> A good one I beleeve thee.
>
> (117–20)

Only in Valentinian's lascivious rhetoric—his bawdy reference to women's holding the hammer and to Eudoxa's opinion of Aecius's "lusty" soldiership—is a sexual liaison implied: the general's unswerving loyalty to the emperor makes an affair with the empress unthinkable. The speech does, however, indicate a closeness and admiration in their relationship, a loving connection between them that exists outside the ties of marriage or family.

As Rome's Empress, Eudoxa occupies the public space necessary for such a relationship. Her presence is not confined to family, nor her virtue to chastity. Although she wishes for death, she does not commit suicide over her husband's murder; neither does she run Gertrude-like into the arms of another man. Eudoxa is rather a woman of worldly experience, visible intelligence, and wry wit—an effective if surprising challenger to Maximus. Maximus, who has successfully used the players' theatrical authority over the text to fulfill his ambitions, believes he can continue to cast and script the people around him. Eudoxa, he assumes, will play true to stereotype: the silly widow easily seduced by overlavish praise and protestations of love. With the revenger's blind assumption that only men are capable of competing with him, Maximus woos her with a trite story that even he knows is unconvincing—he wishes "my joy, and wine had fashiond out / Some safer lye" (5.6.27–28). As he authors his wife and friend once more to suit his plot—Eudoxa's beauty was his motive for arranging Lucina's rape, Aecius's execution, and Valentinian's murder—he never entertains the possibility that before him is a woman with a mind and conscience of her own.

In their contest, Eudoxa's invisibility is her advantage. Letting him shiver, pitifully if unwittingly exposed, behind the thin fabrications of his courtship, she acquires the player's unseen second body, cleverly assuming as her disguise the role he has written for her. To this point, Maximus alone has commanded the liminal space between play and audience. Now, however, Eudoxa upstages him. Her response to his plot is so incredulous and exaggerated that it is clear she has penetrated his disguise. As we watch her elbowing him out of his special relationship with the audience, controlling the scene by allowing him to believe he controls it, theatrical authority shifts to her. With unmistakable irony, she asks him whether a face

> Long since bequeath'd to wrinkles with my sorrowes,
> Long since razd out o'th book of youth and pleasure,
> Have power to make the strongest man o'th Empire,
> Nay the most staid, and knowing what is woman,
> The greatest aym of perfectnesse men liv'd by,
> The most true constant lover of his wedlock,

(Such a stillblowing beauty, earth was proud of)
Loose such a noble wife, and wilfully;
Himselfe prepare the way, nay make the rape?
Did ye not tell me so?

(9–18)

Almost half of her long, disdainful, disbelieving question is devoted to the memory of Lucina. In his new love story, Maximus has authored his chaste wife as a whore; Eudoxa restores her to the beautiful, perfect, constant, noble woman Maximus would say he pandered for love and state. Playing the widow, she protests she will reward his efforts with her obedience and even her life:

I am me thinkes too much in love with fortune;
But with you, ever Royall Sir my maker,
The once more Summer of me, meere in love,
Is poore expression of my doting.

(48–51)

In a mimeticism he fails to recognize, she acts the woman of his fantasies, a perfectly submissive, malleable creature to his "maker."

At Maximus's coronation, Eudoxa casts off that narrowly defined female role to reveal herself as author, actor, and interpreter of a play that erases Maximus's construct of rewarded betrayal. Her didactic drama is, in fact, a revision of Lucina's, with Eudoxa in the role of avenger, a disinterested, independent arm of justice who will restore order and hope to Rome. Lucina's death signaled Astraea's departure from earth; Eudoxa's victory is the goddess's triumphant return. Her persona is androgynous. As a woman who fulfills Lucina's definition of their sex, she devotes herself to reconnecting what Maximus has severed—the ties between heaven and earth, between people's actions and their fame. In cultural terms, however, she is also male: she murders Maximus, bravely faces the consequences of her actions, and speaks before the men of Rome to explain:

Make no tumult,
Nor arme the Court, ye have his killer with ye;
And the just cause, if ye can stay the hearing:
I was his death; That wreath that make him *Cesar*,
Has made him earth.

(5.8.60–64)

By taking action and responsibility, she is more manly than the revenger, hiding behind puppets and arrases. When the soldiers respond to her confession with "Cut her in thousand peeces" (64), she exhibits the rationality and command customarily accorded men—"Wise men would know the reason first" (65), she prompts—and prefaces her statements by invoking their manhood: "And waigh my reasons well, if man be in you" (70).

Her challenge to "wise men" brings Affranius to her side. Already predisposed to her reading of events, he slips into her text, beginning their androgynous collaboration by using his privilege as a man to open public space for her voice to be heard. His thoughts have been given shape by the only woman in the assembly, who is also the only other man. Like Elizabeth with her courtiers and poets, Eudoxa welcomes male participation in her theater. She does not hesitate to use the moment he has cleared for her, staking her own claim to authority as Lucina did, by exercising the right to name: "This *Maximus* . . . / Was to his Country, to his friends, and *Cesar* / A most malitious Traytor" (78, 82–83). She reconnects Maximus to the hierarchy he abjured and that now, reinvoked, gives him his proper title.

Although her use of Adam's authority meets resistance from Sempronius, who reminds her of her sex and place with "Take heed woman" (83), she does not relinquish control of the scene. Her quest for justice demands that she restore Maximus's victims—and Rome—as well as Maximus himself to their true meaning. In her speech, Aecius lives again as the empire's great general, not the dangerous rebel of Maximus's revenge plot:

> Brave *Aecius*
> (Whose blessed soule if I lye shall afflict me,)
> The man that all the world lov'd, you adoard,
> That was the master peece of Armes, and bounty,
> (Mine own griefe shal come last). . .
>
> (84–88)

After revealing the epitome of Roman honor and manhood beneath the mask of treason Maximus had written as Aecius, Eudoxa proceeds to uncover the base treachery hidden beneath Maximus's mask of Roman honor and manhood:

> This Souldier [Maximus], this your right Arme noble *Romans*,
> By a base letter to the Emperor . . . ,

Was cut off basely, basely, cruelly;
(Oh losse, ô innocent, can ye now kill me?) . . .

(89–90, 93–94)

Through emphatic repetition, she lays Maximus bare for all to
see: his self-serving, his cruelty, his plotting. After an emotional
exhalation of grief, she turns to Valentinian, whom she pronounces, in the context of Maximus's plot, "the poor Stale my
Noble Lord, that knew not / More of this villaine, then his forcd
feares" (95–96) and who died for his mistake. Climactically, she
focuses on Lucina:

> Nay his wife,
> By heaven he told it me in wine, and joy,
> And swore it deeply, he himselfe prepard
> To be abusd. . . .
>
> (100–103)

By exposing Maximus's contemptuous lie, Eudoxa restores Lucina
to the "ever living fame" that unites her with a matriarchy of
virtuous women.

Eudoxa's performance intricately blends female and male roles.
She is goddess and executioner, weeping mourner and cool plotter; she combines rational address and passionate aside, argument and feeling. Proudly, she confesses sole responsibility for
Maximus's death and presents herself for judgment with dignity,
but she asserts her own judgment as primary: "These are my
reasons *Romans*, and my soule / Tells me sufficient; and my deed
is justice: / Now as I have done well, or ill, look on me" (106–108).
Eudoxa's soul has already rendered a verdict. She has authored
the new text in the interests of truth, and it is now up to her
audience to embrace or reject it.

Again, Affranius responds to her cue. As her artistic collaborator, he pronounces the verdict by naming her "a piece of justice":
"*Romans*, she is righteous; / And such a peece of justice, heaven
must smile on" (110–11). He completes the action she initiated
by seconding her verdict: Maximus deserved death; she does not.
Responding in kind to her androgyny, he abandons the superior
position accorded men. He "must kneele" (113) to her, he says,
even if all the others bend their swords on him. In that kneeling,
Affranius signifies willing submission to Eudoxa as the person
who has reunited divine and worldly authority and returned justice to Rome. Like the Lady and Govianus, Eudoxa and Affranius

become androgynous co-authors of the play's final moments and of the future.

The play does not end with gynecocracy—Sempronius revives the connection between political authority and maleness by calling for them to pray and then choose another Caesar. The government of Rome, and the Jacobean England in which *Valentinian's* representation of it was staged, remains in the hands of men. The play, however, challenges the connection between maleness and authority. At closure, Eudoxa is central and connective on a stage of soldiers and senators. A female monarch represented as aging, fearless, just, and without consort, Eudoxa evokes the androgynous Elizabeth. Both are women who can be female and male in gender and heal the split between heavenly and earthly authority created by men who define male gender in opposition to women. Unlike the tyrant and the revenger, Eudoxa shares with the players who write her not only the mastery of plot but also the androgynous capability she will share with Affranius.

Feminized Women: *The Maid's Tragedy*

In *The Second Maiden's Tragedy* and *Valentinian*, the androgyny of heroines and heroes alike confirms essential biological difference between the sexes while denying, or creating the possibility of denying, the gender roles based on them. Women adopt male behavior and postures without social opprobrium because men have cut the tie between their given right to command and the religious ideology that grants it to them, a crossing of gender lines that allows men to expand the definition of maleness to include the woman's part. Eudoxa and the Lady define themselves and, as the players' surrogates, author climactic action within their dramas because the governing male texts are not consonant with divine authorship. Like the players with whom they share subversive and marginal space, they are lawfully unlawful. When they unlock their spaces and open their mouths, they are spiritually and, in their echoes of Elizabeth, historically authorized. The players, in turn, profit from lending dramatic authority to their heroines because they are able to share the heroines' justification of political transgression, notably the presentation of regicide and of androgyny.

Evadne, however, has no culturally acceptable grounds for her seizure of authority. The virtuous women of revenge tragedy assert control of their bodies in order to withhold them from tyrants. Evadne's declaration of ownership is a seizure of capital goods, her sexual autonomy a negotiation of profit from the female body—an objectionable blurring of categories even if the body is her own. In abandoning the connective and transformative force of *Valentinian*'s women, Evadne loses the vindicating ideology that permits her virtuous counterparts to speak, command, even kill with moral impunity. Like the tyrant she uses and emulates, and like the revenger she will become, Evadne removes herself from the human community. As misogynistic as her male counterparts, she abuses her sex to become as male as they—asocial, self-authoring, godlike, and, finally, isolated and self-defeating.[7]

Evadne is, in fact, the age's bad dream of the will to power operating through an irresistible and unrestrained female sexuality. As a woman, she is strikingly attractive: the King desires and dotes on her; Amintor is not averse to throwing over Aspatia for her; Melantius accuses her of charms that could "inflame a kingdom" (4.1.21); the Gentlemen of the Bedchamber engage in lascivious fantasies about her. When she is not playing a public female role, however, that complexion and carriage are contradicted by a characteristic curtness of speech. Evadne is as impatient and imperious as her voice, which both Amintor and the King ineffectively try to force into conformity with her looks. She uses her seductiveness to control her world by choosing, or at the very least accepting, the man she will favor sexually, and she will choose him according to what he can give her, not for himself and certainly not for her family.

Evadne's femaleness is a tool of power rather than a connective force. In contrast to Lucina, whose model is her mother, and to Eudoxa, who champions Lucina, she forges no ties with women. She is as indifferent to her abuse of Aspatia as to the pain she causes Amintor in marrying him for her own credit (3.1.255). The only tie she acknowledges, her single utterance before the masque, is with the brother she effusively, if with ambiguity, welcomes to court: "O my dearest brother, / Your presence is more joyful than this day / Can be unto me" (1.2.115–17). Without the authority of principle that made Lucina and the Lady unalterable, Evadne shifts and turns with the winds of power. To the men who wield it, she plays a complementary female role—mistress to the King, penitent to her menacing brother—but she mimics what she covets, first adopting the absolutist presumptions and bantering manner of the King, then embracing Melantius's stern and brutally coercive patriarchalism. Even when Evadne believes she is taking the woman's part in order to author herself, she is a male-authored text.[8]

She defends her illusion of control with Amintor on their wedding night. She will certainly not accept him as her master, which is clear from her flat "No" to his asking, on finding her outside their room, whether she has come to call him. Evadne follows that denial with others as blunt, and while she briefly and half-heartedly attempts to sidestep rather than refuse his advances, protesting she is not well, she grows quickly impatient with even the pretense of submission. She is not Amintor's bride, she is the King's mistress and, like the tyrant who rules not for but as God, she has made a borrowed authority her own. Amintor is her subject; he must define himself in her anger and scorn, not she in his fantasy of marital love.

Evadne's performance with her bridegroom is a stunning verbal display of dominance. She lashes out: "Why, it is thou that wrongst me, I hate thee" (2.1.183); sneers: "A maidenhead, Amintor, / At my years?" (194–95); contradicts and corrects: "Think you I am mad, / Because I speak the truth?" (199–200); derides: "but it was the folly of thy youth / To think this beauty, to what hand soe'er / It shall be called, shall stoop to any second. / I do enjoy the best . . ." (293–96); insults: "What did he [the King] make this match for, dull Amintor?" (306); taunts: "Why should you fill yourself so full of heat, / And haste to my bed? I am no virgin" (313–14). Most eloquent of all, perhaps, she patronizes: "I pity thee" (329). Her behavior is not androgynous but, in the terms of the culture, male: she is the sexually experienced lover and he the naïve virgin; she will dictate the terms of their marriage, and he must follow them.

Confirming the antitheatrical fear that actors of a role, like Antonio of *The Tempest*, cease to distinguish between what they are and what they play, Evadne extends her reversal of gender from the hapless Amintor to the King himself. When she meets him on the morning after her wedding, she abuses him verbally and threatens him sexually. Believing she has cuckolded him, the King recalls the excessive—and therefore, he concludes, unfeminine—quality of her oaths: "So great that methought they did misbecome / A woman's mouth" (3.1.166–67). In characteristic style, Evadne flatly contradicts him: "I never did swear so: / You do me wrong" (168–69). Her candor is startling: she did not vow to love *him*, she says, but never to love "A man of lower place." Were he to fall from his height,

I bade you trust
I would forsake you and would bend to him
That won your throne. I love with my ambition,
Not with my eyes.

(172–75)

Her ceasing to love him, she says, would "more afflict / Your body than your punishment can mine" (181–82). When she must respond to his jealous threat that he will disgrace her, she hales Amintor before him to confess that they did not, indeed, consummate their marriage. She feminizes both men, although she elevates the King by feminizing Amintor to him.

While Evadne can play the man with Amintor, who submits to political ideology, and with the King, who submits to sexual desire, she does not succeed with Melantius, who accepts neither her pretense of femaleness—her blushing and bashfulness (4.1.2, 4)—nor the assumption of maleness beneath it. In their struggle for control of the text, Melantius has all the advantages: their shared familial history, which her affectionate greeting to him suggests is powerful; his devotion to Amintor over any familial tie to her; her ignorance that Amintor has confessed to him; his coldness to the weapons that bring Amintor and the King to their knees; and, decisively, his body's superior strength. On her side, Evadne trusts to the name of king—her card to play when and if she must—to stop Melantius from using force against her. Her hand, however, is already weakened by her acceptance of and complicity in the discourse of male domination, and Melantius holds the trump card in his rejection of the political authority she relies on to support her reversal of sex and gender.

Lucina could resist the attempt of Valentinian and his bawds to force her words to their meaning; the Lady and Eudoxa were able to replace a misogynistic discourse with one that empowered them. All three obeyed not men but a principle of authority that privileged but also encompassed men; they valued their bodies not as the property of worldly power but as their own to command within a larger, unalterable structure. For Evadne, however, physical power *is* authority: her female body's power over men—her ability to "afflict" the King by withholding sex—and the male body's power over women: "I am gone," she tells Amintor when he becomes menacing; "I love my life well" (3.2.280–81). Androgynous collaboration is never a possibility; she will fight for the right to be male according to her definition of gender, which coincides with the King's and her brother's as well as with Amintor's.

The terms of her struggle with Melantius, therefore, are those of the tyrant and revenger. Only total victory, with the loser feminized by the victor, will suffice. As her weapons in the struggle, Evadne brings what she has acquired from her role as king's mistress—the imperatives of social class and absolutist politics. Melantius, however, controls the compelling, misogynist structures of the military and the family. Her authority is supported by political ideology, his by tradition and force. In the face of his display of dominance in locking the door behind him, Evadne takes the offensive, declaring that she would not care if her faults "were written here, here in my forehead" (4.1.29). She counters his seizure of her quarters and his naming her "foolish woman" and "fool" (22, 26) by asserting her right to name and command him: his attack is "saucy" (32); he must leave her quarters: "Look you intrude no more. There's your way" (33).

Her claim to a position that allows her mastery over him, however, is bluff, words without performative power. Her resort to pretense and lie when he threatens to tread upon her (34–35) and orders her to hear and speak his words, and "without enforcement" (39) tacitly recognizes his superior position in their contest. In comparison to him, she is in fact small and weak. Despite her snobbish posture of social superiority—she dismisses the report as spread by "base people" (43)—Melantius can seize her, call her "wretch" (45), command her to identify her seducer, and erase her authority at its source by naming her lover, as he has named her, "fool." "I come to know that desperate fool that drew thee / From thy fair life: be wise and lay him open" (46–47).

What keeps Evadne from capitulating quickly is the belief that the force of absolutism will control Melantius as it did Amintor: like the tyrant, she trusts the superior strength of political ideology. Rather than commanding him in the King's name as she did Amintor, which would constitute obeying Melantius's command to "lay him open," she assumes the voice of the King and speaks as if the taboo against regicide protected her. Melantius is an upstart subject whom she will put in his place: "Unhand me and learn manners; such another / Forgetfulness forfeits your life" (48–49). Only his relationship to her saves him: "You are my brother, that's your safety" (58); if he persists, she will have him whipped (66); any claim to extend his area of authority to her is ludicrous: "Get you to your command, / And there preach to your sentinels, and tell them / What a brave man you are. I shall laugh at you" (66–68). Melantius denied her authority by isolating her within her private quarters; she denies his by isolating it within the army. Her derisive courtly laughter, deflating his martial gravity, mocks the very site of his manhood.

As heady and even appealing as Evadne's combative posture is, it is based on the misogynistic values she shares with her brother: the lust for absolute authority that privileges power and identifies weakness with women. The contest between them will, finally, be the trial of physical strength she cannot win. As Melantius bluntly points out, her "great maintainers are not here"; she has no hope of escape; and no one has the courage to oppose him (77–83). Evadne plays for time—"Let me consider" (86)—but she does not drop the royal mask. Her mocking dismissal of Melantius's wish that their father be restored to flesh ends in Melantius's unsheathing his sword and threatening to rape her with it. His physical domination of her is total, and she has no other level of response. He can not only kill her but also write the act she would call murder—"You will not murder me!" (99)—on her "branded flesh" (108). To his "Wilt thou bend yet?" (109), Evadne responds with her characteristic monosyllable, her world of curt *no*'s transformed to a simple "Yes" (110).

Once enclosed in Melantius's discourse—"I am miserable!"; "I have offended, noble sir, forgive me" (112, 113)—she switches position in the binary gender system they share. Unable to dominate, she becomes an obedient tool, a child-woman who accepts a man's right to author her because he has the strength to do it. Chaste to his sword, silent to his voice, and obedient to his will, she kneels and, under further threat, speaks what he has demanded to know. Abandoning on his command even the absolutist ideology for which she had bartered her body, she swears to kill the King, and, with a sudden awareness of women, she asks that "all you spirits of abusèd ladies / Help me in this performance!" (169–70). The category of abused lady to which she now consigns herself is, in fact, no more than a validation of women's ignorance and powerlessness.

The apparent discontinuity in her character is a shift from one misogynistic text to another. As royal mistress, Evadne tried to rise above "all weaknesses of nature / That make men women"; (Melantius, 4.1 94–95) as penitent, she incarnates those failings and becomes the perfect proof and signifier of male superiority. She cannot escape Melantius's authorship of the woman's part. If she accepts her liaison with the King as her choice, she is a sinner who verifies her sex's inherent corruption. If the King seduced her, she is a victim who is guilty of colluding in her crime and so a verification of both female vice and female weakness. Evadne may, simultaneously or alternately, be sinner or victim, roles that both insist on and deny her agency in the decision to take the King as her lover, but neither role exculpates her.

Constructed without will or agency, the feminized Evadne cannot even repent effectively without a man's forgiveness. Amintor's arrival brings her again to her knees, where she remains for 260 lines, reducing the rich, fluid relationship between men and women to the gendered poles of good and evil. Her life is "leprous" (198); Amintor is "an innocent, / A soul as white as heaven" (218–19). It is a smooth transition from accusing herself to accusing all women by way of extension and explanation. So estranged is she from her own sex and so trapped within Melantius's script that she cites a general "all" as source of the truth that women use their knees and tears to dissemble—"As all say women can" (222).

She will not, like that "all"-authored woman, make excuses for what she has done. Instead, she hyperbolizes her wickedness:

> I do appear the same, the same Evadne,
> Dressed in the shames I lived in, the same monster.
> But these are names of honour to what I am:
> I do present myself the foulest creature,
> Most poisonous, dangerous, and despised of men,
> Lerna e'er bred or Nilus. I am hell,
> Till you, my dear lord, shoot your light into me,
> The beams of your forgiveness. I am soul-sick,
> And wither with the fear of one condemned
> Till I have got your pardon.
>
> (226–35)

The monster Evadne, the "-est" and "most" of all that is harmful, becomes evil's site and synecdoche—"I am hell"—not herself a demon, who can effect evil, but the dark space inhabited by demons, Lear's sulphurous pit. Her misogyny is relentless: false women are "cozening crocodiles" (247); Evadne cannot do any good "because a woman" (255). To be saved by her "dear lord," she must despise herself and demean her sex, attributing to women the sins of humanity as she pleads for Amintor to become her personal harrower and savior.

If androgyny stretches humankind, essentialism shrinks it, and Evadne's parody of sinful womanhood certainly reduces both herself and Amintor. The man who broke his vow to Aspatia and then rationalized his deceit now magnanimously adopts the role she has constructed to complement hers and becomes the flat, flattering image she offers in her distorting glass. He can forgive Evadne on the grounds that "that devil King" tempted her "frailty" (263). After all, frailty's name is woman, and he, ennobled by the cloak of virtue she has cast over him, can generously bid her rise. Amintor's finding the real devil—a rival man—does not, of course, erase Evadne's sin. His "charity" will go with her, and he will not take vengeance on her, but he cannot embrace her as his wife (269–71). If only, Amintor piously wishes, the priest who married them had given them "equal virtues" (275).

In transforming herself into Amintor's dark and defining female opposite, Evadne has conflated two desires—winning her bridegroom's forgiveness and killing the King—but those ends involve a conflict of gender: to become the perfect woman who will be Amintor's wife, she must embrace the revenger's role and destroy her enemy:

> Thus I take leave, my lord,
> And never shall you see the foul Evadne
> Till she have tried all honoured means that may
> Set her in rest, and wash her stains away.
>
> (279–82)

Technically, it is Melantius and not Evadne who authorizes and commands the regicide, he who writes her as the sullied, expendable medium for the restoration of his and Amintor's honor. Evadne is to be female to their male, the vehicle of their meaning who definitively repudiates the King's political and sexual authority and displays justice at its most poetic: as she was his agent against them, she will be theirs against him; as he unmanned and feminized them, she will unman and feminize him.

Evadne's speech, however, culminates in her embracing the revenger's, not the avenger's, identity. Focusing on her own injuries, she separates the guilty but penitent "I" saved through Amintor's grace from the "foul Evadne" who intends to effect her own redemption, creating a second body able to rival and defeat the tyrant King. That second Evadne is not Eudoxa but Maximus: a killer empowered as a victim, a "monster," wild and trapped outside the walls of human community. As a revenger, Evadne will leap the boundaries of gender she has just repented crossing and become transgressively male again, a reversal of gender underscored by the theatrical allusiveness of the revenge scene: like Hamlet observing Claudius praying, she considers whether she should kill the King as he sleeps, opting, however, to "lay before him / The number of his wrongs and punishments" (5.1.31–32);[9] like Othello, she comes upon her victim sleeping; like Montsurry assaulting Tamyra, she repeatedly stabs her immobilized victim, interspersing torture with commentary.

It is Melantius's maleness Evadne replicates in her revenge. She abandons the style of the King, whose authority crumbled in her brother's grip, and forces him to play both the feminized Amintor and the feminized Evadne. Adopting her brother's strategies of dominance, she responds to the King's summons by locking herself and him within his private quarters. She has severed the connection between his political and natural bodies and reduced him to the mortal shell lying on the bed before her. Because she is biologically a woman—her encounter with Melantius was an emphatic reminder—she must also erase the advantage of his body's physical advantage: "I dare not trust your strength; your grace and I / Must grapple upon even terms no more" (36–37).

Like Melantius, too, she uses the power to name as her signifier of authority, overwriting the King's text with her own. He is not her monarch and lover; he is the seducer of her innocence. She is not his subject and mistress; she is the revenger come to win back her "fair name" (63). Evadne establishes herself by refusing to respond to his "Evadne," his "Queen of Love" (50): "I am not she, nor bear I in this breast / So much cold spirit to be called a woman" (65–66). To be a woman is to lack the spirit necessary to perform her act; she will become the pitiless tiger (67–68), so wild that she is outside humanity itself.

Her victory requires her to convince the King that he does not and cannot write this scene, a belief he gives up no more readily than Amintor did with her or she with Melantius. When, like Amintor, he instructs her that she is "too sweet and gentle" to "mean this" (74, 73), she repudiates his Evadne and substitutes her own: "No, I am not," she responds; rather, she is the "blowing rose," and she has come to kill the "foul canker" (74–78) that destroyed her. Physically and verbally disempowered, he can only deny her text:

> *King.*   No!
> *Evadne.*   I am.
> *King.*   Thou art not!
>   I prithee, speak not these things; thou art gentle,
>   And wert not meant thus rugged.
>
>   (83–85)

The King has lost control of her shape and voice and, because his role is defined by hers, of his own as well. She has made him her creature, reshaping his body and now commanding his voice—"Stir nothing but your tongue, and that for mercy / To those above us" (86–87)—while she forces him to hear hers. He is "a shameless villain,"

> A thing out of the overcharge of nature,
> Sent like a thick cloud to disperse a plague
> Upon weak catching women; such a tyrant
> That for his lust would sell away his subjects,
> Ay, all his heaven hereafter.
>
> (91–96)

Ineffectually, the King falls back on the political identity that should command her collaboration in his fantasies—"Hear, Evadne, / Thou soul of sweetness, hear! I am thy King" (96–97)—but she empties that title of its authority and replaces it with her own:

> Thou art my shame. Lie still; there's none about you
> Within your cries; all promises of safety
> Are but deluding dreams. Thus, thus, thou foul man,
> Thus I begin my vengeance.
>
> (98–101)

Melantius may teach Evadne how to act the man, but she betters the instruction. It is she who writes, stages, directs, and performs the scene; she who deprives the King of motion, command, and volition; she who renders him chaste, silent, and obedient to her; she who makes her knife his lover. Evadne authors each stab wound, writing his name and the names of her play's cast of characters on his body. Earlier, she had inscribed the words *foul* and *monster* on herself; now he is the "foul man" and "monster" (100, 105), the scapegoat who must die to cleanse her of sin. The next two thrusts bear the names of his now triumphant victims—"This for my lord Amintor, / This for my noble brother." The last and mortal wound, however, is for her and from her: "this stroke / For the most wronged of women" (110–12).

Evadne's faith in the physical power that writes itself on the body deludes her into believing that she has established the meaning of her act, that despite her bloody assault, she is a "weak catching," "wronged" woman, a blown rose. In her heady moment of victory, however, she overlooks the contextual meaning of her act, which closes around her as soon as she leaves the scene of her revenge. Those who arrive to witness its bloody remains foreground the problem: "who can believe / A woman could do this?" (5.1.128–29) asks First Gentleman; Cleon cannot believe that the gentleman's "her"—"there her woeful act / Lies still" (130–31) refers to the "traitor": "Her act! A woman!" (131). Dividing herself into bloody revenger and submissive wife and sister has created a glaring contradiction between the gender of Evadne's act and the gender it aims to achieve. The King's crimes against men are her justification for revenge, but her crime against him has not absolved her guilt. In the eyes of her male audience, Evadne has revealed herself as the monster she thought to kill with the King.

The men she is ostensibly avenging will respond in the same way. Bathed in blood and holding the phallic weapon, a euphoric Evadne greets her husband: "It is Evadne still that follows thee, / But not her mischiefs" (5.3.110–11). She believes she has freed herself and him from the past; that she has successfully rewritten their wedding so that the contrast between her superficial beauty and interior ugliness is now reversed, and he will find her, "beauteous with these rites," "fair" (117, 116). Yet when she gave him the power to absolve and redeem her, she ceded authorship of herself to him. His construction of her act will not concur with hers but with the gentleman's and Cleon's. Powerless to effect her desire and at the mercy of the man to whom she surrendered authority over herself, Evadne is a pathetic figure. Her voice pleads for forgiveness, for Amintor to take her to his bed (150–51). Her body tries to seize what she desires, but she cannot force him. She begs, "Take me home" (155), and falls to her knees, but in that act of submission, Amintor sees only a refutation of the female gender she enacts: "Thy knees are more to me than violence; / I am worse than sick to see knees follow me / For that I must not grant" (159–61).

Evadne makes a last, tangled attempt to reconstruct herself as a woman: "Amintor, thou shalt love me now again. / Go, I am calm. Farewell, and peace for ever. / Evadne, whom thou hat'st, will die for thee" (167–69). In death, however, Evadne is still the woman who insisted on dominating her world. Once more, she has reversed roles with Amintor, wooing his love by forcing hers on him. Her protestation that she will die for him may be the exhalation of a feminized woman killing herself for love, but it is also the statement of a savior, the redemptive male role in which she had cast Amintor. In the attempts to return her body to a man's ownership, Evadne again crosses the boundaries of gender as she plunges the knife that destroyed the King's offending body into herself. In no one's eyes but her own does the act make her the woman Amintor will love. Both he and Melantius rewrite her text, Amintor pledging love to Aspatia as he dies, Melantius crudely dismissing Evadne's sacrifice as a "thing to laugh at in respect of this" (264).

Evadne occupies the ambivalent role of the genre's male revengers, whose contest with tyranny is a struggle for authority. Like them, she remans herself to unman a tyrant, and, like them, she prompts both sympathy and revulsion in the act. Hers is never the affirmation of her sex that allows a blurring of gender but, rather, a rigid definition of both sex and gender and a reconnection of each to the other. A woman who has played the man to become a woman, Evadne finds herself locked outside the home where she begs Amintor to take her. She dies wild and unmourned, neither woman nor man.

At first glance, Aspatia is Evadne's opposite. She begins as a feminized figure, the abused and lovesick lady Evadne enacts as her final identity. Opposite, too, is her death: she expires in Amintor's arms and not, like Evadne, on her knees before him; she is dressed as a man and not as a woman, although the only blood on her soldier's costume is her own while Evadne is stained with the blood of the King. Apparently contrary, too, are Evadne's misogyny and Aspatia's misandry: "But man— / O, that beast, man!" (2.2.26–27). In response to the manservant who denies her access to Amintor until bribed, Aspatia articulates her view of the insurmountable gulf between men and women:

> There is a vile dishonest trick in man,
> More than in women. All the men I meet
> Appear thus to me, are harsh and rude,
> And have a subtlety in everything,
> Which love could never know; but we fond women
> Harbor the easiest and the smoothest thoughts,
> And think all shall go so. It is unjust
> That men and women should be match'd together.
>
> (5.3.22–29)

Women are fond, easy, and smooth; men are dishonest, harsh, rude, and subtle.

Opposites, however, are always reversible. Women, in Aspatia's view, are also culpably gullible—"be more than women, wise; / At least be more than I was" (14–15)—the natural victims of men, who, while predatory, are also clever and powerful. In this play where the sexual binary is affirmed, where no one explores the promising, androgynous world beyond sexual essentialism, Aspatia and Evadne are equally trapped in the assumptions that provide grounds for both misogyny and misandry. Both search for authority futilely in the failed, reductive maleness of tyrant and revenger, responding to feminized submission by creating an empowering authorial identity.[10]

Aspatia shapes her given role as abandoned woman into a public art form. The suffering maiden is not just a ventriloquized production of the female role men have written for her but a living hyperbole that absorbs other human art into it. We first see the appropriative power of that construction as Aspatia participates in the preparations for Amintor's wedding night with Evadne. In song and speech, she dominates the scene, centering herself and marginalizing the couple: her song celebrates woman's constancy in the face of men's deception—"*My love was false, but I was firm*" (2.1.76); her speech absorbs Evadne into her category of lovelorn women and translates the wedding of Evadne and Amintor into the funeral of Aspatia, complete with instructions on how to mourn her.

> Bring each a mournful story and a tear
> To offer at it when I go to earth;
> With flattering ivy clasp my coffin round;
> Write on my brow my fortune; let my bier
> Be borne by virgins that shall sing by course
> The truth of maids and perjuries of men.
>
> (102–7)

Aspatia lays claim to her public meaning, like Evadne with Melantius, by asking that her fortune be written on her brow. Her body becomes the quintessential expression and monumental repository of maids' truth and men's perjuries in story and song, the work of art that speaks for eternity of her silenced will.

Her attempts to shape her powerlessness into a public role succeed in empowering her by recentering the male text on the woman's part, as she does with Antiphila's needlework depicting the legend of Theseus. Here she authors herself as the bereft Ariadne. Even though Antiphila objects that the changes will "wrong the story" (2.2.57), Aspatia insists on dictating the images. There must be quicksand beneath the shallow water; her face must be Ariadne's; her body will be the "wild island" of Naxos. Usurping Antiphila's authority over the work, Aspatia

writes it to monumentalize herself—"strive to make me look /
Like sorrow's monument" (73–74). As with the tales and songs
at her funeral, she draws and absorbs the legend until Ariadne
disappears into Aspatia, who becomes the sole embodiment of
woman betrayed.

When grief does not consume her life, Aspatia actively seeks
the posthumous culmination of her art. In her final attempt to
bring the world under her authorial control, she cross-dresses,
insisting on a female persona even in male garb and arrogating
to herself the authority of the gods: the heavens must forgive her
because they have "put a woman's heart into my breast" (5.3.4).
Like Evadne, Aspatia is trapped in a contradiction, yearning to
be the woman Amintor loves but functioning as a man to achieve
that end. Evadne, the King's blood literally and figuratively cov-
ering her female dress, lifts the knife against herself; Aspatia,
dressed as her brother with the "womanish" face (1.1.109),
chooses to receive the blow from Amintor's sword. Yet while that
choice makes her sexually female, she must provoke it by playing
the aggressor, striking and kicking him into action. When Amintor tires of being an unwillingly passive victim—"A man can bear /
No more and keep his flesh" (5.3.95–96)—he takes the action that
will utterly destroy him as a man; Aspatia, on the other hand,
has "got enough, / And my desire" (103–4).

As Aspatia, Evadne, and Amintor mingle in death on the blood-
stained floor of the stage, their physical positions restore orthodoxy to the play's representations of gender. Both women are
lower than Amintor—Evadne kneels, then lies dead at his feet;
the virtuous Aspatia is elevated briefly by Amintor's arms but
falls as well to the ground. The rivals for his love in murder and
suicide predecease him, the tainted Evadne expiring before the
faithful Aspatia. When Melantius finds the heap of bodies, he
elevates only Amintor's, dismissing the others as irrelevant to the
central tragedy, which is played by men. Yet the semiotic reitera-
tion of the sexual binary at play's end does not and cannot erase
its reversals within the play.

The Maid's Tragedy's problematic presentation of gender and its
relationship to sovereign authority, both in theory and in history,
is perhaps best displayed in the play's opening masque.[11] Cynthia, that echo of Elizabeth, enters in response to Night, her fellow Queen. Cynthia denies the tale of her love for Endymion:
"Ease and wine / Have bred these bold tales; poets when they
rage / Turn gods to men, and make an hour an age" (1.2.165–67).
We are reminded of historical change, of shifts in styles between

generations and royal courts. At the end of the masque, that chaste luminary relinquishes her power, as Elizabeth did, to the sun god. The reign of a queen, whose light shines brightly in darkness, is given to a king, who is by definition light itself. On the surface, the masque is a compliment both to the King in the small world of *The Maid's Tragedy* and to the King in the greater world of England. Viewed from that perspective, it affirms James's sense of male privilege; it presents him with a display of male love; it presents women as threatening competitors who are contained at the end. Yet Cynthia has been called by Night to celebrate a marriage that is a sham. Arranged by a tyrant, that is, a man who has turned himself into a god, it violates all principles of light as truth. We are left remembering the reign of another monarch of another sex, with another set of public and private values, and another style of theatricality.

Virtue and Authority

Evadne's assumption of absolute maleness does not free anyone from the restrictive social behavior identified with biological sex. It does not permit men and women the freedom to embrace either gender without fear of humiliation and abuse. Rather than dissolve the binary, she reverses the poles of authority—and only for herself. The consequence for men is a deeper, more defensive commitment to male superiority because, unlike Affranius and Govianus, they are disgraced by their subjection to her and cannot transvalue subjection itself. Ultimately, Evadne precipitates a violently conservative reaction that separates the sexes even more definitively and, at the same time, reunites sex and gender in the glorification of men and the dishonoring of women.

Revenge tragedy's chaste heroines dissolve the knot of misogyny, break the male-authored triangle of rivalry and violence, and establish the possibility of an androgyny that both affirms the difference between the sexes and challenges its connection to gender. They understand gender as a function of a greater order with primary and, when necessary, exclusive demands on their obedience, accepting male control of their bodies only if men validate that order and women's reading of it. Paradoxically, then, those women we would see as victims—Lucina, the Lady, and potentially Eudoxa—have a dignity and conviction that ennobles them while the seemingly revolutionary Evadne is, in fact, trapped and helpless in her dedication the power.

The authority of women in these plays is a consequence of their dedicating their bodies to heaven's uses, but the concept embodied by their chastity or virginity is far more encompassing than a physical technicality. It is virtue, an inclusive term that involves commitment to the common good. Aemilia Lanyer, dedicating poem after poem in her *Salve Deus Rex Judaeorum* to virtuous women—one "To all vertuous Ladies in generall"—uses virtue as Lucina does, to signify connection: between her and the King of whom she writes, between her and the women for whom she writes. Women's bodies ensure the continuation of life and the continuity of human history, and they are, therefore, to be protected against any who would abuse or misuse them. Unlike the Tyrant, whose self is based on differentiation from all others, the heroines understand the self, in Ricoeur's terms, *as* another (1992).

Historically, to establish their right to assert and protect themselves, women have relied on a virtue rooted and enacted in the female body but belonging to the ungendered soul. Caroline Walker Bynum writes eloquently of ascetic women of the late middle ages who deprived their bodies of food in order to merge with a divinity represented by Christ. While men mapped the world as dichotomous, which made their embrace of femaleness a reversal, religious women like Julian of Norwich, saw a "continuity of self" with the divine (1987, 289–90) that annihilated worldly identity, including distinctions of gender. For the Lady, Lucina, and Eudoxa, that continuity of self extends from the divine to the human and natural worlds. Men, even absolute monarchs, are those worlds' caretakers, and their commands can be ignored if they endanger their charge; women, marginal to men's political concerns, are in their own eyes the holding, linking center of all that is. The authority of a king or a father can be challenged, but women's authority, as they define it, is unassailable.

Chaste women, then, are not merely self-deluded inscriptions of a male text. They are the unalterable and transformative representatives of a community that extends through them from the material to the spiritual, and their androgyny strongly affirms the female part of that community. Even in a secular and relative world, their definition of sex and gender has great force because it places women at the center of the great rhythms of nature and history. The heroines of these plays, arguably dated by their adherence to virtues no longer universally honored, nonetheless merit study in the strategy they use to oppose unjust authority. They find their voices in the gaps of authority created by the assertion of absolutism, demonstrating that a discourse need not imprison those it relegates to submission if they counter it with an opposing discourse. In the seventeenth century, the political world denied women authority, but the theology that allowed Protestants to combat repressive monarchs granted them equality of soul.

Like a palimpsest emerging from a painting, Elizabeth is discernible as the shadowy, reinforcing background of the heroines' determined and authoritative chastity and, in an extension into the political, of Eudoxa's statecraft. Elizabeth represented her virginity as the sign of service to God and her people, fashioning herself as the living current between the two worlds. For Lanyer, she is the exemplary principle of connection for all humanity:

> . . . [her] worth did bind
> All worthy minds so long as they have breath,
> In linkes of Admiration, love and zeale,
> To that deare Mother of our Common-weale.
> ("To the Ladie *Elizabeths* Grace," 4–7)

A woman writing in praise of another woman, Lanyer authors Elizabeth as gloriously embodying a maternal authority that, like Lucina's mother, binds and transforms others, an authority perceived in the "worthy minds" of those who serve her. As the Lady stated, "It is the mind that sets his master forth."

It was, of course, men who wrote and played these female characters: Francis Beaumont, John Fletcher, Thomas Middleton, perhaps William Shakespeare, along with their collaborators and actors. Players were susceptible to the generic woes of nonphallic men in an age that gendered powerlessness female, and, like the women with whom they were compared, they were required to understand power more accurately than those who wielded it. Subordinates, as Giddens notes, might be better able to penetrate "conditions of social reproduction than those who otherwise dominate them" (1979, 72).

Suspected and attacked for moving outside their sex and social position, the players represent women, suspected and attacked on the same grounds, as heroically challenging criminal authority. As they explore assumptions about gender through the figures of tyrant, revenger, and heroine, the players expose the limitations and extremes of traditional male definition and represent women as embodying a fidelity to principle that men can, without shame, adopt as well. The revenge tragedy of this era pits the authority of the state, wielded in its crudest form by the tyrant, against the authority of theatrical representation, wielded by the player-revenger, but they sacrifice both to a good represented by heroines who, given heaven's authorship and authority, prove successful authors of change. Like the heroines they create and perform, the players use an empowering discourse to counter a disabling one.

Although elevating the terms of this highly subversive genre to a level above politics has clear political advantages for its playwrights and actors, it is misleading to attribute that upward sweep and the consequent idealization of virtuous women exclusively to motives like fear and cynicism. In revenge tragedy's insistent pursuit of justice, the players use female voices to speak for an Astraean principle against the brutality of a corrupt and very explicitly male world. That those women's voices are androgynous, even if their assumption of maleness is forced by circumstance, is both apology and affirmation of the players' necessarily androgynous profession.

6

The Duchess of Malfi

The Duchess of Malfi cannot be reduced to a dramatic subgenre, but its kinship to revenge tragedies written during the same politically turbulent years of the early seventeenth century is immediately striking. Ferdinand and the Cardinal, although they do not explicitly invoke the absolutist ideology that cloaks Emperor, Tyrant, and King, function theatrically like their fellow tyrants. They recognize no familial or personal authority that debars theirs, and they use the misogynistic signifiers of gender to construct themselves as absolute: women are whores and witches; men cuckolds, panders, and intelligencers. Bosola and Antonio attempt to maintain a private, independent maleness beyond their reach, Antonio as a husband and father, Bosola as a seller of professional services, both as virtuous men, but neither can entirely escape his inscription in the brothers' tyrannical text. Bosola, however, dies struggling against it, forming with Antonio a fraternity based on admiration for a woman.

That woman proves the tyrants' most dangerous and effective rival. The Duchess offers the play's only alternative to the pathological male authority of Ferdinand and the Cardinal. As both widow and prince, she is androgynous: a sexually experienced woman, a financially independent inheritor of patriarchal wealth, and a female regnant. Elizabeth healed the inherent division between her female natural body and her male political body with the powerful combination of monarchy and virginity. She was, despite opposition, able to choose manless womanhood in order to strengthen her political position. The Duchess, however, is a Jacobean woman who, like Lady Arbella Stuart and Penelope Rich, does not choose the unmarried state. She has no desire to confront her brothers openly, knowing she will lose any worldly battle she fights against them, but she never doubts her right to choose her husband and shape her life.[1]

In this highly metadramatic play, where the contest for authority is a struggle for authorship of the text, the Duchess is the final victor. Her murder, designed by her brothers to prove their absoluteness, serves not only to refute it but also to dismantle the analogy between maleness and the authority on which it is based. Ferdinand and the Cardinal determine the play's action, but the Duchess determines its meaning.

The Fratriarchy

The play's flimsy, after-the-fact rationalization of Ferdinand's and the Cardinal's malevolence has produced a large body of compensatory explanation. Materialist readings predictably politicize the metaphysical, Frank Whigham, for example, viewing Ferdinand's torture and murder of his sister as a nobleman's response to a crisis of class (1991). Psychological analyses focus on Ferdinand's obsession with the Duchess, some connecting it to sadism, lycanthropy, and necrophilia, most focusing on incest.[2]

Their villainy is explicable as well in the political and theatrical discourses of tyranny, as the play's repeated use of the word indicates. For an English audience of that time, the Aragonian brethren would evoke the particular tyrannies of Catholic Europe and the national pride of Protestant England's successful resistance to them. James's pacifism did not, after all, erase the memories of Spanish invasion, papal intervention, commercial competition, and colonial rivalry. Allusively both Spanish and Italian, Ferdinand and the Cardinal represent a secular and religious oppression that casts its shadow over the current King of England.

Within the play, Ferdinand and the Cardinal are complementary figures.[3] Ferdinand, Antonio tells us, functions in and through others' bodies: he "speaks with others' tongues, and hears men's suits / With others' ears" (1.1.173–74). Except in the person of his brother, he allows no subjectivity, as Wells notes, outside his own (1985, 70). He functions only as a compelling and controlling figure in the *theatrum mundi* that is himself: an actor who holds the attention of audiences onstage and off; a director who cues and manages his actor-surrogates; an audience who closes the circle by witnessing the plays he has set in motion.

The Cardinal, a tyrant's tyrant, is the master playwright who directs his brother's performances. As Cardinal, he is the manifest presence of a timeless institution, an upstage figure who inhabits the isolated public plane of icon and emblem and who, like an absolute monarch, believes himself personally unassailable. Beneath those institutional signifiers, however, the Cardinal styles himself the *sui generis* author of his own authority, an invisible presence behind the furthest reaches of theatrical space. From that vantage, his public, official role as Cardinal functions, like the revenger's disguise, to veil the playwright behind it. He is not always successful, as his failure to bribe his way to the papacy demonstrates, but he nonetheless presumes authorship of all texts, using theatrical strategies to preserve the illusion that his fallible, criminal life is divine, that he supersedes the institution that authorizes him.

Like their fellow theatrical tyrants, the princely brothers require men and women alike to acknowledge their maleness as absolute. Horning Castruccio—tyranny's eponymous male servant—is an important element in the Cardinal's pleasure with Julia: "Thou art a witty false one:— / I mean to him" (2.4.5–6). With Julia, and women in general, the Cardinal's will to absolute control takes the shape of contemptuous indifference. He takes pleasure not in his mistress but in his ability to lock that clever tongue in her mouth and force her to speak his words if she speaks at all. When she attempts to fight back by accusing him of inconstancy, he deftly turns her argument back on her: she is concerned about his constancy because she has "approv'd / Those giddy and wild turnings" in herself" (11–12). Because she is a woman, she is *a priori* false; because she is a woman he has seduced away from her husband, she has proven herself false. Even the tears to which he reduces her he writes as hypocrisy; they will "fall into your husband's bosom" (22) when she returns to him. Julia cannot defend herself because she has no self beneath the roles he authors: a falcon or elephant, a puppet who kisses him on command and thanks him for freeing her into the prison of his absolutist fantasy (27–36).

Ferdinand requires a more public acknowledgment of his mastery, forcing the men around him into ventriloquism or silence. Although not himself a cuckolder, he uses his brother's sexual exploits against Castruccio to ridicule him. He bridles the tongues of Roderigo and Grisolan when they dare to laugh at Silvio's witticism, an especially dangerous sign of independence because it comes at the expense of Ferdinand's horse: "Why do you laugh? Methinks you that are courtiers should be my touch-wood, take fire, when I give fire; that is, laugh when I laugh, were the subject never so witty" (1.1.122–25).

Like Valentinian with Lucina and Melantius with Evadne, he ignores the irrelevant, insubstantial matter of the spirit and establishes the material conditions that grant him the right to own and name others. With Bosola, he presumes, at first correctly, that the desire for position will be stronger than that something "call'd a soul" (4.1.123). Bosola, however, is a difficult subject. He has constructed himself as a soldier—manly, independent, inherently virtuous, and loyal to his own codes—the equal, in his own eyes at least, of the princes who employ him. When summoned, he does not defer to the great duke but, instead, levels the hierarchy separating them: he speaks with mimetic, distancing irony—he was "lur'd" (1.1.231) to Ferdinand like a hawk to his future master.

When Bosola uses the metaphor of witchcraft to describe Ferdinand's intent—"It seems you would create me / One of your familiars" (258–59)—Ferdinand revises "familiar" to "such a kind of thriving thing" (261), explicitly linking the reward of prosperity on Bosola's surrendering his manhood. As a simultaneously neutered and ambiguously gendered "thing," Bosola can, like Piato, serve as female to his master and male to others when his master allows. Although both men underestimate the depth and tenacity of Bosola's commitment to the nonmaterial world of virtue, Bosola here takes the title and name Ferdinand has given him: "The provisorship o'th'horse? say then my corruption / Grew out of horse-dung: I am your creature" (286–87). Bosola has become Ferdinand's thing, a homunculus modeled in excrement as a smaller version of his creator and master.

Ferdinand's world is densely populated with male creatures, but the only woman in it is his sister and, as we learn only after her death, his twin. While he shares the Cardinal's general view of women as lesser beings who serve best as puppets, monuments, or corpses, Ferdinand is far more threatened by them. The Cardinal dismisses women as inferior liars and manipulators, but Ferdinand recognizes, indeed is obsessed by, their subversive, sexual power, which he identifies as witchcraft. Reserving her femaleness in all its aspects for the devil, the witch not only evades men's control but, more unthinkable, becomes male to the men of her human family, feminizing them. The tyrant's power to turn independent beings into creatures animated by his will is, as Bosola's metaphor for Ferdinand implies, itself a form of witchcraft; women, born with the power to give life and, through commerce with demons, able to acquire the power to shape creatures to their will, are ominous rivals. The Duchess is just another Julia to the Cardinal, a woman his language and intellect can readily contain; to Ferdinand, however, she is a fearsome, uncanny enemy.

When, in the siblings' only appearance together, the Duchess tries to penetrate the barrier of their language with her own, "Will you hear me? / I'll never marry:—" (1.1.301–2), the Cardinal interrupts to stuff his words into her mouth like a gag:

> So most widows say:
> But commonly that motion lasts no longer
> Than the turning of an hour-glass—the funeral sermon
> And it, end both together.
>
> (1.1.302–5)

Having wrapped her in his proscriptive misogyny, he fades upstage and offstage. Ferdinand, however, remains to tie the knot of disobedience, witchcraft, and incest around his sister's throat: "they whose faces do belie their hearts / Are witches, ere they arrive at twenty years— / Ay: and give the devil suck" (1.1.309–11).

Notably, Ferdinand's witch is not a crone but a young woman like his sister, a potential wife and mother. The Duchess, who could "like the irregular crab" go her own way and think she "goes right" (319–20), must be kept in her place by the threat of "my father's poniard" (331), the signifier of maleness he will use again to assert his authority over his sister. Ferdinand juxtaposes the avenging patriarchal phallus in his hand to "that part which, like the lamprey, / Hath ne'er a bone in't" (336–37). Although he disingenuously glosses the boneless part as the tongue—in itself an accusation that women enjoy and usurp the male prerogative of language—his essential meaning is as clear as he would wish it. If she dares use her body without his presence in the form of permission, the hard steel of patriarchal authority will castrate the man she chooses, in his imagination a demon lover and child, and assume his rightful place inside her. It is Melantius again, threatening to make his sword his sister's lover.

Like Melantius, too, Ferdinand must confront his failure to block access to his sister's body. On hearing she has borne a child, he visualizes her as a garrison town with passageways, managed by "cunning bawds" (2.5.9), leading to her. She has rejected and mocked him—"Excellent hyena!" (39)—in illicitly creating her own world, which she has furnished with some "strong thigh'd bargeman" or "some lovely squire" (42, 44), and populated with their issue. The Duchess is no longer the female principle, the sister, wife, mother, and daughter within his encompassing maleness, but definitively, dangerously, demonically Other. In separating herself from him and becoming the rival author of his life, she has, like the witch, become male to his female and subjected him to the sexual authority of another man, in effect cuckolding him and making him female both to her and the man who embraces her sexually. He has become Castruccio.

While the Cardinal will deal with her audacity in the public world outside the Duchess's realm, Ferdinand seeks her in Malfi and, penetrating her most inward space, her bedroom. Appearing in her mirror, he replaces Antonio's image and overshadows hers, wordlessly placing his father's poniard in her hand. She exists only to read and obey him: he does not look at her directly and, when he speaks to her, it is behind the simultaneously distancing and enclosing imperatives of patriarchy. Ignoring her "hear me" (3.2.73), he addresses her through an apostrophized "Virtue" (72); when she persists, he commands her silence: "Do not speak" (75). Her attempt to break out of his moralistic context and tell her own story—"I pray sir, hear me: I am married" (82)—is not language to him, only the cacophonous howls and hoots of predatory night creatures: "The howling of a wolf / Is music to thee, screech-owl, prithee peace!" (88–89).

From his remove, he pronounces judgment, beginning with the man she calls her husband. He first commands the hidden Antonio not to make himself known lest the violent consequences damn them both, then grants permission for him to remain: "Enjoy thy lust still" (98). Consciously or inadvertently, it is unclear which, Antonio obeys and, in that obedience, confirms Ferdinand's mastery of his marriage's physical space and the marriage itself. Antonio has become his creature—like Bosola, a man only when his master permits.

Having demonstrated his authority over the man to whom she has dared subject him, Ferdinand turns to his sister. She may have assumed her brother's sex in authoring her life, but she will not, he tells her, be able to play the man by protecting her lover:

> If thou do wish thy lecher may grow old
> In thy embracements, I would have thee build
> Such a room for him as our anchorites
> To holier use inhabit: let not the sun
> Shine on him, till he's dead; let dogs and monkeys
> Only converse with him, and such dumb things
> To whom nature denies use to sound his name;

Do not keep a paraquito, lest she learn it.
If thou do love him, cut out thine own tongue
Lest it bewray him.

(100–109)

Like Antonio, she must live always within the prison that is Ferdinand, doing his bidding even when she attempts to do her own. She must be male to her husband, enclosing his body, closing his mouth, and locking him in her house, making him into her woman while she, locked and silenced within her brother's world, her tongue cut out by the poniard in her hands, is again Ferdinand's. He has overturned her reversal of gender by feminizing her to him and feminizing her husband to her. In the mounting aggression of her implied accusations and in her insistence on writing herself as a woman with "youth, / And a little beauty" who has chosen to follow nature and custom by marrying rather than remain "cas'd up, like a holy relic" (139–40), Ferdinand finds his suspicions confirmed: "So you have some virgins / That are witches" (140–41).

In contrast to Ferdinand, the Cardinal will address the question he coolly posed—"What to do?" (2.5.29)—in the exaggeratedly public, upstage space of public ritual. There, in the distancing spotlight of the dumb show, he transforms himself into the enforcing arm of the patriarchy he embodies, effecting a metamorphosis from Cardinal to soldier as he exchanges the androgynous costume and sexually undifferentiated signifiers of his religion for the physical hardness of sword, helmet, shield, and spurs. The site of the Cardinal's reification of male authority is a shrine consecrated to Mary, Christianity's apotheosis of womanhood as loving mother and merciful intercessor. Whatever the Duchess's motive for pilgrimage, she stands on that sacred ground as a mother whom tyranny has deprived of shelter, her family a replica of the holy family at Christianity's heart.

The pilgrims note the widening gap between the church and state that support the Cardinal's tyranny and the authority on which his and their right to govern rests. Ancona had no right to "determine of a free prince" (3.4.29), the pilgrims agree, nor was there justice in the Pope's seizure of Malfi. For an English audience, the Cardinal is clear confirmation of the tyranny of the Papacy and the political states under its control. The pilgrims also bear witness to the discrepancy between the Cardinal's "too cruel" actions (27) and his clerical role. His performative gesture in wrenching the ring from the Duchess's finger may uncreate her domestic world, but it also casts doubt on his right to the authority he wields and on a maleness that, like his brother's, appropriates in order to silence principles culturally and theologically ascribed to women. In anathematizing the Duchess and shutting the gates of sanctuary against her, the Cardinal has publicly severed himself from the root of his authority and, simultaneously, deracinated the authority.

Ferdinand's enactment of his authority similarly calls into question the familial relationship on which his right to command his sister rests. In brutally transforming the loving, fertile world the Duchess created into his theater of revenge, he exposes the madness woven into the cloth of absolutism: "Curse upon her! / I will no longer study in the book / Of another's heart" (4.1.15–17). He will erase that threatening Otherness by forcing her into his darkness to experience his godlike mystery and power: he is not what he seems; she cannot compass him (3.1.84–86). He appears in his play only as a disembodied voice that vanishes and leaves behind the proof of his art's triumph over hers—the waxwork corpses, the prop hand she was to believe his now matched to the artificial body from which it was taken. He had imagined feeding her child to its father; now he compels her to reabsorb the lives she shaped in that space. Erasing her roles as wife and mother will, he believes, restore her to the total femaleness she must embody for him.

Ferdinand must, of course, reject Bosola's plea to be allowed to assist her penitence because it introduces an outside spiritual dimension into his dark prison: "Damn her! that body of hers, / While that my blood ran pure in't, was more worth / Than that which thou wouldst comfort, call'd a soul" (4.1.121–23). To recognize her soul is to allow her an area of authority over which he has no control. Yet his reducing her to a body, and finally to a lifeless body, proves his own destruction. Ferdinand assumed that, once she was dead and unable to cling stubbornly to her independent existence, she would be safe to look at. What he sees, however, is not a submissive part of himself but her staring eyes. She is not "what / [He'd] have her" (4.2.256–57), not one of his sculpted imitations of death, a stage prop he can manipulate and replace, matter he can animate and render inanimate.

Her life was not, after all, his, and her death places even her body forever beyond his reach. Against his will, she attains for him the objective reality he disallowed her when she was alive, and her separateness carries the magic he had always feared, the power to possess him: "Cover her face: Mine eyes dazzle: she died young" (264). Having once seen her, he can never again choose not to see her: "Let me see her face again:— / Why didst not thou pity her?" (272–73). By the scene's end, Ferdinand is off to "hunt the badger, by owl-light," a "deed of darkness" (334–35).

Like Valentinian, the King, and the Tyrant, Ferdinand and the Cardinal die at the hands of a rival male, but the "cause on't," as Ferdinand rightly says, is their sister (5.5.71). In death, the Duchess exposes the poverty and impotence of their reduction of human life, male and female, to buyable, manipulable, coercible matter. Her tenacious adherence to the full range of her humanity explodes their small world of tyrant-gods and subject-creatures and deconstructs the gendered binary that supports their dominance. Within their own definition of gender, it is they who are feminized, not she. The Duchess's absence from their material world isolates them within their deficient natures, and they become the subjects of the tyrannies they had practiced on her, cornered and locked in their private spaces and silenced by the refusal or inability of others to hear them. They take her place to become not what she was but what they wanted her to be— caught, mad, and damned.

The Cardinal's blindness to motives other than the baits of the world—greed, envy, ambition—and his inability to acknowledge others as equals results in his fatally misjudging, as Maximus did, the force of opposition. Like the King with Melantius, he is too arrogant to detect the presence of other playwrights and actors. As Julia, Bosola, noblemen and courtiers, and even Ferdinand elude his control, he sees his private space become the public arena where he tangles in the coils of his own plots.

Julia is his first failure. When she pries into the Duchess's death, the Cardinal, in what he enjoys as a master stroke of irony, forces her to kiss the poisoned Bible that will make good her vow not to betray him. Yet Julia, by faithfully adhering to his construction of her as unfaithful, turns the irony on the ironist. The Cardinal has not, after all, contained the "witty false one" (2.4.5). Julia pays with her life, but she has cuckolded the cuckolder, staged the master stager to the audience of her new lover.

The Cardinal's authority continues to unravel: his failure to control Julia means he has lost control of Bosola as well. Even though he is forced by her ruse to bargain with Bosola as an equal—"Very well, / Now you know me for your fellow murderer" (5.2.295–96)—he persists in claiming the shaping power of a god: "I'd make you what you would be" (117). With his professed ignorance of the Duchess's death revealed as a lie, he resorts to promises, offering Bosola fortune and honors (302, 304), then employment: "What need we keep a stirring of't, and make / A greater smother? thou wilt kill Antonio?" (309–10). He is incapable of perceiving that Bosola now shapes himself, obeying the conscience that the Cardinal has bid him throw to the devil.

As it does with Julia, the Cardinal's supercilious, predatory irony with Bosola turns on him: to win his intended victim's trust in their supposed partnership, he gives Bosola the "master-key to our lodgings" (327–28), which makes Bosola "master" of the spaces it safeguards. The Duchess's jailer is now his, and it is he who plays the woman's role he had written for his sister, howling (5.5.13) and, as Bosola backs him into the female space of Julia's room, begging for mercy. Subjects and servants have become his masters: the would-be god kneels to his creature; the cuckolder submits to another man. The Duchess bravely kept her silence in the knowledge that none but the mad would answer her; the Cardinal calls desperately for the aid his own plot has precluded—"Shall I die like a leveret / Without any resistance? help, help, help!" (45–46)—only to have a madman respond and aid his murderer.

The basis of authority has steadily shifted to the female even as gender itself—female and male—is redefined: Julia transfers allegiance from the Cardinal to herself and shares it with Bosola; Bosola, once the misogynistic servant of male authority, serves the Duchess. In denying the Cardinal mercy, Bosola cites as his authority yet another female figure: "when thou kill'd'st thy sister, / Thou took'st from Justice her most equal balance, / And left her naught but her sword" (39–41). At the last, the Cardinal must acknowledge that female authority as superseding his: "O Justice! / I suffer now, for what hath former been: / *Sorrow is held the eldest child of sin*" (53–55). He cheers himself with the thought that at least she has served Bosola fairly as well, and, with a final bow to the only community he understood, asks that they look to his brother. In death, the exposed tyrant wishes again to be unseen: "and now, I pray, let me / Be laid by, and never thought of" (89–90). Save for a brief comment from Pescara, the Cardinal's final request is obeyed.

Ferdinand too experiences the ironic turning of his predatory nature on himself. The Duchess was able to withstand his assaults on her mind, but he has no defense against the assaults coming from within him. He enters the world of physical and mental darkness he created for her: "apoplexy," "frenzy" (5.1.58, 59), "lycanthropia" (5.2.6). The human who would be divine is a wolf who cannot be human. Ferdinand, who recognized no compass or boundary, who contained others, is now physically and mentally enclosed within his transmogrified body. The witchcraft of his tyranny created an unnatural, fleeting illusion of divine dominance. Now, as a hybrid creature unnaturally created by his own witchcraft, he restores nature to itself. Helplessly subject to the truth of his own being, he must obey the necrophagous nature that commands him to bring to light what was buried, and, in that obedience, to serve justice.

Ferdinand dies believing he is on a noble field of battle, but, like his brother, he is trapped in the private lodgings from which there is no escape. In his hallucinatory struggles, he is as he has always been, affecting godlike superiority to humanity while sinking to its bestial component. When he inflicts wounds on his brother and Bosola, he is a philosopher moralizing the deaths of Caesar and Pompey and sententiously declaring that "pain many times is taken away with the apprehension of greater" (5.5.59–60); when he is wounded, he is an animal: "Give me some wet hay, I am broken-winded— / I do account this world but a dog-kennel: / I will vault credit, and affect high pleasures, / Beyond death" (66–69). In the wilderness of madness, he is a horse proudly sneering at a world of dogs and a great prince, "vault[ing] credit" and "affect[ing] "high pleasures" in the other world.

The Cardinal comes to recognize Justice shaping his ends; Ferdinand, too, emerges briefly and partially from the tangle of his mind to bear witness to the shift of authority to the female: "My sister! O! my sister! there's the cause on't" (71). Widening the scope of his inquiry into cause, he reaches a conclusion: "*Whether we fall by ambition, blood, or lust, / Like diamonds, we are cut with our own dust*" (72–73). Perhaps naming what he sees as the immediate causes of the three siblings' demise—the Cardinal's ambition, his blood, and the Duchess's lust—or perhaps commenting in general on human weakness, Ferdinand at last reabsorbs his nemesis into himself and then identifies his destruction as self-destruction. It is the only wisdom his nature can embrace.

Bosola and Antonio: In the Courts of Princes

Bosola and Antonio are, at first glance, classic representations of revenge tragedy's misogynistic revenger and androgynous hero. Like Melantius, Bosola eschews women as corrupt inferiors to position himself in the exclusively male world of institutional authority. As long as he defines his manhood in terms of service within a system that places men in command, even if those he serves are tyrants, he can suppress issues of conscience and morality and pursue personal gain. Antonio, on the other hand, acknowledges sexual difference but does not presume the superiority of men to women. He neither predicates his maleness on an opposition to women, nor does he shun the private spaces identified with them. Although he profits, temporarily, from his marriage to the Duchess, he espouses and acts on principles other than personal aggrandizement. Like Affranius, his speeches and actions demonstrate a commitment to family, community, state: the virtues of connectedness that, in revenge tragedy, are embodied in women but valued by all.

Beneath these differences, however, is the intimate bond created by the potentially feminizing role they share. Like women, Bosola and Antonio occupy a subordinate position that gives them greater understanding of the people and structures that control their lives than those in command. Neither can rely on his own efforts to achieve worldly success. Their public maleness— Bosola as provisor of the horse and Antonio as steward—and their even greater private maleness as intelligencer and husband are gifts bestowed by superiors, and they rise and fall with those they serve.

The play represents both men largely in women's company and, in fact, as achieving subjectivity through women. Antonio, except for his scenes with Delio and Bosola, shares his onstage moments with the Duchess, Cariola, and his children; Bosola, despite his attempts to distance himself from everything female, is thrust into a prolonged and transformative intimacy with the Duchess. For Antonio, there is no conflict between closeness to women and manhood. For the misogynist Bosola, however, the recognition of the Duchess not only as a person in her own right but as a person like him[4]—and better than he—effects radical change in his understanding of the relationship between gender and authority. Although at his death he will posit sin and weakness as female, he takes up his sword in the name of women— the Duchess, Julia, Justice herself—to combat the male tyranny he once served.

Another Voyage

More than ambition draws Bosola into Ferdinand's service. Like Ferdinand, Bosola abuses women in order to remain a man in his own eyes; in their shared misogyny, they are natural allies against the Duchess. Ferdinand and Bosola both believe men must control women, which means invading their rooms and bodies—with apricots; if necessary, with a poniard—to reveal and punish their sins and to keep them from practicing the witchcraft that unnaturally empowers them at men's expense. While Bosola does not erase the threat of feminization by devouring all that is female, he does, like Melantius, identify the tears he sheds over the Duchess as male, explicitly denying either their origin in or connection to women: "This is manly sorrow: / These tears, I am very certain, never grew / In my mother's milk" (4.2.361–63). If Bosola lies, he is a woman's child; if he pities, he is a man.

As profound, and as conflicted, as his brotherhood with Ferdinand are his ties to Antonio. Despite the apparent opposition of malcontent and idealist, the two men share the strong bonds of class and gender. Both are educated and militarily trained men whose function is to serve the nobility. Both, moreover, are intelligent and ambitious, and, when they are not actively competing, they express admiration and sympathy for one another. Most significant of all, both count themselves men because they are virtuous. Because they represent the warring interests of Ferdinand and the Duchess, however, they are rivals of one another rather than of their masters, and, with the state governed by a woman, they vie for no less than male dominance in Malfi.

Bosola's rivalry with Antonio, however, melts into kinship when the Duchess accuses and dismisses Antonio. Bosola assumes that she is deflecting her guilt onto her loyal servant, just as the Cardinal did with him. Under these fraternal circumstances, Bosola reconstructs the Duchess's unmanly bawd as the man to whom other men would have prostituted their daughters and made intelligencers of their firstborn (3.2.232–33). Inspired by self-pity and hatred, he can indulge in hyperbolic praise of a man of his own class while lashing the ingratitude of princes. Antonio is not merely a brother but also an *alter ego*: a "poor gentleman" (241) who is "too honest" (243), "an excellent / Courtier, and most faithful, a soldier that thought it / As beastly to know his own value too little / As devilish to acknowledge it too much" (250–53). The Duchess's disingenuous objection that Antonio was "basely descended" (258) exposes even more nakedly his deep sense of grievance and draws him into a statement that, in its vision of community, reiterates Antonio's opening speech:

> . . . an honest statesman to a prince
> Is like a cedar, planted by a spring:
> The spring bathes the tree's root, the grateful tree
> Rewards it with his shadow: you have not done so;
> I would sooner swim to the Bermudas on
> Two politicians' rotten bladders, tied
> Together with an intelligencer's heart-string,
> Than depend on so changeable a prince's favour.
>
> (262–69)

In his image of cleansing water—here a spring—that connects and mutually nourishes prince and statesman, he echoes Antonio's depiction of ideal governance.

By the time Bosola intercepts the Duchess after her unsuccessful flight to Ancona, however, he has returned to an *a priori* misogyny that, in assigning the Duchess's choice of husband to her female weakness in judgment, denies his bond with Antonio. The man he has praised as a gentleman, courtier, and soldier he now denounces as a born coward—"This [refusal to meet the Duchess's brothers] proclaims your breeding" (3.5.52); the Duchess is to forget "this base, low fellow," "One of no birth" whose virtue is "A barren, beggarly virtue" (117, 119, 122). Bosola reconnects his maleness to his masters', supporting the class structure that subordinates him to them rather than challenge the principle of male dominance that subordinates women—and men like Antonio—to him.

Yet Bosola also struggles to free himself from that imprisoning analogy linking birth, wealth, and male gender. In the new spirit of capitalism, he fashions himself as an independent and equal party to a contract. By setting a price on his services—the reward he demands after the Duchess's death indicates a negotiation between him and Ferdinand subsequent to their initial arrangement—Bosola attempts to control the terms of his labor: he will be Ferdinand's creature only for the duration of the contract and only in the service of his own interests. If he is a seller of services rather than a permanent lackey of the great—a creature—he can suppress recognition of the subordinate and dependent position he will always occupy in the aristocratic hierarchy he has invoked against Antonio.

Like Govianus and the Lady, Bosola sees manhood as attending to business, and for him as much as for them, the true business of men is virtue. For the Bosola who sincerely believes himself a soldier and moralist, to be manly is to be courageous in the service of a just cause. Most of his audience—including the Cardinal,

Ferdinand, and Antonio—believe him an ambitious, hypocritical pretender, but Bosola does not, in fact, abandon his principles. He simply convinces himself that a just cause cannot arise in his corrupt world. When it does, and when it sweeps aside his misogynistic premises that men, even tyrannical men, are always superior to women, he can no longer ignore his conscience.

The pressure of his experience as the Duchess's jailer and executioner provides the radical experience that destabilizes Bosola's understanding of gender. First, those roles separate him from the outside male world and immerse him in the private world of women. He is confined with the Duchess and, although we see him in their company only when he orders them killed, with Cariola and the children. The Bosola who invaded the Old Lady's closet and penetrated the Duchess's pregnant body finds himself living within female space.

Further disturbing his conventional ideas about sex and gender is the dangerously uncharted nature of the role he plays there. He occupies the intimate space properly filled by a husband or brother, yet he is neither. With her husband a waxen corpse and her brother a disembodied voice and dead hand, he is the only man physically present. Bosola is at once manned and unmanned. He has absolute authority over the Duchess, but only as long as he is absolutely obedient to Ferdinand. The master-servant bond between him and the Duchess is reversed and male dominance restored, but his ability to see himself as manly is weakened by the insistent likeness of their positions. He shares the Duchess's imprisonment, as unable to escape as she and, culturally, as much a woman.

The confrontation between his premises and his experiences forces an unwilling and resistant Bosola to reconsider the automatic connection between sex and gender, especially between maleness and virtue. As he is increasingly drawn into the Duchess's world, he must question two assumptions: first, that she deserves punishment because she is unchaste and disobedient and, second, that Ferdinand as her male relative is entitled to exact it. Unlike Ferdinand, who will not "study in the book / Of another's heart" (4.1.16–17), he has studied the Duchess for hours, noting her sorrow, her musings, her silence that "expresseth more than if she spake" (10). He cannot withdraw from her, and her behavior, which he praises to Ferdinand as "so noble / As gives a majesty to adversity" (5–6), does not confirm the natural superiority of maleness or even preserve the distinction between the sexes.

Unable to change Ferdinand's course or alter the terms of their agreement, Bosola succeeds only in seizing partial theatrical control from Ferdinand by authoring disguises that will execute the Duchess for his master, bring her the "comfort" (137) for which she has begged, and minister to the soul Ferdinand would deny. Bosola's disguises are also barriers erected against the searing closeness that has forced him to see her as the *I* to whom he has responded with *I*, as a woman who is as human and trapped as he is, not a distanced and mythicized Other.

His recourse to theatricality, however, grants him neither authority nor protection. Even as he attempts to bury subjectivity— both hers and his—in the formalities of rhyme and ritual, he is unable to withdraw from their dialogue: "Doth not death fright you?" "Yet, methinks, / The manner of your death should much afflict you, / This cord should terrify you?" (4.2.210, 213–15). He cannot stop testing the courage he has found so startling, and he cannot stop listening for the voice that will confirm it. He fulfills his contract with Ferdinand by executing the Duchess, and he performs the priestly function he has devised to mollify his conscience, but he cannot break free of his transformative bond with the noble, resolute woman he has come to know and admire.

The definitive shift in Bosola's allegiance from male to female authority—or, more precisely, from reliance on a concept of manhood based on both social hierarchy and the economics of service to one based on a liberating commitment to virtues he has always presumed the property of men—occurs when Ferdinand reneges on their agreement. It is Ferdinand's reversal, his stinging accusation that Bosola should have pitied her, that turns Bosola irrevocably from the corrupt men he has served so well. At first, when Ferdinand reels from the sight of his twin's dazzling face—"she died young" (264)—Bosola tries to recreate their male bond against female frailty: "her infelicity / Seem'd to have years too many" (265–66). Ferdinand, however, has slipped out of their shared misogyny and out of the bargain negotiated on its basis. In replacing the promised reward with a pardon for the act he now calls murder, he destroys Bosola's last remaining tie to a male hierarchy that, no matter how corrupt, he could convince himself was superior to women.

As Bosola hears Ferdinand transform the Duchess from a lustful, disobedient woman into his innocent twin and "dearest friend" (280), he watches the axes of authority diverge. The aristocratic hierarchy that Bosola had defended and served and that had, in its own interests, temporarily elevated him above the

Duchess and Antonio, now puts him firmly back in his place. He is stunned by his "golden" folly: "I stand like one / That long hath ta'en a sweet and golden dream: / I am angry with myself, now that I wake" (323–25). At his feet is the woman who gave a deserving man her princely hand in marriage; at his side is the tyrant who will not fulfill a nobleman's obligation to a loyal servant:

> . . . sir,
> I serv'd your tyranny; and rather strove
> To satisfy yourself, than all the world;
> And though I loath'd the evil, yet I lov'd
> You that did counsel it; and rather sought
> To appear a true servant, than an honest man.
>
> (328–33)

Bosola will dismiss this protestation as "painted honour" (336), but "love" accurately expresses his profound attachment to all that Ferdinand represents.

Bosola's *I* has now definitively split in two: the ungendered and dependent "true servant" is, like a woman, one who "strove" to "satisfy" the man he served; the "honest man," on the other hand, is an explicitly male self that Bosola constructs as antecedent to and independent of that social role and that is paradoxically closer in kind to the woman he helped kill than to the man who ordered her death. Because Bosola's "honest man" eliminates difference from women as defining maleness, however, it is for him a more dangerously feminized self than his "honest servant." Anxiously, he separates himself from femaleness in general, as Melantius did, by locating the tears he sheds for the Duchess's second death within a discourse that constructs them as "manly sorrow"; they are "penitent fountains" he should not have allowed to be "frozen up" while she was living (365–66). Yet he cannot withdraw from his dialogue with her or from the knowledge that the virtue he associates with honesty has not only proven separable from gender but is, in fact, what makes him a man.

In his farewell to the Duchess, Bosola continues that dialogue, his deferential, tender "I" directly addressing her "thee":

> Come,
> I'll bear thee hence:
> And execute thy last will; that's deliver
> Thy body to the reverent dispose

Of some good women: that the cruel tyrant
Shall not deny me.

(368–73)

His role in Ferdinand's revenge drama released them both from the delimiting gender constructs that govern social relationship between the sexes. The disturbing intimacy he experienced with a woman who was neither his wife nor sister he can now attribute to a common humanity where the authority to name—to call Ferdinand "tyrant" as he, following her authority, now does—is based on virtue. With the Duchess as his kindred sufferer, Bosola's general view of women alters. Dropping accusatory, defensive harshness as his sole and habitual response to them, he accepts and seeks out the "good women" on whom he will, in obedience to her request, bestow her body.

Serving the Duchess rather than her brothers places him outside the male hierarchy that has bound him to his murderous life, and that exile grants him freedom to act independently. Disguised, like Melantius, as his former self, Bosola is able to penetrate and destroy the interior world of male power that he now finds as pernicious as he had once found the female body. He rejects the Cardinal's display of absolute authority—in the threat to have him "hew'd in pieces"—and declares himself beyond the tyrant's control: "Make not yourself such a promise of that life / Which is not yours to dispose of" (5.2.293–94).

His response to Julia also marks the change in his definition of himself as a man. She epitomizes the sexual corruption Bosola's misogyny had initially extended to all women, but instead of reviling her, he makes her an accomplice in his war against the Cardinal's tyranny. The Duchess too was constructed as sexually transgressive, and he had found her both innocent and noble. Bosola uses Julia to further his own plot—even vowing to be her "loyal servant" (211) when, in a parody of maleness, she threatens him with a pistol and promises to maintain him—but when she meets her death at the Cardinal's hands, he sincerely laments: "O foolish woman, / Couldst not thou have poison'd him?" (286–87). He attributes to Julia the folly he associates with women, but he uses the eloquent conditional to grant her the independence and agency, qualities he valorizes as male, sufficient to kill their common enemy. Human evil has broken free of simple sexual difference and come to rest on male tyranny.

In the play he writes to bring moral closure to theirs, however, Bosola is still a revenger, a victim rewriting himself as a man in the shape of his oppressor. He is unable to find the self-abandonment necessary to taste the cup of penitence that "throws men down, only to raise them up" (5.2.349). He has shared with the Cardinal and Ferdinand the tyrant's isolating, narrowing, anticommunal absorption with the self, and he has accepted the misogynistic split between male dominance and female subjection through which absolute male authority displays itself. He cannot entirely escape that shared world and its destiny, sincerely remorseful as he would like to be. Bosola is not only penitent and guilty but also aggrieved and betrayed. Ferdinand's—and the Cardinal's before and behind him—failure to acknowledge his maleness by honoring their bargain relegated him to the female world of his victim, and although he has discovered his virtuous manhood there, he cannot entirely suppress the need to seek satisfaction for that violation.

Yet while Bosola cannot be merely an avenger, seeking or supporting justice as Eudoxa and Affranius do, he also cannot be merely the solitary, solipsistic revenger who wrenches scenes and characters to his will. Like the genre's androgynous men, he has discovered he is a man not because he is other than a woman but because he wields the sword Justice left behind after the Duchess's murder had taken "her most equal balance" (5.5.40). Like both Govianus and Affranius, he accepts co-authorship of the play's events, shaping events that will be reshaped according to a greater design. The spirit of the Lady was Govianus's collaborator in the play of justice; Bosola writes his in the name of the woman who haunts him still and of the virtue she has come to represent.

The revenger Bosola is plunged with his fellow revengers into an impermeable darkness that does not allow him, any more than it allows Ferdinand, to distinguish a brother from a traitor. Contrary to his will, he collaborates again with the Cardinal, killing Antonio just as, later, Ferdinand will kill the Cardinal. The avenger Bosola, however, does not accept that "direful misprision" (5.4.80) as his inability to become other than the tyrants' creature. Instead, he emphatically reiterates the *I* that refuses connection to his former masters: "I will not imitate things glorious, / No more than base: I'll be mine own example" (81–82).

The doubleness of Bosola's final role, of his ineradicable egocentrism struggling to create a community of virtue, comes to rest on the fundamental question of gender. Looking into the great vault of his death, he meditates for the last time on "this gloomy world":

> In what a shadow, or deep pit of darkness,
> Does womanish and fearful mankind live!
> Let worthy minds ne'er stagger in distrust
> To suffer death, or shame for what is just—
> Mine is another voyage.
>
> (5.5.100–105)

Again, Bosola both assumes and destabilizes the opposition between the sexes. Like the revenger and tyrant, he distinguishes invidiously between maleness and femaleness, proclaiming "mankind," "womanish," which he equates with "fearful." Women are associated with the "deep pit of darkness," the shadow world that impresses itself on "mankind," who becomes "womanish" as a result. Yet Bosola also separates sex from gender by allowing fearfulness and courage to apply to either sex. Within the overarching "mankind," a male-gendered but inclusive word for humanity, both men and women can be "womanish" or manly. Like the androgynous heroes, Bosola breaks with tradition in understanding that the opposition between men and women does not apply to individual men and women: his only experience of enlightening courage is the Duchess of Malfi, who, as a fearless woman, is both male and female. Courage does not apply to the bawling, mad tyrants nor to Antonio or himself.

As Bosola struggles to climb, or at least see, out of the dark pit that closes over him, he reaches beyond the oxymoron that deconstructs gender—"womanish" "mankind"—to the perfectly linked, ungendering "worthy minds." In ascending to "mind," the Lady's term for a more elevated category of humanity, Bosola abandons worldly ambition that ends irrevocably in that "deep pit of darkness" and transposes himself onto another vertical axis. He cannot follow the Duchess, who ascends to the immaterial world with which the worthy mind is linked. As a revenger, Bosola is struck down in the dark chaos he helped create, tangled and implicated in death, as he was in life, with tyranny. But in death, he aspires to another reality, one he can glimpse if not reach, where he will be thrown down to be raised up. The quondam misogynist's closest kin in his conflicted, tortured farewell is neither the Cardinal and Ferdinand nor even Antonio. It is Julia, a woman who also served tyranny for personal advantage. Julia dies, going she knows not whither (5.2.288–89); Bosola's death is "another voyage."

Antonio: "for ever falling"

Antonio, like Bosola, maintains an uneasy balance between the public service that contains and defines him as a man and the private, independent, and presumably prior male identity that sees and judges those he serves. For both, that balance is made even more precarious by an intimate and covert marriage to authority that at once suppresses the virtue that makes them men and also requires them to play, at first and always in part, a female role within the relationship. Their liaisons with Ferdinand and the Duchess at once validate and undermine them. Antonio's path is, in fact, a mirror image of Bosola's, identical but reversed. The cynic of the play's opening is at the end a determined author of justice; the idealist becomes a fatalistic plotter whose half-hearted plan to survive is a blueprint for suicide.

Antonio arrives in Malfi not, as Bosola does, from enslavement but from the court of a "judicious king" (1.1.6), the French monarch who enacts divine absoluteness rather than his own. The king's aim is to establish a "fix'd order" (6) by cleansing his court of corrupting influences, "which he sweetly terms / His Master's masterpiece, the work of heaven" (9–10). In praising that "common fountain" as a source of cleansing, circulating water, Antonio espouses for the play as a whole a standard of government based on reciprocity and commonalty, a political ethos always potentially in conflict with absolutist theory. The brothers, who equate position with privilege, are, in contrast, "plum-trees, that grow crooked over standing pools" (49–50), their thirst to keep all to themselves resulting in a malformed and malforming stagnancy.

In revenge tragedy, these two constructions of government are tied to competing views of gender: the tyrant and revenger, like the Duchess's brothers and the misogynist Bosola who serves them, identify absolute political rights with maleness; the androgynous man subordinates politics to a hierarchy of justice and virtue that allows him to accept women as equals and, under some circumstances, superiors. In valuing the common good over individual power, such a man accepts the concomitant loss of autonomy and control without believing it diminishes his manhood and without, therefore, having to separate himself from women. Rather than insist on authority and authorship, he collaborates with the woman who takes control of the script from the plays' tyrants and writes himself, as Affranius and Govianus do, into her play.

In many ways, Antonio is the most fully drawn—and the most conflicted—of the genre's androgynous male heroes. He flourishes within his secret marriage, his male sexuality enhanced rather than diminished by its carnivalesque reversals of gender and class. In public, however, he determines to remain the Duchess's steward, a role that makes him publicly submissive to her even as he commands those below him in the court. His judgment of human government in terms of its closeness to heaven's order and its capacity to benefit an entire society goes hand in hand with a political and social conservativism. Antonio is neither a monarch like Govianus nor a soldier like Affranius. He is a man of the court: like Bosola, he affirms the principle of hierarchy even when it produces tyrannical leaders who have ceased to do the work of heaven and even though it maintains his inferiority to them. By position and inclination, he neither can nor would attempt to close the gap between the ideal and its perversion with revolution.

Antonio's idealism is not naïveté, however. He sees the corruption and menace of the Duchess's brothers unflinchingly: the "melancholy churchman" who "strews in his way flatterers, panders, intelligencers, atheists, and a thousand such political monsters" (157–58, 161–63) and the "perverse and turbulent" Calabrian Duke (169). So accurate an assessment of the world's governors produces a respectful, cautious, and potentially timorous—in essentialist terms, female—approach to their destructive capacity. Antonio's general wariness extends to other servants as well. Any bridge between the private and the public—even personal friendship—is a risk for a man whose life depends on princes. Antonio is quick to believe that Delio and Cariola would betray him; he knows that while servants may censure their masters to one another, ambition and fear overwhelm class solidarity. A suspicious fearfulness is, in fact, as integral to his nature and training as his conservatism, and it dominates the public and colors the private half of his dangerously divided life.

Antonio's will to serve a woman rather than her powerful male relations as Bosola does is radical precisely because it is conservative, a Jacobean throwback to the Elizabethan court. When describing the Duchess's "noble virtue" (201), he bestows on her the late Queen's ability to turn captivating words and vivifying looks into tools of princely authority. He does not embrace the misogynistic ideology that would confine female sexuality within silence and immobility. When he limns the Duchess's character for Delio, he praises her both for her eloquence—"her discourse, it is so full of rapture / You only will begin then to be sorry / When she doth end her speech" (190–92)—and also for the accompanying language of her eyes: "She throws upon a man so sweet a look, / That it were able raise one to a galliard / That lay in a dead palsy" (195–97). He acknowledges the prevailing misogyny—both within and outside the play—by hastening to transform the Duchess's voice to virtue and her "countenance" to "continence": "There [on her countenance] speaketh so divine a continence / As cuts off all lascivious, and vain hope" (199–200). His praise, however, replaces misogyny with the old-fashioned and, in Elizabeth's day, politicized language of courtly love, where fervent admiration for virtue is erotically charged and indistinguishable from physical attraction.

The Duchess, however, is no Elizabeth. She summons and woos him, making him an offer he can resist but not refuse. Like Ferdinand with Bosola, she has decided her servant's fate—to be "lord" of the "wealthy mine" that she is (430, 429)—without his knowledge or consent. Antonio's response is characteristic: hesitancy and caution. His vertigo at being suddenly elevated so far above his station, added to his inability to make his own choice or weigh the risk of marriage to himself or to the Duchess, produces a self-protective withdrawal, a timidity culturally attributed to women. Antonio does not seize her proposal aggressively but rather exaggerates the acceptably submissive part he plays opposite her. Like a knight before his lady, he falls to his knees; the Duchess must order him to rise (415, 419). Later, he trembles before her (450); he accepts her kiss, she says, like a child eating sweets (466); he kneels again at her command and, when she calls Cariola out from behind the arras, he responds with a startled, fearful "Hah?" (476). Antonio considers her dangerous brothers; she dismisses them with reckless courage.

Yet Antonio, like Bosola, is not merely a victim of coercive authority. He, too, embraces his superior's proposal out of an affinity with the proposer. His strong attraction to the Duchess, disguised as courtly compliment in his description to Delio, is revealed again when he addresses her as "your beauteous excellence," a hint she is happy to pluck out of his formal greeting— "Beauteous?" (368). Moreover, while she raises the issue of marriage—"If I had a husband now" (382)—it is Antonio who transforms the hypothetical *if* into an imperative—"Begin," he tells her when she asks which good deed she should first remember, with the sacrament of marriage (385–86)—before returning to the conditional mode: "I'd have you first provide for a good husband, / Give him all" (387–88). Nor does he let the subject drop as she jokes about winding and wedding sheets, and he responds at length, if not quite to her purpose, when he answers her inquiry about what he thinks of marriage.

Antonio is keenly aware of the social codes that bar their marriage, protesting his social inequality and unworthiness and denouncing ambition: that man "That, being a-cold, would thrust his hands i'th'fire / To warm them" is a fool (427–28). The Duchess counters his defensive timidity, however, by appealing to a maleness that exists independently of class. Antonio has already defined himself to her: "Were there nor heaven nor hell, / I should be honest: I have long serv'd virtue, / And ne'er ta'en wages of her" (438–40). By conflating that virtue with maleness and, therefore, with position, the Duchess untangles the knot of honesty and ambition that tightens around Bosola's throat. Antonio is not required to accept the analogy that ties political authority to gender because he is already on the ungendered spiritual axis to which Bosola aspires at play's end. The Duchess convinces him that he can enter into his contract without violating his dedication to principles that make him honest and, therefore, manly. In fact, the Duchess emphasizes his sexual dominance, raising him not only to her level but above it: "Go, go brag / You have left me heartless" (448–49), she tells him, and begs him to love more than fear her.

Yet Antonio cedes to her the authoring of their actions, and she demonstrates her mastery even as she shares it with him. She instructs him to "lead your fortune by the hand, / Unto your marriage bed" (495–96) and assures him that her words, which he tells her "should be mine" (472) are indeed his: "You speak in me this, for we now are one" (497). Antonio collaborates with her on the play she had the audacity to write for them both, but it is still she who speaks the lines she has written for him.

Predictably, marriage compromises Antonio's manhood, unsettling the balance between his public and private lives and altering both. He tries to bring those lives into conformity by gradually acquiring land and titles, presumably with support from the Duchess, but the futility of his effort is signaled by Bosola, who exposes what he, like Antonio before him, recognizes as ambition. Bosola mocks Antonio's parvenu attempt to ennoble himself through a newfound "cousin-german" duke and reveals the grounds for Antonio's new air of superiority: "O sir, you are lord of the ascendant, chief man with the duchess" (2.1.96–97). The "graver heads" who do not condemn the Duchess outright as a strumpet see that Antonio has grown "to infinite purchase / The left-hand way" (3.1.28–29).

The only defense against the public world's rewriting of them as strumpet and blackmailer is for Antonio and the Duchess to make public their democracy of virtue. Ideal social institutions, as Antonio has established in his image of the French court, are communal and circulating. To avoid their own destruction, he and the Duchess, who cannot shape themselves to the traditions of the world, would have to bring new life to the stagnant pools of authority and shape the world's traditions to them. Antonio, however, cannot adopt a husband's traditional role as head of household: for him, public authority belongs to the Duchess. He will not even alter the fashion of remaining covered in the ducal presence.

Because the fertile blurring of distinction between classes and genders that makes their marriage politically and sexually revolutionary never bears fruit as an alternative public world, Antonio is only what the Duchess will call him in jest—a lord of misrule. When the fragile coexistence between their world and the brothers' shatters, he has no stable male role in which he can act with honesty and, therefore, manliness. He meets the crisis of the Duchess's induced labor with indecision, panic, and withdrawal. Bosola has the clear advantage when they meet in the night. Antonio cannot control the "mole" who "undermines" him (2.3.14); the "fellow" whom he has presumed his inferior "will undo" him (29). His constant asides in this scene reveal a man literally beside himself, unable to hide the now pervasive fear that Bosola immediately detects in his face and body (11–12): "you sweat: / You look wildly" (19–20).

Neither Antonio's presumption of authority nor his direct and false accusation of Bosola succeeds in closing the gap that has opened in his sense of himself as a man. As a husband, he is supposed to protect his wife and family, which means he must lie; as the servant of virtue, he must tell the truth. In fact, he can do neither: his nose bleeds, and he drops the horoscope. Delio, after the night's crisis has ended, asks Antonio whether news of the Duchess's children has reached the Cardinal, and Antonio replies with a casual, now familiar expression of apprehension— "I fear it hath" (3.1.18).

The belated consequence of Antonio's panic is Ferdinand's appearance in Malfi. Despite that ominous presence, however, Antonio insists on taking his place in the Duchess's bed, where he and she subvert the social codes they have been unable to reform or overturn, parodying the outside world's dangerously sterile institutions and transforming them into erotic foreplay. The Duchess plays hostess of an inn—Antonio will "get no lodging here tonight" (3.2.2); he counters with his own playful imperative: "I must lie here" (7). She archly challenges and usurps his claim to command—"Must?"—identifying him as "a lord of mis-rule" (7), which prompts him to the teasing role of a "labouring" man glad when his "task's ended" (18, 20). Even Cariola is included in the general blurring of classes and genders. She can substitute for either: like Antonio, she is the Duchess's servant and sometime bedfellow; like the Duchess, she is a woman.

Antonio, delighted to be the lover, confidante, and friend of both women, freely answers their questions and asks his own. The man some say "was an hermaphrodite" (220) is unthreatened by women's speech, their sexuality, even their displays of temper: "I love to see her angry" (57). Antonio's androgynous maleness cannot, however, withstand the public world's intrusion. It is unclear whether Antonio might have intervened between his wife and brother-in-law, but even if he did not hear Ferdinand's direct threats or feel the full weight of the Duke's official male domination, he is sufficiently stunned by the breach in the wall between the worlds to respond with his fearful, ineffectual public mien.

He emerges with a pistol, admits to having seen "this apparition" (142), and, driven again to distrust a friend, turns the gun on Cariola. His aggression, however, is strictly verbal. He wishes that "this terrible thing would come again, / That, standing on my guard, I might relate / My warrantable love" (147–49), but he does not follow Ferdinand. When the Duchess shows him the poniard, he wishes again, this time she would have "fasten[ed] the keen edge in his rank gall" (154), a foreshadowing of Bosola's response to Julia's death, but he does not take it for his own use. The knocking at the door brings him back to the panicky alarm with which he greeted Cariola's unexpected entrance into the betrothal scene: "How now! who knocks? more earthquakes?" (155). As always, Antonio leaves their defense to the Duchess, who authors a second failed story of theft.

Their exposure means the end of Antonio's divided life, and with it comes a recognition of hopelessness, a pervasive fatalism that couples unattractively with a raw instinct for self-preservation. The man whose survival has always depended on the will of others attempts to teach the Duchess, accustomed to exercising her will over others, what he understood from the first: "you see what pow'r / Lightens in great men's breath" (3.5.1–2).

He continues to acknowledge her as author of their lives, accepting her plan for a defensive separation and retreat, but he also knows that hers is a lesser authority than Ferdinand's and the Cardinal's. Antonio is torn between his reassurance—to her and himself—that she "counsel[s] safely" (60) and the knowledge that there is no "safely," that he and she must now act the roles assigned them in her brothers' play.

His fatalism does not, however, alter his commitment to the principles he shares with the Duchess. Like her, he continues to separate worldly power from heaven's authority and the service of virtue from service to corrupt princes. Faced with imminent destruction, he turns from the institutions of the world, perfectible but corrupted, to the perfect structures of the next, from the work of heaven to heaven itself. Where once he asked that he and the Duchess not be divided, he now reads their separation as heaven's hand taking them apart like a broken watch or clock "to bring't in better order" (65). As he follows the Duchess's script, he knows he is enacting the script that embraces it and her brothers' as well: "be of comfort! / Make patience a noble fortitude, / And think not how unkindly we are us'd: / *Man like to cassia, is prov'd best, being bruis'd*" (72–75).

The Duchess is not ready for such cold comfort, but resignation is the only solace he can offer: "Heaven fashion'd us of nothing; and we strive / To bring ourselves to nothing" (82–83). Antonio's way out of the moral wilderness in which she cast them both is to return to his first identity and preach the stoicism of the powerless. He continues to see her as the author and chief actor of their play, telling her to save her little ones from the tiger (85–86) as he had before wished for her to turn the knife on Ferdinand, but he has also already withdrawn from their union. Beneath his stoicism is still the fearful *I*: "My heart is turn'd to a heavy lump of lead, / With which I sound my danger" (91–92).

That stubborn note of self-interest and self-pity reveals the depth of his deep connection to Bosola. The *alter egos* crossed over when Antonio, in defense of himself, spoke the malcontent's text and Bosola, in defense of Antonio, the idealist's. After the Duchess's death, Bosola authors himself as a man with purpose and conviction; Antonio wanders aimlessly. He has no wife, no home, no public service; he must bear silent witness to his lands being given to Julia. As Bosola frees himself from his former servitude to great men, Antonio becomes supplicant and servant, his one attempt to author his life a plan to throw himself on the good will of the Cardinal. It is the place Bosola began.

While waiting to implement his plot, Antonio is drawn to the world of ancient ruins and uncanny echoes, the space of human history caught, as he is caught, between the corrupt and the pure, the ephemeral and the fixed. From that perspective, he can remark to Delio that "all things have their end: / Churches and cities, which have diseases like to men, / Must have like death that we have" (5.3.17–19). From Antonio's now liminal life, he can observe the inevitable destruction of human institutions. The Cardinal and Ferdinand, the churches and cities over which they hold absolute sway, are equally diseased and doomed.

The Duchess's echoing voice, occupying the same present and absent space as the ruins, attempts to lead him to the safety he had once valued. As in life, she reaches out to write the script— "*O, fly your fate!*"—which he accepts as written by "necessity": "you'll find it impossible / To fly your fate" (34–35). The sound of her voice tugs him briefly back to the memory of their happiness, but the reminder of his marriage and children merely makes his plight, trapped between worlds, more intolerable:

> Come: I'll be out of this ague;
> For to live thus is not indeed to live:
> It is a mockery, and abuse of life—
> I will not henceforth save myself by halves;
> Lose all, or nothing.
>
> (47–51)

The stoic's ability to endure is at an end. Situating himself in the diseased continuum of human history, Antonio sees his life as an ague in which no one is either finally dead or fully alive. While he consoles himself with the dignity accorded by suffering— "Though in our miseries Fortune have a part, / Yet in our noble suff'rings she hath none— / Contempt of pain, that we may call our own" (56–58)—he is impatient for it to be over. The lost man is determined to find a way home.

With one blind thrust, Bosola, the amanuensis of Antonio's play of necessity, fulfills that wish. Antonio's desperate "hope of pardon" (5.4.45) becomes irrelevant as he finds his way and recovers himself as a man, without deception or pretense. To Bosola's catechistic "What art thou?" he answers, "A most wretched thing, that only have thy benefit in death, / To appear myself" (48–50); to "Where are you, sir?" he responds, "Very near my home" (50–51). Antonio spends his last moments reviewing his courtier's history, denouncing ambition, the "quest of greatness," and seeing those who succumb, as he in part did, as "follow[ing] after bubbles, blown in th'air" (64, 66). Rising up from the sea of stoic truisms is his pointed last line: "And let my son fly the courts of princes" (72). The ambiguity of that startling pronouncement, including as it must not only the courts of Ferdinand and the Cardinal but of the Duchess as well, puts his life and marriage into a final perspective. Whether in that moment of death he sees his Duchess wife as an agent or victim of the world that destroyed him is unclear, but he does read in his own life as a courtier a fate he would keep from his son: the understanding that a man cannot remain "myself" in the courts of princes.

The inability of Antonio to write a play that validates him as a man in his own terms, indeed his inability to believe he either can or should author it, makes him a weak and passive figure. His androgyny, unlike Affranius' and Govianus', exerts a healing, comic force only in the imperiled inner sanctum of his marriage, where he flourishes as a lover, husband, and father. In public, he relinquishes authority to his wife and, beyond her, to the tyrants who clearly govern the world. He is, in the public arena, culturally female. His single attempt to shape his life's events, his futile plot of reconciliation, failed before he could put it into effect. Antonio's initial vision of a fixed order that purges the corrupt comes to fruition, just as Bosola's revenge effects a justice beyond his ability to plot it. The cost, however, is appallingly high. Antonio's ability to transcend the cultural strictures of gender and form a fruitful, androgynous union with the Duchess gives the play its only hopeful, brilliant moments, but it cannot save them or the play from tragedy.

Diamond and Pearl

To the Duchess of Malfi's brothers, she is the sexually undependable carrier of the blood, a figure of great subversive potential whose inherent wildness must be forcibly contained. To Bosola, she is initially a weak, corrupt biological inferior, the sluttish mother who demonstrates the impropriety of female rule over men. To Antonio, she is the beautiful, well-spoken, virtuous ideal he admires as his prince and the exciting, aggressive, fertile woman he loves as his wife. By the play's end, she is her brothers' nemesis, Bosola's angel of innocence, and Antonio's fateful echo.

The Duchess is as multiform as the actor who assumed the voice and costume of her sex and class and as the playwright whose authority in the playhouse gives her authority within the play. Written as a biological female whose public, political body is male and played by a biological male whose public, theatrical body is female, the character reflects and, in her heroism, transfigures the suspicious sexual indeterminacy of the players' profession. Like another female regent and player, the Duchess is a male woman, but she is not a virgin queen whose solitary asexuality keeps institutionalized misogyny at bay. She is sister and wife as well as prince, commander and commanded, a figure whose theatrical fluidity shapes itself to the role demanded of her even as she writes and attempts to live the role she desires.

In her double gendered and ambiguously ranked position, the Duchess shares common ground with the nonruling men of her society as well as with the players who enact her. As monarch and woman, however, she is simultaneously above and below those men, her anomalous status reflected in the contrasting initial relationships Antonio and Bosola forge with her. As her brothers' haste to feminize her confirms, she is an ideologically unstable and destabilizing figure. For an English audience, her decision to marry only adds to her covert power. Within the new Protestant world where the affective bonds of the nuclear family are being lauded over the kinship bonds of the extended family and where the absolute state is eroding the political rights of ruling clans, a woman who is simultaneously ruler and wife challenges the patriarchal bastions of noble lineage in the state and of male supremacy in the family.[5]

While the Duchess does not choose the role of public reformer, she is in fact the revolutionary figure her brothers fear, unraveling the cultural oxymoron of female regnancy by acting on the presumption and habit of agency identified with her male prerogative. She does not treat her political body as a placeholder for her brothers, nor does she assume her natural body is theirs to command. Her secrecy reveals how well she understands the coercive force behind her brothers' construction of her roles as duchess and sister, but she chooses to live as if the discourses that empower her as ruler and as wife and mother supersede theirs.

Assuming ducal privilege, she hastens to rewrite her female role within the family from sister to wife, erasing the division between her political maleness and her life as a woman by choosing her own husband and establishing the conditions of her obedience. Because her choice of Antonio is a response to her brothers' unnatural and ungodly tyranny, her seizure of familial authority from them is in the heroic vein of her revenge tragedy compeers. Unlike the Lady and Lucina, however, she does not articulate the grounds for her right to disobey them. While her actions suggest that, like Antonio's, her ideal human world is a fertile, living system where virtue resides in accepting the paradigmatic axis proceeding from God, she does not challenge tyranny's improper seizure and misuse of divine authority, nor does she use her political voice to bring Malfi into consonance with the principles she follows in private. For her, the roles of duchess and wife are incompatible neither with one another nor with the virtuous government of the state and human life, but she does not opt to construct a public self that combines them.[6]

Within the play, the Duchess is represented primarily in the domestic world where her theatrical fluidity is unconstrained, but she is also various and mutable in her ducal role. In both, she commands and obeys, acts with certainty and vacillates, charts her own course and craves guidance, enforces and relinquishes her will. For the Duchess, opposition of any kind is indeed metaphysics (Kristeva 1986, 209). Even with the brothers from whom she must hide her radical polymorphism, she is unable to confine herself to a single role. The woman who determines to shape herself as she sees fit cannot consistently and convincingly fashion herself to the submissive role of sister.

Her contests with her brothers, punctuated by scenes of the marriage she authors, are struggles for stage and script, with victory granting authority not only over the immediate meaning of gender and its relationship to authority but over the right to determine meaning. By confining her within their narrative, Ferdinand and the Cardinal subdue the dangerous forces she represents. By writing herself, the Duchess wrests control of their narrative's meaning both within the play and outside it in the widening circle of her theatrical audiences.

Her direct confrontations with her brothers—with the Cardinal and Ferdinand and, later, with Ferdinand alone—chart her increasing inability to stay within the character they have written. In the first encounter, the Duchess attempts to soothe and accommodate them by accepting Ferdinand's nomination of Bosola for provisorship of her horse: "Your knowledge of him / Commends him, and prefers him," she assures Ferdinand (1.1.217–18). Their continued verbal barrage, however, drives her to self-defense and an oblique assertion of authorial presence. When her brothers physically encircle her, Ferdinand arguing that those who marry twice have "livers . . . more spotted / Than Laban's sheep" (298–99), she elevates the vehicle of his metaphor from sheep to diamonds. Using the vague authority of "[t]hey say" rather than affirm her brothers' or assert her own, she declares that diamonds increase in value as they pass through jewellers' hands (299–300). She is, of course, the tenor of both metaphors, and even though she has again suppressed the subjective *I*, Ferdinand recognizes rebellion in her words. Transforming diamonds into whores, he wrenches away the authority she has assumed in creating her own comparison.

The instant Ferdinand exits, the Duchess's first person emphatically reemerges. She may have no power within any discourse of theirs, and she may need to appease them, but she does not presume them politically absolute or morally right. With their departure, she becomes her own author:

> Shall this move me? If all my royal kindred
> Lay in my way unto this marriage:
> I'd make them my low footsteps: and even now,
> Even in this hate, as men in some great battles,
> By apprehending danger, have achiev'd
> Almost impossible actions—I have heard soldiers say so—
> So I, through frights, and threat'nings, will assay
> This dangerous venture: let old wives report
> I wink'd and chose a husband.
>
> (341–49)

The Duchess's model—the man in a great battle who achieves the "almost impossible"—and her position—standing on her royal kindred to climb to her will—are culturally male, as is her dismissal of old wives, those discredited recorders of women's lives. The Duchess does not "fall to action indeed" any more than her twin brother (1.1.92), but she constructs herself as a soldier in a noble cause and, moments later, as an explorer facing "a wilderness, / Where I shall find nor path, nor friendly clew / To be my guide" (359–61). Her *I* is a complex and contradictory mixture of genders and classes, of strength and weakness: *I* is a sister who does not obey her tyrannical male kin and a wife who will write the conditions of her obedience to her husband; a soldier who does not arm herself for the great battle and an explorer who does not forge a path for others to follow. In all her roles, she blurs the boundaries of difference, not transcending opposed categories but deconstructing them.

The Duchess's husband must have the same capacity. Even were it not secret, the nature of marriage between a royal woman and a commoner man would necessitate the redefinition of gender and class that would allow both to play each other's part. In the Duchess's preamble to the marriage proposal, she begins the fluid exchange of roles by dictating her "will," which is to free herself of the need to dictate her will. She wishes to leave her "cares" to a man who would, within their culture rightly, assume them. She announces that he has taken her cares upon him (370) and later identifies that male caretaker, with whom she has already associated him, as a husband: "If I had a husband now, this care were quit" (382). At the same time that she elides the steward's and husband's role, she takes the part of "thrifty husbands"—male stewards—(366) who "inquire / What's laid up for tomorrow" (366–67). She has evened the ground between them: in her male role of Duchess, she is a steward, in her female, a would-be wife. Given the synonymous nature of *steward* and *husband* and the Duchess's leveling and then exchange of their positions, Antonio can indeed write her will by becoming her husband.

When Antonio does not respond as she would wish to her questions—"What do you think of marriage?" and "How do you affect it?" (392, 395)—she becomes a more active wooer, offering him her wedding ring to "help [his] eyesight" (409), telling him she has vowed to part with it only to her second husband (406–7), and placing it on his finger to remove the "saucy, and ambitious devil" he finds "dancing in this circle" (412–13). Finger and ring, phallus and vagina: having played the man, she can become the woman according to the traditional signifiers of heterosexual union. She uses her authority to erase her authority, her voice to give him speech, her body to initiate a mutual embrace.

The reciprocity of the relationship she authors extends to their liberation from the oppressions of her brothers' hierarchy. Willing away Antonio's servitude to her means willing away hers to her dead husband and to the brothers who take up his authority in order to keep her in subjection to them. When she makes Antonio her fellow steward, and when she raises him from his kneeling position because she "cannot stand upright" under that "too low built" roof (417, 416), she not only frees him but grants him the authority to free her. She is her own woman, not the monumentalized female in which she has been cast, "the figure cut in alabaster / Kneels at my husband's tomb" (454–55). No longer does Antonio have to kneel to her; no longer does she, in turn, have to kneel to her husband.

In that freedom, limited to the enclosed intimacy of her family, the Duchess confesses her desire to be a simple, virtuous woman:

The misery of us that are born great—
We are forc'd to woo, because none dare woo us:
And as a tyrant doubles with his words,
And fearfully equivocates, so we
Are forc'd to express our violent passions
In riddles, and in dreams, and leave the path
Of simple virtue, which was never made
To seem the thing it is not.

(441–48)

Yet while yearning to play the woman's part, the Duchess speaks in the monarch's "we" to unlink virtue from the political and religious discourse that empowers tyrants. She wants her authorial powers to replace tyranny, her creation of their marriage to allow a space where truth can be spoken. She holds to the conviction that the direct expression of her admittedly violent passion, like the unadorned and unequivocating service of virtuous space, absorbs all other structures and institutions.

In her ecstatic liberation from a false truth that insists on circumlocution, she appropriates virtue itself, paying the wages Antonio protests he never took: "Now she pays it" (440). Like a Christian reformer, she replaces the Church's empty ceremonies with one that gives truth presence, exchanging vows that refuse gendered postures of mastery and servitude—"What can the church force more?" (488)—and identifies the church ceremony, as she identifies her brothers, with coercion: "How can the church build faster? / We now are man and wife, and 'tis the church / That must but echo this" (491–93). Her assertion of the spiritual primacy of the individual over the church implies her intimate connection to the divine will absent in that corrupt institution, and her fidelity to that greater truth places her, not them, in a position of command. Their political and religious tyranny must fall before the liberty she has opened through the marriage she officiates as her own priest in the name of her own law.

Superficially, the Duchess resembles Evadne in her assumption of aristocratic maleness: she takes control of her body from her male relatives, asserts ownership of herself and her fortune, and plays the man on her wedding night. She does not, however, barter sex for tyrannical authority, nor does she feminize her husband in order to maintain command and control. Like the Lady rather than Evadne, she plays the man in order to make her husband male and feminizes him in order to be female. Her male body does not erase or suppress the woman who occupies it, nor does she relinquish her political maleness even when pregnancy exposes her female body to public gaze and invasion. Instead, she creates a fiction that transforms her confinement within her chambers into the confinement of others within theirs, thereby maintaining the union of her political and natural bodies.

Paradoxically, however—and it is a paradox she will be unable to keep from unraveling into conflict—she keeps the divine principle of harmonious plenitude alive by isolating the marriage that manifests it from the human world. Inevitably, the long life and broad extent of her deception begins, in the metaphor of another player, to color the dyer's hand. Within the revenge genre, her false public image resembles both the duplicitous mask of the tyrant and the doubling disguise of the revenger. While the differences between her and those rivals for absoluteness are as striking as the similarities, she does not occupy the indisputably moral space of the unalterable Lucina, Eudoxa, and the Lady. She has wooed Antonio by authoring a world where the improprieties of their marriage vanish before a spiritual definition of merit, and their marriage is indeed closer to heaven's order than the corrupt world she so sweepingly waves away. Nonetheless, she has chosen a course that necessitates "doubl[ing] with [her] words," and she leads them into that menacing wilderness that is, like the tyrant's and revenger's, both moral and political.

Either in spite of or because of Ferdinand's sudden presence in her court, the Duchess resorts to their conjugal haven where she functions in all her roles without constraint: she abandons the false essentialism that insists on the discontinuity of her two bodies and assumes male or female gender, princely or common status as she wishes.[7] She teases and kisses her husband, who now avidly kisses her in return, brushes and examines her hair for gray as she contemplates ordering the court to powder theirs with arras; she plays hostess and duchess, denying and approving Antonio's request to stay with her that night, and fashions a new marital relationship: "I hope in time 'twill grow into a custom / That noblemen shall come with cap and knee, / To purchase a night's lodging of their wives" (3.2.4–6). The Duchess is joking, but the marriage she has authored allows her the right to deny a husband's claim to her body.

It does not, however, disallow a brother's. Ferdinand's invasion of her sanctuary, like Melantius of Evadne's, not only announces his presumed right but also demonstrates his ability to violate the private female space that is also, barely metaphorically, her body. The wall between her world and his is definitively breached when he overhears her undisguised voice engaged in intimate dialogue with a rival and, just as he had imagined—"Methinks I see her laughing" (2.5.38)—mocking him: "We shall one day have my brothers take you napping"; "I'll assure you / You shall get no more children till my brothers / Consent to be your gossips" (3.2.63, 66–68).

Confronting the apparition of Ferdinand in her mirror, the Duchess moves seamlessly from the private woman, free and laughing in a world where she has unwritten the protocols of class and gender, to the public figure of her birth and title. Relief is her first response to the end of her separated life: "'Tis welcome: / For know, whether I am doom'd to live or die, / I can do both like a prince" (69–71). She acknowledges his ability to command her death, but she will not allow him to ignore her title or diminish her to a parody of femaleness.

Her gestures of obedience—the deferential "sir," the "Pray sir, hear me:—" (73) and "No sir: / I will plant my soul in mine ears to hear you" (76–77)—are preliminary to her announcement that she is married: Ferdinand's "shears do come untimely now / To clip the bird's wings that's already flown!" (84–85). The declaration is neither apologetic nor remorseful. It is triumphant, a substitution of her construction of her life for his. In the face of Ferdinand's threats to her and her unseen husband, she drops even the placating gestures of submission to assert, through the only slightly mitigating form of a question, her rights: "Why might not I marry? / I have not gone about, in this, to create / Any new world, or custom" (109–11). She has, of course. By affirming her princely prerogatives in choosing when and whom to wed, she has flouted his authority. Ferdinand's implacable insistence on his now-confirmed construction of her as shameless and undone draws her even more into the open. Under the flimsy veil of a conditional clause, she challenges him: "You are, in this, / Too strict: and were you not my princely brother / I would say too wilful" (116–18).

Her attempt to slip back into his discourse by adding, in contradiction to her earlier confession of scandal, "my reputation / Is safe" (118–19) fails. She cannot retreat. His continued deafness precipitates the inevitable:

> Why should only I,
> Of all the other princes of the world,
> Be cas'd up, like a holy relic? I have youth,
> And a little beauty.
>
> (137–39)

The Duchess bases her right to author her life on her male body's princely prerogatives and her female body's youth and beauty, an androgyny to which Ferdinand adds the additional, historically evocative element of virginity before transmogrifying it: "So you have some virgins / That are witches" (140–41).

Their conflicting narratives of gender, authority, and transgression, once concealed by the Duchess's secrecy, are now in open confrontation. Ferdinand has already symbolically killed her, absorbing her life into his own by not hearing her voice, by wishing he had not beheld her (96). The Duchess, by insisting that he has no right to entomb her living body, has declared independence of him, an act that, for him, is equivalent to murder. For both, the other's death is a form of purification, yet as much as each desires to restore the solipsistic perfection of their former lives— he by erasing her separateness and she by fleeing his tyranny— their worlds begin to mingle. As she characteristically abandons the public realm to Ferdinand, acting exclusively for and within her family, the public world invades and alters her truth, forming knots of irony when criminal charges usurp the words of marriage vows, betrayal the language of fidelity.

The need to decontaminate her truth, reinforced by her immediate loneliness for her husband, moves her toward the disclosure she still tries to avoid. She asks her officers their opinion of Antonio, searching for an opening or at least an opportunity to speak of him; eager to embrace Bosola as an ally when he unexpectedly praises Antonio, she concludes after the most perfunctory of tests that he is a friend. What seems a fatal last irony, however—that she who has lived by lies is now duped by a lie—instead anticipates the play's final reversal of authority. Bosola's suggestion that she parade before the world what he deems her shameless hypocrisy shows his contempt for her, his link to Ferdinand and not Antonio. Yet the doubleness in his speeches that at once praise and pretend to praise Antonio and the Duchess, like the ironies generated by the Duchess and Antonio's farewell, indicate a matrix for change. The Duchess has exposed herself to Bosola, but she has also exposed Bosola to himself, revealing the buried idealism in his nature, the virtuous man beneath the callous of cynicism. She will be denied refuge, caught, entombed, and murdered, but the principles that formed the basis of her personal narrative have begun to write the larger world and everyone in it.

Her fellow pilgrims at Loretto—the first public audience within the play—are overt indications of that shift. Unlike Bosola and Antonio, they are not tied by bonds of obedience either to her or to Ferdinand and the Cardinal and are, therefore, able to assess the competing claims to authority inherent in the Duchess's roles as a woman and monarch, either governed by men or governing herself and others. Although wondering at the Duchess's matching herself to "so mean a person" (3.4.26), the first pilgrim censures not her but the Cardinal, whose behavior he judges "too cruel" (27), and argues for her rightful independence of Ancona and her brothers: "But I would ask what power hath this state / Of Ancona to determine of a free prince?" (28–29). In response, the second pilgrim iterates the official position, which subordinates the Duchess's political independence to her familial and social dependency:

> They are a free state sir, and her brother show'd
> How that the Pope, fore-hearing of her looseness,
> Hath seiz'd into th'protection of the church
> The dukedom, which she held as dowager.
>
> (30–33)

The first pilgrim is not to be diverted from his argument for the primary authority of her political body—"But by what justice?" (34)—and the second pilgrim concurs: "I think by none, / Only her brother's instigation" (34–35).

In their brief exchange, the pilgrims expose the corruption of their world's political, familial, and spiritual authorities. Moreover, they corroborate the Duchess's view of her privileges: she is a "free prince" over whom neither "free" Ancona, nor Ferdinand and the Cardinal, nor even the Pope has jurisdiction. Those figures do not merit obedience, nor do they have the right to seize Malfi from its legitimate ruler. In the end, the pilgrims express sympathy even for the "mean person" she has chosen to marry: Antonio is *"th'unhappy man"* whose "own weight / Will bring him sooner to th'bottom" of the well (44, 41–42).

With her marriage exposed and officially erased, the Duchess is able to abandon deceit and construct herself openly as she did within her domestic world, accepting and discarding roles, acknowledging and disregarding distinctions of class and gender. The temporal positions of wife and prince are authorized by the atemporal reality whose variety she embodies and mirrors, and she speaks with a conviction whose voice is either female or male, both female and male, and, therefore, neither female nor male.

Everywhere, she finds the transcendent in the immanent: in her son's play with his top, in Antonio's cold farewell kiss. She wishes for her "ruin" to be "sudden" (3.5.97–98) and, later, to "fly in pieces" (106) like a rusty cannon, yet she is still alive, and she also hears and answers the world's call, rejecting Antonio's stoical resignation to affirm the encompassing truth she represents.

In that liminal last stage of her existence, Bosola—enemy and admirer, minister and convert—replaces Antonio as her intimate male partner. In the field outside Ancona, his stubborn attempt to correct the Duchess's errancy drives her to identify, oppose, and correct the evil he has chosen to serve. In his command, "you must see your husband no more" (99), she exposes his appropriation of divine authority: "What devil art thou, that counterfeits heaven's thunder?" (100). When he advises her to forget "this base, low fellow" (117), she angrily wishes for a physical power that could unmask and punish the vizarded liars who surround her: "Were I a man / I'd beat that counterfeit face into thy other" (117–18). Like her princely forebear, Elizabeth at Tilbury, she accepts the cultural premise of women's biological weakness only to dismantle its linkage to moral weakness and cowardice. When Bosola continues to presume the right to admonish her, referring to Antonio as "One of no birth," the Duchess shifts to abstraction, enunciating the principle of ideal consonance between position and merit: "Man is most happy when 's own actions / Be arguments and examples of his virtue" (120–21).

Bosola's sneering retort, that Antonio's virtues are "barren" and "beggarly" (122), effects a final alteration in the Duchess's discursive mode as she eschews both challenge and precept for parable. All her voices—the natural, the political, and the spiritual—speak in her narrative of the dogfish and the salmon: the tale is homely, indeed housewifely (Berggren 1978, 354); it definitively corrects Bosola's misreading of social hierarchy; it takes the parabolic shape of Christ's teachings. It also parallels and corrects the worldly orientation of Ferdinand's moralizing allegory of Reputation, Love, and Death, contextualizing it in terms of eschatological absolutes.

The Duchess's final conflict with her brothers is written, as her earlier struggles have been, in the idiom of theater. In her gift for playing many roles separately and simultaneously, the Duchess is, like the players, closest to the absence of role, the fullness of her life an emptiness that testifies to the spirit. Ferdinand and his brother Cardinal have succeeded in demonstrating their control of the physical manifestations of her authority, divorcing her from her chosen husband and from the signifiers of her political position. Yet the locked inner circle of Ferdinand's theatricality is itself enclosed within the powerfully extending circles of hers. In, and in between, life and death, the Duchess embodies the wholeness that spreads through her up and down the paradigmatic axis. Now unhampered by the debilitating separation of her private principles from her public life, she responds to her brothers' barren tyranny by connecting herself ever more firmly to the sacred plenitude that unifies all life and grants her authority. In the confinement of childbirth, she had confined others; now she imprisons those who would imprison her.

Her gift for play enables her to resist Ferdinand's authoring and, instead, to author first herself and then others. Her response to his play recapitulates the stages of her earlier responses to her brothers, moving quickly from seeming obedience to overt defiance. When he names her children "cubs" and "bastards" (4.1.33, 36), she angrily invokes the spiritual law she has obeyed to correct his conflation of the maternal and the bestial: "Do you visit me for this? / You violate a sacrament o'th'church / Shall make you howl in hell for't" (38–40). Her progeny are licit and sacred; he is the damned soul: "What witchcraft doth he practise that he hath left / A dead man's hand here?" (54–55). Ferdinand, creating an illusion of life from the dead and the severed, is the practitioner of devilish arts, the maker of monsters, not she, whose children are born of a natural, loving union and, therefore, blessed.

The Duchess would like to regain enough control of her body to destroy it: to freeze to death, to swallow coals, or, when Bosola chides her for unchristian despair, to starve (68–69, 72, 76). Yet no more than she could embrace Antonio's stoicism can she abandon the active struggle against her brothers: "I'll go pray: no, / I'll go curse" (95–96). To pray is to seem Ferdinand's penitent, his abject, weeping woman; to curse is to oppose his power. The performative force of the natural authorities she has always invoked live in her voice: she calls on nature to consume them with plagues; on history, the record of the political world, to bequeath them the ill fame of tyrants; on heaven to "cease crowning martyrs" (107) to punish them: "Go howl them this: and say I long to bleed" (109). Behind her curses is the power of a divinely authored system of correspondences that contradicts her brothers' will to isolate and dominate. Her metaphor refuses the script they write by substituting hers: she is the sacrificial, bleeding woman;

her brothers are beasts, without human ear or tongue; Bosola is their animal servant "howling" her message to its masters.

Only to Cariola can she express her apprehension without risking the misogynistic triumph of the male world Bosola serves. It is to servant and friend that the Duchess addresses her worry that her own image may be assuming the shape of his script: "who do I look like now?" (4.2.30). Cariola's response reassures her that she is not the creature of his black art:

> Like to your picture in the gallery,
> A deal of life in show, but none in practice;
> Or rather like some reverend monument
> Whose ruins are even pitied.
>
> (31–34)

Like the tragedy she has asked to hear, the picture and the monument are not holy relics that testify to Ferdinand's divinity. The Duchess has, rather, withdrawn from herself to become the object of her own gaze and the sculptor of her own monument. She grants him the power to make her suffer—she is "chain'd to endure" the tyranny focused on her (60)—but her suffering, like her body, is hers to shape.

The madmen sent to drive her out of her wits make her saner; the relentless pressure on her authority makes her surer of it. "Am not I thy Duchess?" she asks Bosola as tombmaker (134), and when he erases her title by focusing on her natural rather than her political body, noting the lined forehead, gray hairs, and unquiet sleep of "some great woman" (135), she answers her own question: "I am Duchess of Malfi still" (142).[8] She rejects, too, Bosola's construction of the tyrants who torment her as the "princely brothers" (166) whose authority dwarfs and negates hers. Instead, she treats their ironic "present" of death as a sincere gift and returns it with an equally sincere wish whose implications are, however, ironic: "I have so much obedience in my blood, / I wish it in their veins, to do them good" (169–70). Ostensibly, she offers them what they seek, but the "obedience in my blood" is not obedience to them. Moreover, she has so much of "it"—ambiguously blood and/or obedience—that she would like to share it with them: if *it* refers to her blood, she confirms Ferdinand's horror of her contaminating him; if *it* refers to obedience, her wish subjects them to the divine law she obeys. In both cases, the Duchess is not their subject; they are hers.

In death as in life, the genders of her public and private personae are separate and mingled: the male prince clearly inhabits the body of a suffering, grieving wife and mother; the woman exhibits a firmness and courage assigned to men. Ferdinand has not successfully made her the mad, cowering figure his misogyny requires. On the contrary, she is rational and brave: she questions Bosola's change of role from tomb maker to bellman and informs Cariola that it would be futile to call for help from the mad; she is unterrified of death or its instrument and scorns the distinctions of class that would make death more acceptable if it took the form of diamonds, cassia, or pearls. Triumphantly, she takes control of her execution, ordering it halted, like the Lady, while she kneels to show humility before the only authority she accepts as greater than hers and then commanding her executioners to pull strongly.[9]

The Duchess's physical disappearance from the play is gradual: she returns from the dead to utter "Antonio!" and "Mercy!"; her disembodied spirit haunts Bosola, her disembodied voice Antonio. Yet even as her corporeal life fades, her presence strengthens and magnifies, a final demonstration of the almost comical absurdity of her brothers' powers.[10] They become Bosola's "dead walls, or vaulted graves, / That ruin'd, yields no echo" (5.5.97–98); she speaks within a silence beyond death's material ruins.

The Duchess of Malfi is, as the title has always told us, the Duchess of Malfi's play. The temptation to rewrite her story either to save her or to make her an open warrior against male tyranny is great, but she is neither a comic nor an epic figure. She is the tragic heroine she has constructed from the materials of her brothers' theater. Unlike the unalterable Lucina and Lady, who are supporting characters in men's plays, she is her drama's center, the character whose choices arise from a strength that is also weakness and who grows in determination and understanding. In her tragic role, the Duchess is again androgynous: not only a female character who embraces and defies sexual difference but also a woman playing what is traditionally a man's role.

In that double challenge to traditional male gender, she is sister—and brother—to the men who wrote and performed her. Webster, bestowing his theatrical authority on his Duchess, writes her as connecting it to an authority that transcends both his and hers. As his work of art, she becomes her own; as her own work of art, she testifies to his: the mutuality she never found with her brothers or Bosola, or even with Antonio, rests in her final relationship with her author. Like him, she does not obey the syntactic chart of either/or—male or female, public or private, noble or commoner. Character and playwright both understand that the world is, finally, as it is written: that absolute political authority does not exist any more than essential and immutable sexual difference; that absolute authority, if it exists at all, resides with those who write the meaning of their stories.

Coda

The theory that proclaims gender a simple continuation of biological difference is alluringly tidy, but the evidence is against it.
A culture that posits as natural the social and political superiority
of either sex tempts those of that sex to make permanent what
seems promised by the conditional positions they hold. Because
the vast majority of cultures make authority over worldly affairs
a male prerogative, the monsters of injustice, and those who become monstrous in opposing them, are usually men.

The fear of tyranny that accompanied James's attempt to cen-
tralize authority in his person revitalized revenge tragedy and
produced a concentration of tyrant-driven plays in the politically
heated middle years of his reign. Even in those plays, however,
with their cultural presumption of equivalency between sex and
gender, men and women are shown as capable of behavior assigned by theory and custom to one or the other. Govianus, Affranius, and Antonio relinquish traditional male roles to women
without believing they have become less than men; the Lady,
Lucina, Eudoxa, and the Duchess assume authority over men
without ceasing to affirm their femaleness. Characters who insist
on linking biology to behavior and both to authority—Evadne
and the Cardinal, for example—are monstrous in both tyranny
and submission.

Jacobean revenge tragedy, then, while representing misogyny
with chilling accuracy, does not support it. Disrespect for women
as autonomous agents of action is identified with the purveyors
of tyranny and revenge, while heroic women, unsilent and disobedient, restore the ideal to the world of corrupt practice. The
heroines of these plays adhere to what seems an archaic definition
of virtue, but the theological and cultural discourse invoked by
that definition allows them to establish their own authority in the
interstices of male absolutism and to forge alliances with men
who are willing to imagine a world where the face of authority
can belong to either sex.

Notes

Chapter 1. Gender, History, and Jacobean Revenge Tragedy

1. In her work on the seemingly opposed views of women in Ovidian and Petrarchan discourse, Evelyn Gajowsky, for example, extends C. S. Lewis's observation that male idealism and cynicism about women are "twin fruits on the same branch" (1992, 19). See, too, McLuskie (1989, 228), Weil (1982, 148).

2. The definition of authority and its relationship to power is fundamental to this discussion. Like Robertson and Levin (1989, v), I am using Louise Lamphere's distinction between authority and power: "When power rests on legitimacy . . . and when it is exercised within a hierarchy of roles, it is defined as authority" (1974, 99). Leonard Krieger elaborates: "authority is simply constituted power—that is, any capacity to secure obedience or conformity that carries with it some title to do so" (1977, 253). Women had power in the Renaissance family, for example, but men had coercive authority (Jordan 1990a, 4). Michel Foucault's definition of power as immanent in force relations rather than as imposed through a system of dominance and subjugation clarifies the ways power organizes processes and strategies within discourses (1980, 92–93).

3. See Philippe Ariès and Georges Duby for germinal studies of the private and public spheres. I am using *public* to refer to the political space of institutionalized state authority from which women were excluded and *private* to refer to the enclosed domestic space in which they were contained. In theory, men dominated public and private spaces as voices of the governing class and as familial patriarchs.

4. Eve Kosofsky Sedgwick's examination of homosociality and "the relation of sexual desire to political power" (1985, 6) broke ground in connecting male patriarchal relationships with both misogyny and homophobia. As Stanley Chojnacki states, gender must be discussed relationally (1994, 74).

5. Renaissance feminists affirmed their spiritual equality with men, and that affirmation, Constance Jordan notes, entailed "a correlative political status" (1990a, 5). S. P. Cerasano and Marion Wynne-Davies agree: The "new spiritual equality," they write, "carved out a space for female expression that could not be possessed or supervised by men" (1992a, 18). Women could have—I would like to say *must* have—seen the authority of their merit as connecting naturally to political authority, even if they were denied it, and in Queen Elizabeth's forged link between virginity and entitlement to power, they had a functioning model for that belief.

6. I recognize the risk in adopting this view. Carol Cook, in her debate with Jonathan Goldberg, articulates the danger of "[eliding] sexual difference in a way that would disable any genuinely political discussion of gender" (1991, 70); Carol Neely warns that "declaring the end of difference conceals rather than

erases women's subordination" (1988, 13). Yet neither is the tenacious emphasis on difference without risk. Restricting otherness and sameness to the logic of either/or, while a beneficial and certainly necessary rhetorical structure for political action (and its sibling, war), produces an unproductive stalemate when continued on principle.

7. The history of colonialism, for example, is filled with the phenomenon of European men asserting dominance over colonial men by forcing them, as an act of humiliation and oppression, into roles gendered female. The stereotyped attributes of all deemed inferior, whether women or racial "others," are the same (Loomba 1989, 45). In recognizing that fact, however, we must guard against reversing the binary by demonizing the white, male, European Other. As Valerie Wayne aptly puts it, we do not "need a criticism that essentialises white men" (1991a, 154).

8. Ian Maclean's work offers a compendium of analogies, taken from scholasticism and medicine, that presume and seek to demonstrate male superiority to women (1980). For additional commentaries on femaleness in analogic reasoning, see Jardine (1987, 115), Callaghan (1989, 9–27), Newman (1991, 1–31).

9. Mary's sexual notoriety made it difficult for James to assert his title through his father, who was also a descendant of Henry VII.

10. Kari Weil objects to the idealization of androgyny, which she sees as a "conservative, if not a misogynistic ideal" (1992, 2). Androgyny, she argues, is not a union of the sexes so much as a way for men to avoid sexuality with all its attendant fears by appropriating the female Other, a conversion of female to male that renders the female unnecessary. While Weil's objections to women's accepting androgyny as an ideal are compelling, the strong connotation of monstrosity linked to hermaphroditism in the Renaissance militates against its use in a discussion of Jacobean revenge tragedy. I am using androgyny to refer to the claim made by a member of either sex to possess the attributes of both. For a bibliography of texts on androgyny to 1974, see Bazin (1974, 217–35).

11. There is disagreement among critics about how the Cult of Elizabeth fashioned Elizabeth's gender. Philippa Berry challenges Yates and Strong as well as those like Montrose and Tenenhouse who follow their lead in "enabl[ing] Renaissance scholarship to displace the fundamental problem of the queen's gender" (1989, 65). That displacement occurs prominently in feminist writing that treats Elizabeth as token or exception, for example, Jardine (1989, 178) and Callaghan (1989, 150). For the argument that Elizabeth was a pattern for women, see Neely (1991, 8) and Loomba (1989, 110).

12. Church fathers paid virgins the high compliment of calling them "male" or "virile" (Schulenburg 1986, 32), demonstrating how much virginity was still beholden to male discourse (Erickson 1987, 134–35). Women who chose the religious life also referred to themselves as "becoming male," understanding their renunciation of the sexual organs that differentiated them from men as progress toward a higher human form (Miles 1989, 55, 66). The gospels themselves lay the foundation for the concept of "heroic virginity" as male (Miles 1989, 56; Bloch 1991, 107). See too Castelli (1986, 74–75) and Warner (1985, 146–53).

Virginity, however, allowed women some autonomy in a life otherwise dominated by men's control of their reproductive function. Elizabeth's assertion of her virgin state in the first speech of her reign creates "a category of virtue that she herself would define" (Frye 1993, 15). The maleness attributed to virgins was, in Elizabeth's case, enhanced by her political gender.

13. Although customarily distinguished from one another, virginity and chastity are often used interchangeably. The Protestant emphasis on marriage, in conscious opposition to Catholicism's glorification of sexual abstinence, attempted to replace virginity with married chastity as a praiseworthy virtue, especially for women. Yet both terms denoted sexual purity, and the word *chastity* could mean virginity. Elizabeth was both the Virgin Queen and the Queen of Chastity (Pearse 1973, 51), her mythos a "cult of chastity" (Berry 1989, 136).

14. Time-honored though these accounts of Elizabeth's speech and dress at Tilbury are, Frye (1993) and Teague (1992) note there is reason to doubt the historical accuracy of both. Orgel explains the posthumous accounts of Elizabeth dressed in full armor as evidence of "the changing nature of the ideological discourse of gender roles in the period," invented well after the event first as a challenge to James's pacifism and then, in a Caroline engraving, as part of the "politics of nostalgia" (1992, 15). Given the consistency of Elizabeth's self-representation with her words at Tilbury, I am assuming that the queen appeared in a costume suggesting readiness for war and addressed her troops with the words attributed to her.

15. Elizabeth's biographers all attest to the nostalgia that sprang up after her death. "When we had experience of [King James's] government," the bishop of Gloucester wrote, "the Queen did seem to revive. Then was her memory much magnified: such ringing of bells, such public joy in memory of her coronation than ever was for the coming-in of James" (qtd. in Hibbert 1991, 265). See too Anne Barton's "Harking back to Elizabeth: Ben Jonson and Caroline Nostalgia" (1981).

16. Opposing Goldberg's reading, Deborah Shuger argues that the image of a nursing father is a common trope, originating in Isaiah 49:23—"And kings shall be thy nursing fathers, and their queens thy nursing mothers"—and appearing in Andrewes and Hooker (1990, 128–29).

17. Both Gohlke (1980) and Montrose (1983) discuss the desire for male parthenogenesis as founded in a fear of women. Gohlke argues that to author the self, as Macbeth does, is to "eradicate femininity itself" (176). Poets, for example, use a female persona, Lawrence Lipking argues, not to experience Otherness but to control it (1988, 127).

18. Valerie Traub, countering Goldberg's assumptions of James's homosexuality, argues that fondling Buckingham and calling him his wife "held no necessary implication of sodomy" (1992, 106). In this, she follows Alan Bray's discussion of the inevitable distancing of men engaging in homoerotic sex from the demonized sin of sodomy (1982, 92). Bruce Smith also maintains that "a man who had sexual relations with another man" did not think of himself as fundamentally different from his peers" but rather as part of a "general depravity" (1991, 11). While, on the basis of Foucault's *History of Sexuality* (1980), there is general agreement that the term *homosexuality* cannot be applied to anyone who lived before the nineteenth century, Gregory Bredbeck argues against the "paranoia of historicization" that stigmatizes any "effort to examine sexual difference in the past . . . as anachronistic" (1991, xi). He links the terms *homoeroticism* and *sodomy* to discuss male-male attraction in the Renaissance (see, especially, ix–xv, 1–30). Cady cogently argues for "masculine love" as the term for such attraction in the Renaissance (1992). For debate over the possibility of using *homosexual* to describe sexual orientation in early modern England, see Goldberg's *Sodometries* (1992) and *Queering the Renaissance* (1994) and Keith

Thomas's comments on the "orthodox chronology of gay history" (1994, 10), as established by Foucault, that disallows the use of the term.

19. Jenny Wormald hypothesizes that that the difficulty lay in the English taking their new king too seriously. They were uneasy because they did not understand James's love of controversy and his use of writing to clarify his thoughts (1991, 48–49, 52). Nor, she emphasizes, was he the absolute tyrant the English feared he was or was planning to become. Sommerville, however, reiterates the fact that James was the "first monarch in 200 years to dissolve parliaments abruptly" and "to leave any substantial gap between meetings of parliament" (1991, 55); that he informed the Commons, who questioned him about impositions, that as "'it is atheism and blasphemy to dispute what God can do . . . , so it is presumption and high contempt in a subject to dispute what a king can do or say that a king cannot do this or that'" (66); that he tore up the Commons' Protestation on their privileges, written in response to his declaring free speech a right derived from the monarch who could limit or revoke it (67). Perhaps the English misunderstood him, but he certainly gave them grounds.

20. Marcus traces images of Elizabeth like Moll Frith in other genres as well: "The cultural memory for Elizabeth's mannerisms and characteristic strategies was longer than we are likely to find credible, and continued to exert a subtle shaping on stage depictions of female dominance—particularly those with a reformist bent—even decades after her death" (1986, 104).

21. Discussions of the genre have ranged from Fredson Bowers's encyclopedically inclusive, chronologically arranged catalogue of revenge tragedies to Charles and Elaine Hallett's narrower definition of the genre according to its conventions. In this study, I am neither cataloging plays nor tracing conventions but rather concentrating on the Jacobean moment in the genre's history when revenge—enacted or rejected—is triggered by a tyrant's sexual assault on his realm. The plays under discussion fall within two of Bowers's categories: the "Reign of the Villain," which he defines as a "drift towards sensationalism and artificiality" but with the love theme as a motivating factor rather than as a subsidiary element (1940, 155–56); and the "Disapproval of Revenge," in which the interest shifts from the "workings of . . . revenge to the general villainy of action and the evil intrigues of the protagonist" (185), in short where the revenger replicates the tyrant.

22. For an overview of critical and historical views of revenge, see Keyishian (1995, 4–12). It is customary to use *revenger* to designate those figures "retaliating for wrongs done to themselves" and *avenger* those "retaliating for the wrongs and sufferings of others" (2). Because characters like Maximus and Melantius, as well as the revenger's namesake Vindice, view women and, ultimately, other men as adjuncts of themselves, they are never really avenging the wrongs done to others. I therefore term them revengers. The simplification involved in sketching composite characters is necessary at this stage of the discussion to elucidate patterns and structures. These characters are, of course, cultural and authorial fictions, but it is shorter and simpler to use the standard shorthand and write as if they were autonomous: to say, for example, "Govianus believes" rather than "Govianus is constructed to believe."

Chapter 2. The Stage Tyrant and Jacobean Absolutism: In the Throne of God

1. As Heinemann points out, revenge tragedy is political drama (1990, 190). The explicit linking of politics to sex, however, is usually attributed to Beaumont

and Fletcher, although, as Wymer notes, there is a general link in the drama between rape and tyranny (1986, 104). Beaumont and Fletcher developed "the tradition of a sexualized politics in which desire defines sovereignty and tyranny" (Bushnell 1990, 163), with Fletcher's tyrants in particular "express[ing] their disregard for restraints by invading the bedroom" (Turner 1989, 127). See too McLuskie (1989, 195).

2. I am certainly not equating the actual monarchy of James I with the tyrants of revenge tragedy. Speaking for historians, J. H. M. Salmon decries that tendency among theater critics: "Certainly it seems extreme to assert that Whitehall under James I was actually like Rome under Tiberius, but it is understandable . . . that some at the time came to believe it to be so" (1991, 178). The understanding that "some" could "believe it to be so" is precisely what brought popular success to a dramatic genre that exploited the fear. Turner points to the appearance of stage tyrants in the years 1607–12 as "a reflection of discouragement consequent upon a growing acquaintance with James's behavior and an exploitation of anxieties about being trapped under a bad monarch" (1989, 134).

3. Greenblatt has established the reading of early English drama as politically subversive, with tragedy destroying the "fundamental paradigm of the dominant culture" (1982, 7). Moretti argues for the drama's explicit contribution to the execution of Charles I, (1982, 7–8) while Molly Smith sees the drama's "opposition to king and social system" as a broader criticism of "the deviation by society as a whole from desirable norms" (1991, 17). For other discussions of the relationship between the drama and the era's political climate, see Margot Heinemann (1980), J. W. Lever (1971), Stephen Orgel (1991), Albert Tricomi (1989), Robert Y. Turner (1989), and Paul Yachnin (1991).

4. The tyrant's theatrical history of "effeminacy" (see Bushnell 1990, 50–69), a construction that implies he is cowardly, weak, and uxorious, follows him into Jacobean revenge tragedy. Yet the dramatic representation of tyrants is altered both by the political context of debate over absolute authority in the state and by the dramatic context of the revenge genre itself. In the seventeenth century, the tyrannical monarch was defined not by his moral depravity, as he was in the sixteenth, but by his depriving subjects of liberty and property (Bushnell 1990, 39), the rights, as Henry Howard affirmed, of a freeborn people.

Altered, too, after forty-five years of Queen Elizabeth's untyrannical rule and her posthumous glorification, is the automatic identification of femaleness with tyranny. Moreover, with James's jealous hostility to Elizabeth and the country's dissatisfaction with James, the equation of maleness with rational authority did not hold. Elizabeth was certainly an absolute ruler, but it was James who had committed himself to print on the subject and used the case for absolutism to argue against rights granted the English Parliament under common law. The convention of the tyrant's effeminacy, then, becomes loosely associated with the current rather than the former monarch, with maleness rather than with femaleness, a complication that denies the essentialist concept of effeminacy itself.

5. Coppélia Kahn links cuckoldry to the confluence of misogyny, the double standard, and patriarchal marriage, the horns a "defense formed through denial, compensation, and upward displacement" (1981, 121–22). Callaghan enlarges on the psychological reading: the cuckold's horn is "a deformation of the erect phallus," now "useless and misplaced—displayed for all to ridicule on the forehead while the cuckold remains blissfully unaware of it" (1989, 164). For a reading of cuckoldry as a metaphor of "nascent capitalism" (61), see Bruster's "Horns of Plenty: Cuckoldry and Capital" (1992, 47–62).

6. Citations from *The Maid's Tragedy* are taken from the 1988 edition by T. W. Craik.

7. In contrast to the centuries'-old view of the playwrights as hack royalists, Finkelpearl finds "political criticism of court and king was a central urge in [their] most important plays" (1990, 7); Turner (1989) and Bushnell (1990) concur. Fletcher, after all, collaborated with Massinger on a clearly political play, *Sir John Van Olden Barnavelt* (Patterson 1984, 80). For an historical overview of the fate of the playwrights' reputations, see Finkelpearl (1990, 3–7), Bushnell (1990, 159–63).

8. See, especially, Patterson (1982), Bushnell (1990), and Goldberg (1989) for discussions of Roman history used as context for contemporary events.

9. Citations from *Valentinian* are taken from the 1979 edition by Robert K. Turner.

10. Citations from *The Second Maiden's Tragedy* are taken from the 1978 edition by Anne Lancashire.

11. It is notable that the unfaithful Wife of the subplot is given voice and sympathy. Her husband's sexual abandonment and paranoid distrust of her makes him ugly, ridiculous, and, when he becomes his own pander, unmanly. The Wife also effectively defends women against her lover's misogyny: "You say we're weak, but the best wits on you all / Are glad of our advice, for aught I see, / And hardly thrive without us" (4.1.36–38). The Wife's death between the swords of two men does not, despite its signification of adultery, erase either the initial sympathy created for her or the pathos of her struggle to break the identification of men's relationship to women in terms of their relationship to one another.

Chapter 3. The Revenger as Rival Author

1. Hallett and Hallet (1980, 92–95) and Griswold (1986, 62) discuss disguise as a convention of revenge tragedy. The madness, as well as the folly adopted by Antonio of *Antonio's Revenge*, generally gives way to disguises more suitable to a Jacobean court: Vindice's lascivious pander or melancholy malcontent, Melantius's tame soldier-courtier. For the revenger as playwright, see Goldman (1975, 97–99), Hallett and Hallett (1980, 89–93), and Rozett, who identifies that role with the Vice (1984, 183).

2. The recent studies of antitheatricality by Jean Howard and Laura Levine amplify the earlier works by Jonas Barish and Margot Heinemann by concentrating on the connection between hostility to the theater and the disruptions of social and personal identity, in particular sexual identity. Levine hypothesizes that antitheatricality expresses the fear that representations have the power to alter what they represent and, most specifically, to transform men into women. Because the female is "the default position" for men, "there is no masculinity except in the performance of masculinity"—in short, "the terror [is] that there is no masculine self" (Levine 1994, 8–9). Heinemann locates the unease about players in their relative freedom from political and even religious constraint that resulted from the popularization and commercialization of theater (1980). She quotes Cocke's *A Common Player* (1615): "Howsoever he pretends to have a royal master or mistress, his wages and dependance prove him to be the servant of the people" (qtd from E. K. Chambers, *Elizabethan Stage*, iv, 256). Howard sees the antitheatrical fear as emanating in part from the players' ability to write

themselves: "No longer actors in a God-given script, individuals are presented as writing the scripts in which, through studious self-cultivation and artful self-presentation, they will perform" (*Stage*, 35). The players' competition with preachers for audience certainly added to the suspicion that they were infringing on sacred territory (Rozett 1984, 15–24). Heinemann reminds us, however, that Puritan objections to the theater were also very practical concerns over "plague, riots and traffic jams" (1980, 35), with keeping order in a chaotic, tumultuous city (31). See Barish for a bibliography of early commentary on antitheatrical polemic (1981, 82).

3. Griswold notes that madness, like wildness, inspires the horror typical of revenge tragedy by crossing the "line between human . . . and inhuman" (1986, 80).

4. See Abbe Blum's discussion of the monumentalizing impulse in Shakespeare (1990).

5. Bowers (1940), Danby (1952), and Finkelpearl (1990) find Melantius sympathetic throughout the play. Other critics, however, have found more darkness and deceit in the noble soldier, for example Bradbrook (1962, viii), Bliss (1987, 102), Shullenberger (1982, 141).

6. Bruce Smith discusses in general the classical world's praise of male love and its effect on early modern England (1991, 35–40); John W. Wieler focuses on the Stoics' idealization of male friendship in the works of Chapman, especially in *The Revenge of Bussy D'Ambois* (1969, 11–12, 102–8). See Bray (1982), Bredbeck (1991), and Saslow (1986) for a discussion of Renaissance representations of homoeroticism.

7. See Shullenberger (1982, 144) and McCabe (1983, 245) for comments on the sexuality of Melantius's relationship with both Evadne and Amintor.

Chapter 5. "I Am Not to Be Altered": The Authority of Women

1. For a review of psychological and literary discussions of the erotic triangle, see Sedgwick (1985, 21–27).

2. Cross-dressing was often singled out as an especially disturbing signifier of social disorder, as it was in the *Hic Mulier/Haec Vir* controversy. Garber discusses transvestism as an interrogation of sexual categorization in general (1992); Jardine (1987, 141–68) and Newman (1991, 109–27) consider the effects of English sumptuary laws. Within the drama, the players' transvestism has been interpreted as challenging patriarchal assumptions (Belsey 1985, 180; Howard 1994, 93–128; Rackin 1989, 127), as intensifying them (Woodbridge 1984, 154), and as pandering to men's preference for female sexuality in male form (Jardine 1989, 29). Zimmerman argues that "hetero- and homoerotic stimuli for male spectators were mutually dependent," with cross-dressing the signifier of the "Renaissance fascination with sexual indeterminacy" (1992, 56). For an incisive discussion of the connection between transvestism and antitheatricality, see Levine (1994).

3. Hamlet's inclusion of "the lady shall say her mind freely—or the blank verse shall halt for't" (2.2.323) among the stock figures of an Elizabethan repertory company—adventurous knight, lover, humorous man, and clown—is enigmatic but suggestive. The Arden edition dismisses two readings: the role

contained obscenities; the boy playing the lady, forgetting his lines, improvised. The reference may, however, be to a stock figure of an outspoken woman.

4. The customary reading of Lucina as no more than one man's victim and another's motive for revenge decenters her more than the play does. In his overview of *Valentinian*, Squier, for example, never mentions her at all, spending instead a few sentences on Lucinda, the source's raped woman, and focusing exclusively on Maximus (1986). Even Finkelpearl, who does mention Lucina sympathetically, brushes aside the force of her decision to die and gives the agency for that event to Maximus: "he encourages her suicide," and the "well-trained Roman matron agrees" (1990, 215). It is unfair to fault critics who are pursuing other interests for slighting Lucina in their analyses, but in treating her as no more than a pawn in a male struggle, they do duplicate a view of gender that revenge tragedy exposes as destructively limited. Mincoff, although he later trivializes Lucina's suicide as motivated by the fear "she will be pointed at in the streets" (1964, 80), argues for the importance of women's roles in the play (71); Waith notes in passing that Lucina is heroic in her self-defense (1971, 161); Turner finds Lucina's will a match for Valentinian's, her death "hardly a defeat" (1989, 130).

5. Pearse notes that "feminine 'honor' and 'honesty' came to be considered almost exclusively as sexual purity" (1973, 55), a statement that accepts a male view without attempting to ascertain whether women agreed. Certainly Lucina and her chaste sisters—granted, images of women created by men—link the two concepts, but rather than narrow the abstract principle of honor to physical purity, they widen the meaning of physical purity, as did Elizabeth, to a spiritual and cosmic state of virtue.

6. Eudoxa gets even shorter shrift from critics than Lucina. The discussion of revenge customarily ends with Maximus, the theatrical power of Eudoxa's action and speech relegated, if it is mentioned at all, to a tidying up of the plot and a tying up of loose ends. I have no quarrel with those who focus on Maximus as the play's central figure or on the plight of subjects under tyranny as its governing theme. That Eudoxa is a pivotal figure, however, is signaled by Fletcher's radical alteration of the character he found in his source. Procopius's Eudoxa invited the enemy Vandals to assist her in ousting Maximus and, in consequence, destroyed Rome; Fletcher's Eudoxa plans and executes Maximus's demise alone and, with Affranius, saves Rome—and the play.

7. Evadne has her share of supporters: Farley-Hills declares her "not unsympathetic" (1988, 181); Shullenberger, avoiding the equivocating litotes, treats her murder of the King as "an act of tragic courage: daring, representative, and necessary" (1982, 155). The more common response, however, is disapproval, often significantly marked by adjectives that suggest Evadne's lack of conformity to a positive female image and her gravitation toward a negative male one: "violent, amoral and ruthless" (Bradbrook 1962, viii); "powerful and sadistic" (Finkelpearl 1990, 191); "a study in radical perversity" (Danby 1952, 193). Molly Smith makes the reversal of gender explicit in discussing Evadne as the woman-on-top. Citing the King's plea for her to be gentle and not rugged, Smith notes the "implication . . . that she has usurped an essentially male quality, that of rugged boldness" (1991, 145), an identification of male gender made even more emphatic by gentleman of the bedchamber's incredulity at a woman's committing the murder.

8. Shullenberger brilliantly delineates the "fatal split in [Evadne's] consciousness": "An independent, sexually aggressive woman, she is utterly dependent

on the masculine hierarchy for her status in the court. In choosing the king for her lover, and vowing to have no one less than a king, she binds herself to the power of place in the patriarchal system. . . . Yet [although she knows that system is "merely a distribution of power"] in placing herself as a dependent within that system, she implicitly consents to its authority, and sets herself up for its judgment of her sexual audacity" (1982, 148). Her "sexual authority" (147) is then meaningless.

9. For a fuller discussion of the parallels between *The Maid's Tragedy* and *Hamlet*, see Squier (1986, 92, 98–99).

10. The two heroines are, in fact, usually read as opposites, but the good girl–bad girl opposition does not account for Aspatia's resemblance to Evadne in seizing authorial control of the world around her. Shullenberger (1982, 152–53) and Bliss (1987, 105) comment on Aspatia as an artist.

11. Sarah Sutherland offers a review and classification of readings of the masque to 1983 (1983, 62–74). For relevance of the masque to the play, see Neill (1970, 111–35), Farley-Hills (1988, 179–80), Shullenberger (1982, 134–40), Finkelpearl (1990, 206–21), and Smith (1991, 143).

Chapter 6. *The Duchess of Malfi*

1. Forker compiles a sizable list of her English contemporaries who married for love and whose marriages disregarded social inequalities, including Anne More's to John Donne (1986, 299–300). Bradbrook offers the Rich-Blount union as "possible endorsement" (1980, 146); Steen, detailing the striking parallels between the plight of Arbella Stuart and the Duchess, uses public reaction to Stuart's marriage to assess probable response to the Duchess's, concluding that some in the audience would have been ready to "condemn her, some to cheer her, and most to pity her" (1991, 76).

2. See, for example, Forker's discussion of sadism (1986), Mitchell and Wright's of lycanthropy (1975), and Wilkinson's of necrophilia (1981). Forker also provides a history of critical debate on Ferdinand's incestuous desire (1986, 563 n.19).

3. The brothers' halves of that being have been variously identified: passion and intelligence (Brown 1976, xli); feverish egoism and deficiency of normal feeling (Ornstein 1960, 146); appetite and will (Best 1987, 17). For a comprehensive enumeration of their complementary traits, see Forker (1986, 316).

4. One can see the likeness of Bosola and the Duchess in many ways: in their shared images of madman and galley slave (Pearson 1987, 77); in their obstinacy and tendency to change the roles they play (Best 1987, 26); in their "struggle for self-realization and enriched humanity" (Bliss 1983, 139). The sexual difference that initially overwhelmed Bosola's ability to recognize kinship has become irrelevant.

5. A number of Jacobean discourses grant the Duchess authority in her world. Rose finds the Duchess inscribed in the Protestant discourse that idealizes marriage (1988, 162); she also reads the Duchess's widowhood as the "symbolic equivalent of the [female comic hero's] androgynous disguise" (165). Jankowski adds "the long humanist tradition that placed importance on nobility of character and validated a woman's right to choose a husband" (1992, 170). Jankowski, however, reads the Duchess as punished for her attempt to act on that perceived right, to create a concept "in which men and women are compan-

ions, equal partners, friends, and lovers" (179). Jardine's and Desmet's views are even darker: for Jardine, the play "ritually exorcis[es]" "the spectre of real female strength implicit in the inheritance structure" (1987, 127); for Desmet, the Duchess is systematically denied the authority of "both sovereignty and respectable female roles" (1991, 82); she and women in general are encompassed and excluded by the rhetoric of the "Woman Controversy" (88).

6. In any discussion of the Duchess's public and private selves, the emphasis should be on her inability and unwillingness to separate the two. The Duchess is, as Lord states, a spirit of greatness *and* of woman, a union of opposites (1976, 316); Webster, says Forker, insists on "both her public image as regnant princess and her private personality as wife and mother" (1986, 323). To focus on her private world is to treat her as a housewife in over her head, as Bliss does: "hers is no heroic passion. Her true context is the private and domestic sphere of wifely devotion" (1983, 148). To focus on her "greatness," on the other hand, is to risk dismissing her as no more than an irresponsible leader. As Jankowski says of the Duchess after her brothers' exit from Malfi, "the "boundaries of [her] two selves are perpetually slipping" (1992, 188).

7. Antonio's inferiority in rank and his superiority in gender, Wells points out, creates a "dissonance" that allows them "to play the relations of subordination off against each other, so that neither character is subsumed by the other" (1985, 68).

8. The antiliberal humanist reading of this greatly admired line seems excessively, stingily ideological: "I am Duchess of Malfi still" "fits very easily into a bourgeois liberal notion of the autonomous integrated subject asserting individual rights against antiquated and oppressive systems" (McLuskie 1985, 88).

9. Her death, like her life, mingles contrary elements in her nature: "she commands her executions . . . yet she assumes a posture of humility" (Bliss 1983, 156). Some critics emphasize that humility and its religious implications: Mulryne (1960, 215), Gunby (1970, 197), and Baker-Smith (1970, 226) read her ending as explicitly Christian; Ornstein declares this "vain, willful girl" the only character in the play "to move out of self, to turn her thoughts outward upon those she loves and upward in serene religious faith" (1960, 148); Bradbrook finds her using the language of religious experience although, she cautions, "there is nothing doctrinal about it" (1980, 152). Others see the commanding prince: Best remarks that Christian humility is accompanied by scorn for the evil destroying her (1987, 22); Leggatt, who finds her still arrogant, notes that she forces her executioners to change position to accommodate her (1988, 160). In facing death, she prefigures Charles I: forced to bow before the assumed authority of her executioners, she maintains her male identity as prince by bowing instead to the authority of God.

10. Even the dramatic mode shifts. Pearson has commented on the fifth act's increase in comic and tragicomic incidents (1987, 80); Bliss on its ironic structure (1983, 166); Codden on its "parodic theatricality" (1993, 15).

Works Cited

Amussen, Susan D. 1985. "Gender, family and the social order, 1560–1725." In *Order and disorder in early modern England. See* Fletcher and Stevenson 1985, 196–217.

Ariès, Philippe. 1989. Introduction to *Passions of the Renaissance.* Vol. 3 of *A history of private life.* Edited by Roger Chartier. Translated by Arthur Goldhammer. Cambridge: Cambridge University Press.

Ashton, Robert, ed. 1969. *James I by his contemporaries.* London: Hutchinson.

Baker-Smith, Dominic. 1970. "Religion and John Webster." In *John Webster. See* Morris 1970, 105–208.

Barish, Jonas. 1981. *The anti-theatrical prejudice.* Berkeley: University of California Press.

Barroll, Leeds. 1991. "The court of the first Stuart queen." In *The mental world of the Jacobean court. See* Peck 1991, 191–208.

Barton, Anne. 1981. "Harking back to Elizabeth." *English Literary History* 48: 706–32.

Bazin, Nancy Topping. 1974. "The concept of androgyny." *Women's Studies* 2: 217–35.

Beaumont, Francis, and John Fletcher. 1988. *The Maid's Tragedy.* Edited by T. W. Craik. Manchester: Manchester University Press.

Belsey, Catherine. 1985. "Disrupting sexual difference." In *Alternative Shakespeares. See* Drakakis 1985, 166–90.

Bergeron, David M. 1991. *Royal family, royal lovers.* Columbia: University of Missouri Press.

Berggren, Paula S. 1978. "'Womanish' mankind." *International Journal of Women's Studies* 1: 349–62.

Berry, Philippa. 1989. *Of chastity and power.* London: Routledge.

Best, Michael R. 1987. "A precarious balance." In *John Webster's Duchess of Malfi. See* Bloom 1987, 13–29.

Bliss, Lee. 1983. *The world's perspective.* New Brunswick, N.J.: Rutgers University Press.

———. 1987. *Francis Beaumont.* Boston: Twayne.

Bloch, R. Howard. 1991. *Medieval misogyny and the invention of Western romantic love.* Chicago: University of Chicago Press.

Bloom, Harold, ed. 1987. *John Webster's The Duchess of Malfi.* New York: Chelsea House.

Blum, Abbe. 1990. "'Strike all that look upon with mar[b]le.'" In *The Renaissance Englishwoman in print. See* Haselkorn and Travitsky 1990, 99–118.

Bowers, Fredson. 1940. *Elizabethan revenge tragedy*. Princeton: Princeton University Press.

Bradbrook, M. C., ed. 1962. Introduction to *Beaumont & Fletcher*. New York: Dutton.

———. 1980. *John Webster: Citizen and dramatist*. New York: Columbia University Press.

Braunmuller, A. R., and Michael Hattaway, eds. 1990. *The Cambridge companion to English Renaissance drama*. Cambridge: Cambridge University Press.

Bray, Alan. 1982. *Homosexuality in Renaissance England*. London: Gay Men's Press.

Bredbeck, Gregory W. 1991. *Sodomy and interpretation*. Ithaca: Cornell University Press.

Bridges-Adams, W. 1957. *The irresistible theatre*. Cleveland: World.

Brown, John Russell. 1976. Introduction to *The Duchess of Malfi*. See Webster, xvii–lxii.

Brown, John Russell, and Bernard Harris. 1960. *Jacobean theatre*. New York: Capricorn.

Bruster, Douglas. 1992. *Drama and the market in the age of Shakespeare*. Cambridge: Cambridge University Press.

Bushnell, Rebecca. 1990. *Tragedies of tyrants*. Ithaca: Cornell University Press.

Butler, Judith, and Joan W. Scott. 1992. *Feminists theorize the political*. London: Routledge.

Butler, Martin. 1984. *Theatre and crisis, 1632–1642*. Cambridge: Cambridge University Press.

Bynum, Caroline Walker. 1987. *Holy feast and holy fast*. Berkeley: University of California Press.

Cady, Joseph. 1992. "'Masculine Love,' Renaissance Writing, and the 'New Invention' of Homosexuality." In *Homosexuality in Renaissance and Enlightenment England. See* Summers 1992, 9–40.

Callaghan, Dympna. 1989. *Woman and gender in Renaissance tragedy*. Atlantic Highlands, N.J.: Humanities Press.

Castelli, Elizabeth. 1986. "Virginity and its meaning for women's sexuality in early Christianity." *Journal of Feminist Studies in Religion* 2: 61–88.

Cerasano, S. P., and Marion Wynne-Davies. 1992a. "'From Myself, My Other Self I Turned.'" In *Gloriana's face. See* Cerasano and Wynne-Davies 1992b, 1–24.

———, eds. 1992b. *Gloriana's face*. Detroit: Wayne State University Press.

Champion, Larry S. 1977. *Tragic patterns in Jacobean and Caroline drama*. Knoxville: University of Tennessee Press.

Chojnacki, Stanley. 1994. "Subaltern patriarchs: Patrician bachelors in Renaissance Venice." In *Medieval Masculinities* 7. Edited by Claire A. Lees. Minneapolis: University of Minnesota Press.

Christianson, Paul. 1991. "Royal and Parliamentary voices on the ancient constitution, *c.* 1604–1621." In *The mental world of the Jacobean court. See* Peck 1991, 71–95.

Claridge, Laura, and Elizabeth Langland, eds. 1990. *Out of Bounds*. Amherst: University of Massachusetts Press.

Coddon, Karen. 1993. "*The Duchess of Malfi.*" *Madness in Drama* 15: 1–17.

Collins, Stephen L. 1989. *From divine cosmos to sovereign state.* New York: Oxford University Press.

Cook, Carol. 1991. "Straw women and whipping girls." In *Shakespeare Left and Right. See* Kamps 1991, 61–77.

Craik, T. W. 1988. Introduction to *The Maid's Tragedy. See* Beaumont and Fletcher, 1–46.

Danby, John. 1952. *Poets on fortune's hill.* Port Washington, NY: Kennikat Press.

Desmet, Christy. 1991. "'Neither Maid, Widow, nor Wife.'" In *In another country. See* Kehler and Baker 1991, 71–92.

D'Ewes, Sir Simonds. 1974. *The diary of Sir Simonds D'Ewes 1622–1624.* Edited by Elisabeth Bourcier. Paris: Didier.

Drakakis, John, ed. 1985. *Alternative Shakespeares.* London: Methuen.

Duby, Georges. 1989. "Introduction: Private power, public power." *Revelations of the medieval world.* Vol. 2 of *A history of private life.* Edited by Roger Chartier. Translated by Arthur Goldhammer. Cambridge: Cambridge University Press.

Erickson, Peter. 1987. "The Order of the Garter, the cult of Elizabeth, and class-gender tension in *Merry Wives.*" In *Shakespeare reproduced. See* Howard and O'Connor 1987, 116–40.

————. 1991. *Rewriting Shakespeare, rewriting ourselves.* Berkeley: University of California Press.

Farley-Hills, David. 1988. *Jacobean drama: A critical study of the* professional drama, 1600–25. New York: St. Martin's Press.

Farrell, Kirby, Elizabeth H. Hageman, and Arthur F. Kinney, eds. 1988. *Women in the Renaissance.* Amherst: University of Massachusetts Press.

Ferguson, Margaret W., Maureen Quilligan, and Nancy J. Vickers, eds. 1986. *Rewriting the Renaissance.* Chicago: University of Chicago Press.

Finkelpearl, Philip J. 1990. *Court and country politics in the plays of Beaumont and Fletcher.* Princeton: Princeton University Press.

Fletcher, Anthony, and John Stevenson, eds. 1985. *Order and disorder in early modern England.* Cambridge: Cambridge University Press.

Fletcher, John. 1979. *The Tragedy of Valentinian.* Edited by Robert K. Turner, Jr. Cambridge: Cambridge University Press. Vol. 4 of *The dramatic works in the Beaumont and Fletcher canon, 1966–* , gen. ed. Fredson Bowers.

Forker, Charles R. 1986. *Skull beneath the skin.* Carbondale: Southern Illinois University Press.

Foucault, Michel. 1979. *Discipline and punish.* Translated by Alan Sheridan. New York: Vintage.

————. 1980. *The history of sexuality.* 3 vols. Translated by Robert Hurley. New York: Vintage.

French, Marilyn. 1983. *Shakespeare's division of experience.* London: Sphere Books.

Frye, Susan. 1993. *Elizabeth I.* New York: Oxford University Press.

Gajowsky, Evelyn. 1992. *The art of loving.* Newark: University of Delaware Press.

Garber, Marjorie. 1992. *Vested interests.* New York: Routledge.

Giddens, Anthony. 1979. *Central problems in social theory.* Berkeley: University of California Press.

Gohlke, Madelon. 1980. "'I wooed thee with my sword.'" In *Representing Shakespeare. See* Schwartz and Kahn 1980, 170–87.

Goldberg, Jonathan. 1989. *James I and the politics of literature.* Stanford University Press.

———. 1992. *Sodometries.* Stanford: Stanford University Press.

———, ed. 1994. *Queering the Renaissance.* Durham: Duke University Press.

Goldman, Michael. 1975. *The actor's freedom.* New York: Viking.

Greenblatt, Stephen, ed. 1982. *The forms of power and the power of forms in the English Renaissance.* Norman: University of Oklahoma Press.

Griswold, Wendy. 1986. *Renaissance revivals.* Chicago: University of Chicago Press.

Gunby, D. C. 1970. "The Duchess of Malfi." In *John Webster. See* Morris 1970, 179–204.

Hallett, Charles A., and Elaine S. Hallett. 1980. *The revenger's madness.* Lincoln: University of Nebraska Press.

Harvey, Elizabeth D. 1992. *Ventriloquized voices.* London: Routledge.

Haselkorn, Anne M., and Betty S. Travitsky, eds. 1990. *The Renaissance Englishwoman in print.* Amherst: University of Massachusetts Press.

Heilbrun, Carolyn. 1973. *Toward a recognition of androgyny.* New York: Knopf.

Heinemann, Margot. 1980. *Puritanism and theatre.* Cambridge: Cambridge University Press.

———. 1990. "Political drama." In *The Cambridge companion to English Renaissance drama. See* Braunmuller and Hattaway 1990, 161–205.

Henderson, Katherine Usher, and Barbara F. McManus. 1985. *Half humankind.* Urbana: University of Illinois Press.

Hibbert, Christopher. 1991. *The virgin queen.* Reading, Mass.: Addison-Wesley.

Howard, Jean E. 1994. *The stage and social struggle in early modern England.* London: Routledge.

Howard, Jean E., and Marion F. O'Connor, eds. 1987. *Shakespeare reproduced.* London: Routledge.

Ingram, Angela J. C. 1987. *In the posture of a whore.* 2 vols. Salzburg: Institut für Anglistik und Amerikanistik Universität Salzburg.

James I. 1918. *The political works of James I.* Edited by Charles H. McIlwain. Cambridge: Harvard University Press.

Jankowski, Theodora A. 1992. *Women in power in the early modern drama.* Urbana: University of Illinois Press.

Jardine, Lisa. 1987. "The Duchess of Malfi." In *John Webster's The Duchess of Malfi. See* Bloom 1987, 115–27.

———. 1989. *Still harping on daughters.* 2nd ed. New York: Columbia University Press.

Jordan, Constance. 1990a. *Renaissance feminism.* Ithaca: Cornell University Press.

———. 1990b. "Representing political androgyny." In *The Renaissance Englishwoman in print. See* Haselkorn and Travitsky 1990, 157–76.

Kahn, Coppélia. 1981. *Man's estate.* Berkeley: University of California Press.

Kamps, Ivo, ed. 1991. *Shakespeare left and right.* London: Routledge.

Kastan, David Scott, and Peter Stallybrass, eds. 1991. *Staging the Renaissance.* London: Routledge.

Kehler, Dorothea, and Susan Baker, eds. 1991. *In another country.* Metuchen, N.J.: Scarecrow Press.

Keyishian, Harry. 1995. *The shapes of revenge*. Atlantic Highlands, N.J.: Humanities Press.

Kimbrough, Robert. 1990. *Shakespeare and the art of humankindness*. Atlantic Highlands, N.J.: Humanities Press.

Krieger, Leonard. 1977. "The idea of authority in the West." *American History Review* 82: 249–70.

Kristeva, Julia. 1986. "Women's Time." In *The Kristeva reader*. *See* Moi 1986, 187–213.

Lamphere, Louise. 1974. "Strategies, cooperation, and conflict among women in domestic groups." In *Woman, culture, and society*. *See* Rosaldo and Lamphere 1974, 97–112.

Lancashire, Anne, ed. 1978. *The Second Maiden's Tragedy*. See *The Second Maiden's Tragedy*.

Lanyer, Aemilia. 1993. *The poems of Aemilia Lanyer*. Edited by Susanne Woods. New York: Oxford University Press.

Leggatt, Alexander. 1988. *English drama*. London: Longman.

Lever, J. W. 1971. *The tragedy of state*. London: Methuen.

Levin, Carol and Karen Robertson, eds. 1991. *Sexuality and politics in Renaissance drama*. Lewiston, N.Y.: Edward Mellen Press.

Levine, Laura. 1994. *Men in women's clothing*. Cambridge: Cambridge University Press.

Lipking, Lawrence. 1988. *Abandoned women and poetic tradition*. Chicago: University of Chicago Press.

Loomba, Ania. 1989. *Gender, race, Renaissance drama*. Manchester: Manchester University Press.

Lord, Joan M. 1976. "*The duchess of Malfi*." *Studies in English Literature* 16: 305–17.

Maclean, Ian. 1980. *The Renaissance notion of women*. Cambridge: Cambridge University Press.

Marcus, Leah. 1986. "Shakespeare's comic heroines, Elizabeth I, and the political uses of androgyny." In *Women in the middle ages and the Renaissance*. *See* Rose 1986, 135–53.

McCabe, Richard A. 1983. *Incest, drama and nature's law*. Cambridge: Cambridge University Press.

McLuskie, Kathleen. 1985. "Drama and sexual politics." In *Drama, sex, and politics*. *See* Redmond 1985, 77–91.

———. 1989. *Renaissance dramatists*. Atlantic Highlands, N.J.: Humanities Press.

Miles, Margaret. 1989. *Carnal knowing*. Boston: Beacon.

Mincoff, Marco. 1964. "Fletcher's early tragedies." *Renaissance Drama* 7: 70–94.

Mitchell, Giles, and Eugene Wright. 1975. "Duke Ferdinand's lycanthropy as a disguise motive in Webster's *The Duchess of Malfi*." *Literature and Psychology* 25: 117–23.

Moi, Toril, ed. 1986. *The Kristeva reader*. New York: Columbia University Press.

Montrose, Louis Adrian. 1983. "'Shaping fantasies.'" *Representations* 44.2: 61–94.

Moretti, Franco. 1982. "A huge eclipse, form and deconsecration of sovereignty," *Genre* 15: 7–40.

Morris, Brian, ed. 1970. *John Webster*. London: Ernest Benn.

Mullaney, Steven. 1994. "Mourning and misogyny." *Shakespeare Quarterly* 45: 139–61.

Mulryne, J. R. 1960. "'The White Devil' and 'The Duchess of Malfi.'" In *Jacobean theatre. See* Brown and Harris 1960, 201–6.

Neely, Carol. 1988. "Constructing the subject." *English Literary History* 18: 5–18.

———. 1991. "Constructing female sexuality in the Renaissance." In *Sexuality and politics in Renaissance drama. See* Robertson and Levin 1991b, 1–26.

Neill, Michael. 1970. "'The simetry, which gives a poem grace.'" *Renaissance Drama* 3: 111–35.

Newman, Karen. 1991. *Fashioning femininity and English Renaissance* drama. Chicago: University of Chicago Press.

Orgel, Stephen. 1991. *The illusion of power.* Berkeley: University of California Press.

———. 1992. "The subtexts of *The Roaring Girl.*" In *Erotic politics. See* Zimmerman 1992, 12–26.

Ornstein, Robert. 1960. *The moral vision of Jacobean tragedy.* Madison: University of Wisconsin Press.

Patterson, Annabel. 1982. "'Roman-cast similitude.'" In *Rome in the Renaissance. See* Ramsey 1982, 381–94.

———. 1984. *Censorship and interpretation.* Madison: University of Wisconsin Press.

Pearse, Nancy Cotton. 1973. *John Fletcher's chastity plays.* Lewisburg: Bucknell University Press.

Pearson, Jacqueline. 1987. "Tragedy and anti-tragedy in *The Duchess of Malfi.*" In John Webster's The Duchess of Malfi. *See* Bloom 1987, 75–86.

Peck, Lina Levy, ed. 1991. *The mental world of the Jacobean court.* Cambridge: Cambridge University Press.

Pinciss, Gerald M., and Roger Lockyer, eds. 1989. *Shakespeare's world.* New York: Continuum.

Rackin, Phyllis. 1989. "Androgyny, mimesis, and the marriage of the boy heroine." In *Speaking of gender. See* Showalter 1989, 113–33.

Ramsey, P. A., ed. 1982. *Rome in the Renaissance.* Binghamton: Center for Medieval and Early Renaissance Studies.

Redmond, James, ed. 1985. *Drama, sex, and politics.* Cambridge: Cambridge University Press.

Ricoeur, Paul. 1992. *Oneself as another.* Translated by Kathleen Blamey. Chicago: University of Chicago Press.

Robertson, Karen, and Carole Levin. 1991a. Introduction to *Sexuality and politics in Renaissance drama. See* Levin and Robertson 1991b, i–xx.

Rosaldo, Michelle Zimbalist, and Louise Lamphere, eds. 1974. *Woman, culture, and society.* Stanford: Stanford University Press.

Rose, Mary Beth, ed. 1986. *Women in the middle ages and the Renaissance.* Syracuse: Syracuse University Press.

———. 1988. *The expense of spirit.* Ithaca: Cornell University Press.

Rozett, Martha. 1984. *The doctrine of election and the emergence of Elizabethan tragedy.* Princeton: Princeton University Press.

Salkeld, Duncan. 1994. *Madness and drama in the age of Shakespeare.* Manchester: Manchester University Press.

Salmon, J. H. M. 1991. "Seneca and Tacitus in England." In *The mental world of the Jacobean court.* See Peck 1991, 169–88.

Saslow, James M. 1986. *Ganymede in the Renaissance.* New Haven: Yale University Press.

Schulenburg, Jane Tibbetts. 1986. "The heroics of virginity." In *Women in the middle ages and Renaissance.* See Rose 1986, 29–72.

Schwartz, Murray M., and Coppélia Kahn, eds. 1980. *Representing Shakespeare.* Baltimore: Johns Hopkins University Press.

Scott, Joan W. "Experience." In *Feminists theorize the political.* See Butler and Scott, 1992, 22–40.

The Second Maiden's Tragedy. 1978. Edited by Anne Lancashire. Manchester: Manchester University Press.

Sedgwick, Eve Kosofsky. 1985. *Between men.* New York: Columbia University Press.

Showalter, Elaine, ed. 1989. *Speaking of gender.* New York: Routledge.

Shuger, Debora Kuller. 1990. *Habits of thought in the English Renaissance.* Berkeley: University of California Press.

Shullenberger, William. 1982. "'This for the most wrong'd of women.'" *Renaissance Drama* 13: 131–56.

Smith, Bruce R. 1991. *Homosexual desire in Shakespeare's England.* Chicago: University of Chicago Press.

Smith, Molly. 1991. *The darker world within.* Newark: University of Delaware Press.

Sommerville, J. P. 1991. "James I and the divine right of kings." In *The mental world of the Jacobean court.* See Peck 1991, 55–70.

Sowernam, Esther. 1985. *Esther hath hanged Haman.* In *Half humankind.* See Henderson and McManus 1985, 217–43.

Squier, Charles L. 1986. *John Fletcher.* Boston: Twayne.

Stallybras, Peter. 1986. "Patriarchal territories." In *Rewriting the Renaissance.* See Ferguson, Quilligan, and Vickers 1986, 123–42.

Steen, Sara Jayne. 1991. "The crime of marriage." *Sixteenth Century Journal* 22: 61–76.

Strong, Roy. 1977. *The cult of Elizabeth.* London: Thames and Hudson.

Summers, Claude, ed. 1992. *Homosexuality in Renaissance and Enlightenment England.* New York: Haworth.

Sutherland, Sarah P. 1983. *Masques in Jacobean tragedy.* New York: AMS.

Teague, Frances. 1992. "Queen Elizabeth in her speeches." In *Gloriana's face.* See Cerasano and Wynne-Davies 1992b, 63–78.

Tennenhouse, Leonard. 1986. *Power on display.* New York: Methuen.

Thomas, Keith. 1994. "As you like it." *New York Review of Books,* 22 September.

Thompson, Ann. 1991. "Are there any women in *King Lear?*" In *The matter of difference.* See Wayne 1991, 117–28.

Tourneur, Cyril. 1966. *The Revenger's Tragedy.* Edited by R. A. Foakes: Manchester University Press.

Traub, Valerie. 1992. *Desire and anxiety.* London: Routledge.

Trexler, Richard C., ed. 1994. *Gender rhetorics.* Binghamton: Medieval & Renaissance Texts and Studies.

Tricomi, Albert. 1989. *Anticourt drama in England, 1603–1642.* Charlottesville: University Press of Virginia.

Turner, Robert K. 1989. "Responses to tyranny in John Fletcher's plays." *Medieval and Renaissance drama in England*: 123–41.

Turner, Robert K., ed. *The Tragedy of Valentinian.* See Fletcher.

Waith, Eugene. 1971. *Ideas of greatness.* New York: Barnes & Noble.

Wallis, Lawrence B. 1968. *Fletcher, Beaumont & Company.* New York: Octagon Books.

Warner, Marina. 1985. *Monuments and maidens.* New York: Atheneum.

Wayne, Valerie. 1991a. "Historical Differences." In *The matter of difference.* See Wayne 1991b, 153–79.

———, ed. 1991b. *The matter of difference.* Ithaca: Cornell University Press.

Webster, John. 1976. *The Duchess of Malfi.* Edited by John Russell Brown. Manchester: Manchester University Press.

Weil, Kari. 1992. *Androgyny and the denial of sexual difference.* Charlottesville: University Press of Virginia.

Wells, Susan. 1985. *The dialectics of representation.* Baltimore: Johns Hopkins University Press.

Whigham, Frank. 1991. "Incest and ideology." In *Staging the Renaissance.* See Kastan and Stallybrass 1991, 263–74.

Wieler, John William. 1969. *George Chapman.* New York: Octagon Books.

Wilkinson, Charles. 1981. "Twin structures in John Webster's *The Duchess of Malfi.*" *Literature and Psychology* 31: 52–65.

Williamson, Marilyn L. 1991. "Violence and gender ideology in *Coriolanus* and *Macbeth.*" In *Shakespeare left and right.* See Kamps 1991, 147–66.

Woodbridge, Linda. 1984. *Women and the English Renaissance.* Urbana: University of Illinois Press.

Wormald, Jenny. 1991. "'Basilikon Doron' and 'The Trew Law of Free Monarchies.'" In *The mental world of the Jacobean court.* See Peck 1991, 36–54.

Wymer, Ronald. 1986. *Suicide and despair in Jacobean drama.* Sussex: Harvester.

Wynne-Davies, Marion. 1992. "The Queen's masque." In *Gloriana's Face.* See Cerasano and Wynne-Davies 1992, 79–104.

Yachnin, Paul. 1991. "The politics of theatrical mirth." *Shakespeare Quarterly* 43: 51–66.

Yates, Frances A. 1975. *Astraea.* London: Routledge & Kegan Paul.

Zimmerman, Susan, ed. 1992. "Disruptive desire." In *Erotic politics.* See Zimmerman 1992, 39–63.

———. 1992. *Erotic politics.* London: Routledge.

Index